Jack the

ALSO BY PATRICK LUCANIO AND GARY COVILLE

*Smokin' Rockets: The Romance of
Technology in American Film, Radio
and Television, 1945–1962*
(McFarland, 2002)

*American Science Fiction Television Series of the 1950s:
Episode Guides and Casts and
Credits for Twenty Shows*
(McFarland, 1998)

JACK THE RIPPER

His Life and Crimes in Popular Entertainment

by GARY COVILLE *and*
PATRICK LUCANIO

McFarland & Company, Inc., Publishers

Jefferson, North Carolina, and London

The present work is a reprint of the library bound edition of
Jack the Ripper: His Life and Crimes in Popular Entertainment,
first published in 1999 by McFarland.

Library of Congress Cataloguing-in-Publication Data

Coville, Gary, 1949–
 Jack the Ripper : his life and crimes in popular entertainment /
by Gary Coville and Patrick Lucanio.
  p. cm.
 Includes bibliographical references and index.

 ISBN 978-0-7864-4045-0
 softcover : 50# alkaline paper

 1. Jack, the Ripper — In literature. 2. English literature —
20th century — History and criticism. 3. English literature —19th
century — History and criticism. 4. English literature — Film
and video adaptations. 5. Whitechapel (London, England)—
In literature. 6. American literature — History and criticism.
7. Popular literature — History and criticism. 8. Popular
culture — History — 20th century. 9. Serial murders in mass
media. I. Lucanio, Patrick. II. Title.
PR478.J34C68 2008
820.9'351— DC21   99-24751

British Library cataloguing data are available

On the cover: The Houses of Parliament, London (Shutterstock)

Manufactured in the United States of America

McFarland & Company, Inc., Publishers
 Box 611, Jefferson, North Carolina 28640
  www.mcfarlandpub.com

To the Memory of
Dutch and Nana
— PJL

and the Memory of
my Dad
— GWC

CONTENTS

Preface   1

   I. The Carnival of Blood   7

  II. Order Out of Chaos   19

 III. Brother to the Darkness   57

 IV. Ripper Redux   85

  V. Apocalypse: Sherlock Holmes Against
     Jack the Ripper   109

 VI. Jack the Ripper in America   133

VII. Post Mortem   155

Appendix: Media Representations of Jack the Ripper   161

Bibliography   177

Index   181

...there are no human laws when you feel yourself in the darkness, when the darkness hides and protects and the outer mask slips off your face and you feel something welling up within you, a brooding shapeless purpose that is brother to the darkness.

— Robert Bloch
"Yours Truly, Jack the Ripper"

PREFACE

Jack the Ripper is a recurring figure in historical studies as well as fictional endeavors. He first tormented the East End of London in the autumn of 1888, and in the century since, numerous books have been written attempting to reduce the Ripper to a known quantity, that is, to unequivocally identify him by name and thereby solve the crimes. But little has been done to amplify the meaning of *Jack the Ripper* in the greater context of cultural significance as expressed through imaginative literature. This book attempts to impart that meaning by surveying the major artistic works about Jack the Ripper and his crimes.

Our purpose is twofold. Our primary objective is to offer a descriptive study of the literature about Jack the Ripper, since little has been done to articulate the Ripper's appearances in various kinds of popular works, both nonfiction and fiction. What is important here is that fictional works have effectively kept the Ripper alive for more than 100 years, and they have done so by consistently following one of two courses of expression. Either they have plucked him out of history to offer biographical novels about his crimes, or they have rendered Jack the Ripper in a more supernatural context. The former works depict Jack the Ripper as an historical figure not unlike Attila the Hun, Genghis Khan, Billy the Kid, or Al Capone. The latter works depict the Ripper's deeds as products of a transcending spirit of inhumanity loose in a civilized world. What all works share, however, is a focus on the acts committed, since Jack the Ripper himself remains the great unknown. Because he escaped apprehension, he remains elusive, and in fact he has derived a good deal of his mythic status simply from his uncanny success in evading capture. Thus he forever remains in the shadows, where only imaginative literature has had the ability to elucidate his meaning to the modern world.

Our secondary objective is to analyze the meaning and value of representative fictional works. In this sense, we see ourselves as very much like the historians known as Ripperologists, such as Donald Rumbelow, Tom Cullen, and

Premier Ripperologist Donald Rumbelow, in a frame enlargement from the ABC television series *Secrets of the Unknown*, explains his theories about the Jack the Ripper case.

Colin Wilson, who discover fragments of Victorian history and use their unique skills to determine the significance of Jack the Ripper in the wider context of criminology and social behavior. In such cases, historical references usually contain commentary on the deplorable social conditions of Whitechapel as well as on the political conditions of Whitehall in efforts to show why a fiend such as Jack the Ripper could have marched against a civilized nation. Similarly, we use our familiarity with Ripper lore to identify the essential elements that give each story its lasting energy. In this effort we work from the perspectives of historian and literary critic, respectively.

It is not, we must emphasize here, our intention to plow the same fields as countless Ripperologists, and thereby argue the guilt or innocence of any particular historical figure. Simply put, we can offer no special insights into the Ripper's flesh and blood identity; we leave this manhunt, which has gone on now for more than a century, to the Ripperologists themselves. But appraising the Ripper's mythic value necessitates an understanding of the facts, and for those facts as well as speculation about identities, we have consistently drawn upon what others have written and said about the Ripper and the crimes. In other words, we have not attempted to reexamine primary sources already well covered by the experts.

On the other hand, we have energetically sought out the fictional representations (including books, movies, television programs, radio programs, and other media) that form the nexus of our argument. We have read, listened to, and viewed as many of the works mentioned as possible because it is only in such a primary experience that we could feel confident we had reached a valid synthesis. We do not pretend to know who Jack the Ripper was, but we do submit that we have learned something significant about what Jack the Ripper represents. In this sense, Jack the Ripper, in the context of the ever changing popular culture, is the touchstone against which civilization measures its tolerance for violence; as Western culture has adjusted its intake of violence over the years, it has reflected that adjustment through artistic representations of Jack the Ripper. Even though the mystery of the Ripper's physical identity has consistently drawn the attention of the public, the *symbolic* Jack the Ripper tantalizes the public even more. This symbolic Jack the Ripper is addressed in the pages to follow.

For purposes of illustration and analysis, we have centered our study on two works that define the two categories of Ripper fiction. For biographical works we use Marie Belloc Lowndes' novel *The Lodger*, and for supernatural works we use Robert Bloch's story "Yours Truly, Jack the Ripper." Using these works as springboards, we then specify numerous secondary titles under each category in an effort to be as complete as possible in revealing the Ripper's literary legacy. We have explored major references, particularly Paul Begg, Martin Fido, and Keith Skinner's comprehensive *The Jack the Ripper A to Z* and Alexander Kelly's *Jack the Ripper: A Bibliography and Review of the Literature*. We have also searched television and radio logs, studio release schedules, newspaper and magazine reviews, and numerous other bibliographies to seek out obscure titles. At times we were successful, such as when we discovered Alfred Hitchcock's radio program *Forecast* and its version of "The Lodger" and actually secured a recording of the program, but all too frequently we could find descriptions of works but no artifact for review. One such instance is the February 17, 1956, episode of the NBC television series *The Big Story* in which host and narrator Ben Grauer recounted a purportedly true story of a "modern day Jack the Ripper" stalking a major American city; the description of the episode is conspicuous but no copies of the program were made available to us. In addition, we were unable to view an episode of the CBS television series *Cimarron Strip* titled "Knife in the Darkness" (January 25, 1968), but we nonetheless were able to base our analysis of the episode on a copy of the shooting script by Harlan Ellison.*

To achieve thoroughness we have included a review of the major works of nonfiction which have offered various theories about the Ripper's identity.

Incidentally, Donald Rumbelow refers to "Knife in the Darkness" as an episode of the NBC television series Cimarron City *(1958). Begg, Fido, and Skinner, obviously restating Rumbelow, also identify the*

Here, we discover a foundation for the many fictional works which have taken their leads from the various assumptions raised by the theorists about the Ripper's identity and reasons for his existence. We are necessarily brief here because our primary objective, as we have noted, is the analysis of fiction, but we need to periodically remind ourselves that Jack the Ripper did not spring from the imagination as did his contemporaries Mr. Hyde and Count Dracula; as abhorrent as his crimes were, the Ripper was nonetheless flesh and blood. But in a very real sense the mystical aura that coalesced around the killer, from the moment that he was invested with that marvelous name of "Jack the Ripper," effectively made the flesh and blood Ripper less and less important. As succeeding decades forced the Ripper into darker shadows of the past, the heretofore knife-wielding thug was subsumed by a wholly symbolic figure who now represents something of what and who we are as a culture. Regardless of the differences that separate the real murderer from the mythical Ripper, both have been historically imbued with a phenomenal ability to strike terror into our souls. Each successful murder increased the terror exponentially, and the most successful creative presentations of the Ripper theme have always centered on that crucial point.

Next, we discuss works whose narratives are obviously inspired by Jack the Ripper and his crimes. Inclusion of specified works was arbitrary; we judged these works by their pronounced affinity with the Ripper murders — such as the *Ellery Queen* radio program "Nick the Knife" — or by a milieu we felt approximated the Ripper's, such as Ray Bradbury's story "The Whole Town's Sleeping." We have purposely left out the so-called "spatter and splatter movies" of the latter part of the twentieth century. It is interesting to note that as Western culture approached the centenary of Jack the Ripper's reign of terror, popular culture grew more and more visceral in its depictions of violence, and concomitantly grew manifestly amoral in its estimation of the causes of such violence.

We have also added a section mandated for inclusion in Ripper lore simply by its existence; if any words can express the truest statement of Victorian attitudes toward virtue and evil, those words are "Sherlock Holmes against Jack the Ripper." Here, we examine the all too sparse body of work that comprises an essentially Victorian vision of apocalyptic confrontation.

Researching the subject has been a monumental task. We have pored over thousands of pages of reference material, viewed numerous hours of film and television programming, and listened to countless hours of radio programming

---

series as Cimarron City. *The possible confusion between the two series is understandable since, aside from the similarity of titles, both series were westerns set in the Oklahoma Territory of the 1890s.* Cimarron City, *starring George Montgomery as Matt Rockford, the city's mayor, and featuring Audrey Totter, John Smith, Dan Blocker, and George Dunn, is an interesting series; it frequently eschewed the usual western narratives for offbeat stories including one called "The Beast of Cimarron" (November 29, 1958) about a phantom-like, brutish murderer loose in the city.*

in an effort to make this study a comprehensive record of Jack the Ripper in popular entertainment. As such, we thank all those who have helped in securing manuscripts, books, films, videotapes, audiotapes, and magazine articles. In particular, we wish to thank John Cooper, David P. Miller, David S. Siegel, Steve Finkelstein, Ian Griggs, Norm Sams, and Nell Williams. Additionally, we wish to express our gratitude to the editorial staff of *Filmfax* magazine, namely Michael Stein, Ted Okuda, and former editor Sharon Lind Williams, who helped get us started on the project. Also, sincere thanks to Barbara Lucanio, Denise Houser, Steve Hahn, Harry Bartell, and Sid Gonzalez, who helped in so many special ways.

It is true to say that audiences have never stopped pursuing Jack the Ripper, a fact that conveys something about Western culture. Should audiences ever suspend the chase, that too would suggest something about our culture, since ultimately the story of Jack the Ripper is also the story of the human passion to voyeuristically follow in the Ripper's footsteps. By examining the Ripper tales in context, readers can enlarge their understanding not just of a social structure, but of the human condition itself. On the one hand, Michael Harrington has keenly observed, in his essay "Victorian Psycho" for the *National Review* (June 23, 1995), that "Jack the Ripper has only a tenuous connection with the Whitechapel murderer. He is more a Gothic monster than a real person … [and] it would all come to an end if he could be identified and found to be as boring and mediocre as most killers are" (38). But Robert Bloch, in a television interview, more accurately depicts the Ripper's sustained appeal and artistic influence by noting that "with that knife … [Jack the Ripper] penetrated the deepest secrets of our own being." Hence, we can say that Jack the Ripper's symbolic identity is revealed here for the first time: He is us.

I

THE CARNIVAL OF BLOOD

In the early morning hours of August 31, 1888, in a lowly part of London called Buck's Row in Whitechapel, Constable John Neil flashed his "bull's eye" lamp into a narrow gateway and discovered the mutilated body of Mary Ann "Polly" Nichols, a 37-year-old prostitute. By the time the coroner's inquest into her death had adjourned nearly a month later, the mutilated body of a second prostitute, Annie Chapman, would be found but a few blocks away from the death scene in Buck's Row. Chapman's murder would join the seemingly unrelated murders of prostitutes Emma Elizabeth Smith and Martha Tabram of April 3 and August 7 in what the *Times of London* reported as throwing "Whitechapel and the whole of the east of London ... into a state of intense excitement." By November 9, the blood of at least four more victims would stain the cobblestone streets of Victorian London, and then the murders would cease as abruptly as they had begun.

The perpetrator of these murders remains unknown, and yet he is the most celebrated killer in the history of inhumanity. Known by no other name except for that which he reportedly gave himself, Jack the Ripper has become a byword for the most vicious and despicable of all criminals, the senseless and wanton sex murderer. It is true to say that unlike the Ripper's contemporary villains in literature, namely Mr. Edward Hyde and Count Dracula, the Ripper arose not from the depths of fiction but from the black soul of inhumanity. As such, the deeds and motives of the villains of imagination pale when compared to the deeds and motives of this singular villain whose victims shed real blood, cried out in real agony, and fell in real death. Jack the Ripper provides the model which all modern serial killers have sought to emulate, and whether consciously or unconsciously Western culture has judged the deeds of the many imitators against the Ripper's own bloody legacy.

As true as this claim is, however, the question remains, Why Jack the Ripper? Why not Dr. Thomas Neill Cream, for instance, the Ripper's contemporary who allegedly murdered four prostitutes in 1892? The question becomes even more perplexing when one considers that, as numerous Ripperologists like Donald Rumbelow and Colin Wilson have noted, the Ripper's actual reign of terror is meager when compared to other serial killings, and amazingly there is no melodrama or glamour to his criminal acts. Essentially, Ripperologists agree that the victims officially number five: Mary Ann Nichols, Annie Chapman, Elizabeth Stride, Catharine Eddowes and Mary Jane Kelly. But there are considerable differences of opinion about including the look-alike murders of Frances Coles, Alice McKenzie, Rose Mylett, Emma Elizabeth Smith and Martha Tabram into the Ripper's registry of horror. Also, Colin Wilson notes, in his introduction to Rumbelow's *Jack the Ripper: The Complete Casebook* (1988), that in many modern murders "the mutilations resembled those made by Jack the Ripper, and often the killers committed far more murders than the Ripper. (The record is probably held by Bruno Lüdke, a mental defective who confessed to eighty-six murders)" (4). Nonetheless, what remains is that the scenes of the crime were always the darkened streets of a lowly section of London, not the manor house of grand melodrama, and the victims were always women of common standing, never ladies of gentry.

What, then, is the Ripper's continued appeal? Paul Begg, Martin Fido, and Keith Skinner, in their comprehensive *The Jack the Ripper A to Z*, rightly claim, echoing Donald McCormick, that a viable reason for the Ripper's resilience is the sobriquet itself (213). This is a salient observation since the appellation Jack the Ripper not only describes accurately the savagery of the crimes, but, more important, instills a certain commonality to the perpetrator; after all, he is merely a "Jack," an everyman, not a Dr. Cream. Tom Cullen notes that, "'Jack' was a popular name with many famous criminals of the past — Jack Sheppard, Spring-Heeled Jack, Sixteen-Stringed Jack, Three-Fingered Jack, and Slippery Jack, to mention a few. 'High Rip' gangs were those who preyed on prostitutes, either in robbing them or in exacting tribute from them" (98).[1] In this sense, Jack the Ripper has transcended mere criminality to become a representation of the dark side of ourselves, and hence the Ripper is no longer somebody, but everybody. The Ripper lives on because we have permanently fixed him and his deeds within our collective minds, as if he and his crimes were products of our imagination since the Ripper's criminal deeds were so wanton and vicious that they defy civilized comprehension.

The answer to the mystery of Jack the Ripper, then, lies in the ambiance of quality or attitude of the Ripper himself. The heinous crimes, coupled with Jack the Ripper's phantom-like anonymity, have effectively transformed an ordinary yet resourceful criminal into a mythic representation of the darkest and most bestial aspect of the human condition. This is what Rumbelow means when he writes that Jack the Ripper has proved to be more of an "eponymous

---

[1]*All Cullen references are from the American paperback edition of* Autumn of Terror *titled* When London Walked in Terror *(1968).*

individual, a human shell without character or identity, than a mere criminal at large" (237). Thus, the appeal of Jack the Ripper originates not so much in the pursuit of his identity as much as it originates in a morbid fascination with his deeds, and it has remained for literary endeavors to sustain the Ripper's magical fascination. It is interesting to note that literary parodies and pastiches of the Ripper and his deeds dramatically escalated over the intervening years at a rate in keeping with the expanding power and diversity of popular entertainment, and as a result it is creative expression that has largely kept the Ripper alive in the public mind for well over 100 years. In this regard, it is not so much *who* the Ripper was — in fact, should the Ripper be unequivocally identified he would lose much of his appeal — that fascinates the public as much as it is *what* the Ripper was and continues to be: a pervasive representation of ancient evil loose in a progressive, technological world. As such, the magnetism that so radically draws us to Jack the Ripper persists in an extensive fascination with the Ripper's bestiality, particularly as that savagery is set against the ever smug advances of civilized order as only the imaginative mind can fathom.

Before we analyze the Ripper's fictional manifestations, however, we must first briefly acquaint ourselves with the various nonfiction works about the Ripper which, though scant, run parallel to the fiction and, often had an influence on the fictional subjects themselves. We need to remember that the Ripper debuts in the press; the Ripper's self-appellation emerges from the infamous "Dear Boss" letter sent to the Central News Agency on September 27, 1888, and published in the *Daily News* on October 1, 1888. In this letter, the Ripper taunts the police before signing the letter with what has become the epigrammatic "Yours truly, Jack the Ripper" (Begg 210). The Ripper was also known infrequently as "Saucy Jack" because, as Begg, Fido, and Skinner note, a postcard included the line, "I was not codding dear old Boss when I gave you the tip, youll hear about saucy Jacky s work tomorrow [*sic*]" (210). Modern Ripperologists agree, however, that this letter along with others, including the brief "From Hell" missive sent to George Lusk, head of the Vigilance Committee, was a hoax penned by a journalist named Best (45).

The Best letter hoax is significant and appropriate since it illustrates the "best" of journalism at the time. As Thomas Boyle has noted in *Black Swine in the Sewers of Hampstead*, newspapers had only recently discovered crime, and by the 1850s crime reportage had grown enormously in quality and quantity (185). What is so interesting about this reportage, including the copious coverage of the crimes of Jack the Ripper, is that what we now so naively revere as objectivity in the press is conspicuous by its absence in these vehemently subjective reports. Specifically, Ripper reportage on both sides of the Atlantic took a distinctive melodramatic edge.

The Ripper's deeds are described with gory detail that far exceeded any published fiction at the time; passages, such as those found in the *Times of*

London, that both detailed mangled viscera and modestly noted that "a more horrible or sickening sight could not be imagined" in the same article frequently infuriated the public. Moreover, the Ripper is described, for American readers in the *New York Times* at least, not as a perpetrator, alleged killer, or even subject, but variously as a "fiend" (September 30, 1888) and as a "master murderer" (October 2, 1888) whose deeds are characterized as a "carnival of blood" (October 2, 1888). Newspapers unabashedly berated the police, arguing, as the *New York Times* did in straight news pieces, that the police "have done absolutely nothing" and that "they confess themselves without a clue ... [and] devote their entire energies to preventing the press from getting at the facts" (September 30, 1888). But despite public censure for its sensational reportage of crime, the newspaper accounts of the crimes nonetheless remained popular with the public, and in this sense the Ripper's reign of terror served only to exacerbate the love-hate relationship between the public and the press, a relationship that remains intact today.

Crime historian Jonathan Goodman, in *Bloody Versicles: The Rhymes of Crime,* has reported that a total of 128 letters and postcards sent to various agencies and individuals claimed credit for the Ripper killings during Jack's murderous run (59). Letters to the press, in particular, appeared designed for publicity's sake alone and the press seemed delighted to publish the material as a public service. The authenticity of these 128 missives has always been a matter of debate, and Goodman reports that Thomas Dutton, a student of microphotography and a friend of Inspector Abberline, one of the key figures in the Ripper investigation, had occasion to examine all 128 communications and concluded that 34 of the notes were genuine. As we have noted, contemporary scholars tend to argue against the legitimacy of most if not all such letters, but nevertheless we are left with the inescapable conclusion that Jack the Ripper was, in today's parlance, a media star. In fact, Jack the Ripper was a creature born of the press, selling newspapers on the strength of his foul work and the attraction of his name alone. Moreover, from 1888 onward, the Ripper has provided entertainment value to the masses commensurate to the changes in entertainment form, from stage through screen, radio, and television to, most recently, the interactive CD-ROM.[2]

The tabloids, of course, were even more vehement in their coverage of the Ripper case, and nowhere is this more apparent than in the notorious and flamboyant *National Police Gazette.* Bill Doll, publicist for movie mogul Joseph

---

[2]*The quintessential CD-ROM has to be RIPPER, produced by Take 2 Interactive, which combines filmic elements with computer graphics to fashion an adult computer game. Contemporary performers Christopher Walken, Karen Allen, Jimmie Walker, John Rhys-Davies, and veterans Ossie Davis and Burgess Meredith star, if one can call it that, in the dramatic portions (with a credited "screenplay" by Dennis Johnson). The story is set in the year 2040 in New York City where a serial killer calling himself "the Ripper" emulates Jack the Ripper's crimes. True to its modern origins, there is plenty of gore (including an autopsy scene) and gratuitous profanity.*

Stylistic design by E. McKnight Kauffer for the 1926 release of Alfred Hitchcock's *The Lodger* succinctly states the press's obsession with Jack the Ripper and his crimes.

E. Levine, distributor in 1960 of Robert S. Baker and Monty Berman's *Jack the Ripper* (1958), describes editor Richard K. Fox as being so taken by the Whitechapel murders that Fox reported each murder with a perverse enthusiasm that could have been matched only by the Ripper's zeal for his own deeds. Moreover, Doll asserts that Fox was so enamored of the Jack the Ripper figure that he christened other killers Jack as well, e.g., referring to a strangler as Jack the Strangler. In 1889, Doll continues, Fox went so far as to publish a pamphlet titled "The History of the Whitechapel Murders" which reportedly carried an open letter to what he deemed the incompetent investigations of Scotland Yard under the title "Where, oh, Where is Jack the Copper?" Fox's enthusiasm for the Ripper waned in 1892, according to Doll, when Fox turned his attention to the Lizzie Borden case, but in 1895 the *National Police Gazette* resurrected the Ripper by publishing a lengthy exposé of a series of murders under the headline, "Is Jack the Ripper in New York?" (Doll 154).

Doll also contends that one of the first theories explaining the Ripper's motivation was espoused by a celebrated writer of fiction, the creator of Sherlock Holmes himself, Sir Arthur Conan Doyle, whose novel *A Study in Scarlet* (1887) had been published recently. Doll claims that Conan Doyle submitted a letter to Scotland Yard speculating that since the victims' dissections were so swift and skilled the Ripper must have possessed medical knowledge, and suggesting that Scotland Yard "employ a new system advanced by a Paris policeman named Alphonse Bertillon who insisted that fingerprints could be used to identify a criminal" (152). Doll even quotes portions of this letter in which Conan Doyle asserts, "The Ripper once contracted some loathsome disease from a prostitute ... [which] ruined his health and perhaps his career as a physician, and he has been driven mad with vengeance against all prostitutes" (152). As probable as this sounds, there appears to be no evidence to corroborate the validity of the letter. Doll's statement is even more suspect when one considers the fundamental error he makes in equating fingerprinting with the Bertillon System, which predated Scotland Yard's adoption of fingerprinting, and was a criminal identification system based upon the taking of precise overall physical measurements. Bertillon believed that no two people would have precisely the same physical characteristics. Begg, Fido, and Skinner, however, in discussing William Stewart's *Jack the Ripper: A New Theory* (1939), laud Stewart's book for advancing "Conan Doyle's suggestion that a midwife could have escaped detection as the Ripper since she would be expected to pass through the streets in a blood-stained apron" (Begg 207); moreover, Rumbelow quotes Conan Doyle's well-known interview with the Portsmouth *Evening News* (July 4, 1894) in which Conan Doyle states that he believed the Ripper to be someone "who had been in America" (239).

The credibility of Doll's "letter" was further undermined by Tom Cullen, who, in *Autumn of Terror: Jack the Ripper: His Crimes and Times* (1965) and its later paperback edition *When London Walked in Terror* (1968), quotes Conan Doyle's son, Adrian, as recalling that Sir Arthur believed, as early as 1888, that the Ripper disguised himself as a woman to escape detection. In a letter to Cullen, Adrian Conan Doyle remembered that his father "considered it likely that the man had a rough knowledge of surgery and probably clothed himself as a woman to avoid undue attention by the police and to approach his victims without arousing suspicion on their part" (191).

Significantly, this theme of "Jill the Ripper" (alternately "Jane the Ripper") was promulgated by Edwin T. Woodhall in *Jack the Ripper: Or When London Walked in Terror* (1937), the first major investigation into the Ripper's identity and his crimes. According to Begg, Fido, and Skinner, Woodhall concluded that the Ripper was a Russian immigrant named Olga Tchkersoff, whose sister, Vera, fell into prostitution after being befriended by Mary Jane Kelly. According to this theory, Vera died following a botched abortion, and Olga went on a rampage slaying prostitutes until she ultimately found the woman responsible for Vera's death, Mary Jane Kelly, the Ripper's official final victim. Similarly,

Opposite: **Cover art for the American paperback edition of Tom Cullen's** *Autumn of Terror: Jack the Ripper: His Crimes and Times* **(London: The Bodley Head, 1965) titled** *When London Walked in Terror* **(1968).**

AVON/V2177/75¢
"Gruesomely Fascinating"
BOSTON GLOBE
When London Walked In Terror
Tom A. Cullen

Stewart's supposition, developed in *Jack the Ripper, A New Theory* (1939), was that Jill the Ripper was a crazed abortionist who exacted revenge on members of her own sex for being betrayed by a married client.

The most startling and certainly the most notorious claim about the identity of Jack the Ripper was made in 1970 by Dr. Thomas Stowell in an essay titled "Jack the Ripper: A Solution?" published in the November issue of the forensic journal, *The Criminologist*. Without ever actually naming the suspected killer — referring to him only as "S" — Stowell argued that Jack the Ripper was HRH Prince Albert Victor, Duke of Clarence and Avondale and eldest son of Edward, the future King Edward VII of Great Britain. Stowell reported that the entire affair was covered up by palace politics. Needless to say, Stowell's claim — reiterated by both Joseph Sickert, Stephen Knight in *Jack the Ripper: The Final Solution* (1976) and by Frank Spiering in *Prince Jack* (1978) — remains controversial despite censure by most Ripperologists. In particular, Sickert's claims of an illicit family relationship to the Duke of Clarence and knowledge of a fanatical conspiracy which spawned the Ripper murders have been makers of especially heated controversy. Sickert's contentions have frequently changed over time and have even been withdrawn and publically reinstated. Knight's theories, based on Sickert's claims, at least have the distinction of intellectual consistency. Nonetheless, Stowell's theory, exacerbated by Sickert's claims and Spiering's book was an international sensation (see Chapter VI). Finally, Begg, Fido, and Skinner write that the theory may have "triggered the international obsession with Jack the Ripper of the past twenty years" (453). More important is that the notion of government cover-up has itself become a pervasive contrivance for those attempting to prove the otherwise unprovable — everything from unidentified flying objects crashing in the New Mexico desert to a conspiracy surrounding the assassination of John F. Kennedy.

The theory that the Ripper was a crazed physician — male or female — has pervaded the speculative history of the Jack the Ripper crimes. Donald McCormick's *The Identity of Jack the Ripper* (1959), which in recent times has been labeled dubious by Ripperologists, postulated a theory partially based on a handwriting analysis of the Ripper's own letters to *The Times*, concluding that the Ripper was a Russian physician named Alexander Pedachenko.[3] Likewise, Conan Doyle's theory of a crazed physician was the impetus for Leonard P. Matters' *The Mystery of Jack the Ripper* (1929), which postulated the theory that the Ripper was a British doctor named Stanley whose son had contracted syphilis from a prostitute named Mary Jane Kelly. Dr. Stanley then took revenge on

---

[3]*Donald Rumbelow is kind to McCormick, saying that his "book is readable" in* Jack the Ripper: The Complete Casebook, *185. Begg, Fido, and Skinner are harsh, writing that, "The consequent impossibility of checking Mr. McCormick's sources, and the variants between the original and revised editions in quotations from the same source ... make* The Identity of Jack the Ripper *a book to be used with extreme caution" in* The Jack the Ripper A to Z, *274–275.*

the prostitutes of London's East End, according to Matters' theory, until he had at last located his intended victim (this theory served as the impetus for the 1960 film *Jack the Ripper*, discussed later).

What we find here in this succinct discussion of nonfiction is actually but a fragment of the Ripper's appeal. The bulk of our knowledge about Jack the Ripper comes not from the historian but from the artist; it is the writer, the dramatist, and the filmmaker who shed light on what the Ripper truly represents. It is important to arm ourselves with a nodding acquaintance of the key theories, plausible and implausible, because these theories frequently provide the scholastic underpinnings for the various media representations of the Ripper.

Interestingly, one of the first artists to gain notoriety concomitantly with the Ripper's reign of terror was the British novelist Robert Louis Stevenson and the American actor Richard Mansfield. Bill Doll claims that the Ripper murders served as the impetus for the financial success of Stevenson's investigation into the nature of evil, *The Strange Case of Dr. Jekyll and Mr. Hyde*, whose publication in 1886, just two years before the killings, was received only moderately by the public. Begg, Fido, and Skinner, on the other hand, assert that the murders caused the financial failure of American actor Richard Mansfield's dramatization of the Stevenson story, which was appearing at The Lyceum Theatre at the time of the Whitechapel slayings (292). Reportedly, newspapers — inspired by Mansfield's acclaimed performance — speculated that the Ripper was a mild-mannered physician by day who became a monstrous murderer by night in the squalid dens of London's East End. The publicity may have spawned a resurgence of sales for Stevenson's book, but public condemnation of the play caused Mansfield to close down his production in October after a ten week run, according to Cullen. He adds that the *Daily Telegraph* claimed Mansfield had "determined to abandon the 'creepy drama,' evidently beloved in America, in favor of wholesome comedy." Moreover, Cullen quotes the paper as noting that, "Experience has taught this clever young actor that there is no taste in London just now for horrors on the stage. There is quite sufficient to make us shudder out of doors" (96). Begg, Fido, and Skinner add that Mansfield was "promptly attacked by philistines who believed that histrionic representation of the transformation from a gentleman to a fiend encouraged serial murder" (294). Interestingly, Rumbelow reports that Mansfield was considered one of numerous suspects, citing a nameless contributor to newspapers who charged Mansfield with giving a too clever performance of Mr. Hyde *not* to be Jack the Ripper (113). Begg, Fido and Skinner, however, deny this (294).

The Mansfield incident is apparently the impetus for Edwin Zbonek's *Das Ungeheuer von London City/The Monster of London City* (1964), a German production based on the novel by Bryan Edgar Wallace, son of the prolific mystery writer Edgar Wallace. In this black and white melodrama scripted by Robert A. Stemmle, reportedly an authority on crime stories, the stage success *Jack the*

Edwin Zbonek's film of Bryan Edgar Wallace's novel was most likely inspired by contemporary suspicions that American actor Richard Mansfield was Jack the Ripper.

Ripper by one Anatole Lestrade is playing at the Edgar Allan Poe Theatre in Whitechapel. Coincidentally, someone is murdering prostitutes in like manner in Whitechapel, which causes Sir George Edwards (Fritz Tillman), a member of Parliament, to call for the play's closing. The producers scream censorship in one breath and the more truthful "blood flows and money pours" in a second breath. The play stars Richard Sand (Hansjörg Felmy), who had at one time played Hamlet, in the title role of the Ripper, and when someone switches a real knife for a prop knife Sand begins to doubt his own sanity. Meanwhile, Zbonek heavy-handedly throws suspicion on Sir George to the point of dressing him in cape and slouch hat, but as the curtain closes on the play and the film, the new Ripper turns out to be Sand's best friend, police surgeon Dr. Michael Greeley (Dietmar Schoenherr), a rival as well for the hand of Sir George's niece, Ann Morley (Marianne Koch). One of the victims is named Elizabeth "Lizzie" Straight, and another is named Evelyn Nichols, obvious references to actual victims Elizabeth Stride and Mary Ann Nichols. *The Monster of London City* was released in the United States on a double bill with Franz-Josef Gottlieb's *Das Phantom von Soho/The Phantom of Soho*, which was also based on a novel by Bryan Edgar Wallace, and featured a similar milieu of sordidness and squalor.

The first author of fiction to exploit the Ripper murders, according to

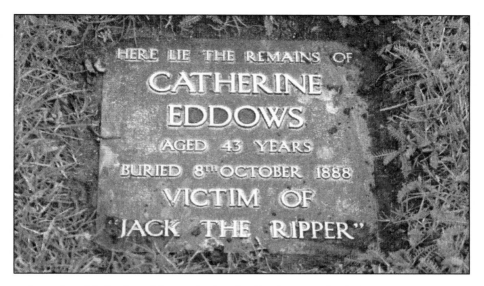

Gravesite of Catharine Eddowes, the fourth official victim of Jack the Ripper, in East London Cemetery. Note that her name is misspelled. (Photograph courtesy of Ian Griggs.)

Rumbelow, specifically the murder of Catharine Eddowes on September 30, 1888, was one J. F., or John Francis, Brewer, who, within a few weeks of the murder, published a monograph titled *The Curse Upon Mitre Square A.D. 1530–1888*. Brewer suggested, Rumbelow writes, that the location of the murder was actually the lost location of Holy Trinity Priory, and that Eddowes fell upon the exact spot where centuries before a mad monk named Martin mistakenly had killed his own sister for profaning the monastery. Brewer writes that, "With a demon's fury the monk then threw down the corpse and trod it out of very recognition. He spat upon the mutilated face and, with his remaining strength, he ripped the body open and cast the entrails round about" (236). In remorse, the monk turned the knife on himself, and Brewer claimed that ever since that night, between midnight and one, a dark young man dressed as a monk can be found in Mitre Square pointing to the very spot where the killing occurred, promising that other killings will follow. Rumbelow adds that Brewer's pamphlet contained "a classic example of bad taste" by carrying a single advertisement: "Warner's Safe Cure for Kidney and Liver Disease."

Rumbelow also cites an 1889 music hall performance based on the murder of Mary Jane Kelly as probably the first entertainment to exploit Jack the Ripper, but we could find no corroborating evidence of this. In addition, Rumbelow reports that the first fictional prose to deal with the Ripper was published in Finland in 1892. In this collection of short works titled *Uppskäraren*, or *The Ripper*, author Adolf Paul offers a first person narrative of how he encountered the Ripper in Berlin, found the Ripper's diary, and then used the Ripper's own words to analyze the murders in terms of what Paul concluded was the Ripper's sexual deviancy. As far as can be determined, Rumbelow is the sole advocate for inclusion of this story into the canon of Ripper fiction, and he indicates that a copy of the book can be found at the Royal Library of Stockholm (236).

It remains, however, for Brewer's pamphlet to serve as a benchmark in Ripper lore because it blurred the distinction between Ripper nonfiction and fiction. Although not a new contrivance since such blending was already apparent in the so-called "sensation novels," which default, as Thomas Boyle tells us in *Black Swine in the Sewers of Hampstead*, to "thrillers with elements of sex and violence" utilizing a true crime milieu (129), the Ripper's reign of terror served as organic nutrient for the ever increasing market. Moreover, the Ripper's popularity in both works of nonfiction and fiction marked the coming of age for the Victorians. Boyle notes how our own popular culture — manifested primarily by film and television — reveals crime-ridden cities with a "legal, political, or social establishment that is tainted or infested with madness and corruption." Boyle then argues that until the sensation novel

> the Victorians had no really comparable tradition of their own. They were barely digesting the news revolution ... and the news, at least, usually had something of an inadvertent quality. With the advent of novels with such content, there was now a body of work that seemed willful in its murderous descriptions.... Certainly, the grip of authority of news and fiction became another, coexistent problem to confront, along with the brazen existence of the novels themselves [128].

One can only extrapolate this point to include the widely vast and various coverage of the Ripper and his crimes. If anything, reportage of the Ripper solidified the vision of his age. As Boyle notes, "newspapers are bringing bad news, news which at once binds the city together and fragments it" (206); moreover, the Victorian "happy ending" was becoming increasingly more elusive. In this sense, the literary works — telling truth about ourselves and not necessarily fact about the Ripper — abrogated the Victorian compromise. At once the works elicited self-recognition that the civilized aren't that far removed from the savage, and collaterally elicited the self-realization that the civilized create a new kind of savagery, an autonomous threat that Joseph Conrad's Kurtz can describe only as "the horror, the horror." If, as Matthew Arnold eloquently noted in "Dover Beach," the sea of faith had withdrawn in melancholy, then Jack the Ripper's chronicle is a reminder not only to the Victorians but to us as well that, as Boyle notes, Darwin's beast proved eternal; that evil is indeed archetypal, and it can never be displaced or supplanted — even by the most civilized of the civilized.

II

Order Out of Chaos

As we have already mentioned, there was no clear beginning or end to the Ripper's reign of terror, and without any conclusion the Victorian public had difficulty forgetting Jack the Ripper. The masses conspicuously preserved the memory of the celebrated serial killer and his abominable crimes. Rather than purging or repressing the emotional legacy of the Ripper from its collective consciousness, the civilized Victorian world seemed to fixate upon and embellish the Ripper's sordid accomplishments. In fact, the Victorian habit of obviating unpleasantness through means of artistic compromise was quickly superseded where the Ripper was concerned. As a result, scarcely a symbol of greater evil had arisen to capture the public fancy as did the Ripper in the waning years of the nineteenth century.

For years after the gruesome death of Mary Jane Kelly on November 9, 1888, speculation abounded every time a particularly brutal murder surfaced. If anything, the facts and speculations about the Ripper and his motives were made to appear even more horrific than the actual crimes themselves. The public seemed to revel in the continuing story, and the press and public eagerly continued to divine the Ripper's murderous handiwork in and around the East End. On February 14, 1891, Frances Coles, a streetwalker known locally as "Carrotty Nell," was found in Swallow Gardens near death with her throat cut. Although she died without naming her assailant, her murder ignited a frenzy both in the press and among the public, all of whom seemed morbidly delighted to have the Ripper back at work; the public marveled that perhaps Saucy Jack was alive and well and had resumed his chosen profession. In addition, reports would place the Ripper in various parts of the world over the next several decades until his further survival became chronologically impossible.

What was becoming increasingly clear was that Jack the Ripper was transcending his own time and place, becoming an international if not timeless symbol for inhumanity. His ghastly charnel house view of life was tapping secretly into our darker side; his viciousness seemed to appeal to Freud's claim about our bestial heritage, our id, that raw untamed portion in all of us which has steadfastly managed to resist the refining influences of civilization. There was even a certain satisfaction — unspoken but dominant nonetheless — with the Ripper's uncanny ability to escape detection and to "get away with it." But the Victorian need for order necessarily led the public to seek a rational explanation for the irrational acts committed by the Ripper, if only to maintain a sort of communal sanity.

As a result of his pervasive grip on the public, the Ripper was forcing the Victorian mind — just as the Ripper forces us today — to look inward for answers to two unrelenting questions: What motivated the Ripper to stalk the streets of Whitechapel in the first place, and, more importantly, just what is there about this particular fiend that fascinates us above almost every other killer in recorded history? Historians and politicians espoused different theories about his origin, and the Victorian press and public alike speculated about the uncanny ability of Jack the Ripper to go undetected. As such, an accomplice was variously suggested, and just such an explanation was supposedly alluded to when the British Home Secretary, Henry Matthews, responded to a question in the House of Commons following the disemboweling of Mary Jane Kelly. Begg, Fido, and Skinner quote Matthews as saying that, "In the case of Kelly, there were certain circumstances which were wanting in the earlier cases and which make it more probable that there were other persons who, at any rate after the crime, had assisted the murderer" (14–15). It has been inferred by some from Matthews' response that the authorities had concluded that the Ripper, though he may have been acting alone, must inevitably have aroused the suspicions of people close to him who were now, in turn, covering for the Whitechapel fiend (15).

Moreover, Queen Victoria, like many of her subjects, took an active interest in the detection and apprehension of the Ripper. In a note dated November 10, 1888, to Prime Minister Lord Salisbury following the murder of Mary Jane Kelly, the Queen chastised London's detectives as "not what they should be." Three days later, in a letter addressed to the Home Secretary, a clearly agitated and impatient sovereign offered a series of personal suggestions to shake the London constabulary into obtaining results; she asked sarcastically, "Has any investigation been made as to the number of single men occupying rooms to themselves? The murderer's clothes must be saturated with blood and must be kept somewhere" (Hibbert 314).

But the answers to such questions would come not so much from the historians and the politicians as much as it would from the creative community. In fact, the artists and writers had taken the premise of unyielding interest in the killer as an established fact, as indeed it is. Quite literally, from the time of the first reports of the Ripper's active presence in the seamier environs of London, the creative side had been fascinated with the whole aura and mystique surrounding Jack the Ripper. Rumbelow remarks that, "What is surprising is just how quickly the public seized on the dramatic possibilities," and then cites Brewer's "piece of nonsense" titled *The Curse Upon Mitre Square A.D. 1530–1888*, alluded to earlier, which appeared in only a matter of weeks following the murder of Catharine Eddowes, according to Begg, Fido, and Skinner (236).

One writer in particular, Marie Belloc Lowndes, made use of the Ripper persona to such an extent that her preeminent novel *The Lodger* has formed the basis of many of the speculative performances depicting the Ripper. Appearing first as a short story in the January 1911 edition of *McClure's* magazine, her story was so effective in reaching the more or less contemporary audiences of the Ripper that she expanded it into a novel, which saw publication two years later. Detective fiction critics Chris Steinbrunner and Otto Penzler describe *The Lodger* as, "A psychological suspense thriller rather than a tale of detection," and they point out that its effect is "more a 'why-done-it' than a 'who-done-it'" (252). It is this approach, they argue, that forms the basis of Belloc Lowndes' best works. With respect to *The Lodger* specifically, the why-done-it hinges on a theme of sexual madness, which registers throughout Ripper lore as it must given the nature of the crimes involved. For Belloc Lowndes, the "why" was a religious fanaticism charged with sexual repression that fed and impelled the actions of the lodger himself. And it remained for Marie Belloc Lowndes to overtly establish this theme thereby setting the principal concern for an entire school of writers caught up in pursuing the Ripper as objet d'art.

At this stage, then, the flesh and blood creature who plunged his knife into five, seven, ten, or twenty ladies of the evening — or "sisters of the abyss," as some Victorians modestly called them — had become irrelevant to the central point. The public had taken to its liking an embellished monster larger than life, one that was capable of transcending life itself as previously stated. What had happened was that we had become fascinated by an effigy which spoke to us of blood and evil in surrealistic terms, and those images figuratively seized us by the throat and forcibly reminded us just how close we remained to our primordial heritage, and that it was only the thin conspicuously woven fabric of civilization that separated each of us from Jack the Ripper.

The Lodger provided one of the earliest and strongest embodiments of this thematic presentation. Although for the purposes of *The Lodger*, Marie Belloc Lowndes elected to anoint her fiend "The Avenger" rather than "Jack the Ripper," there has never been any question as to the Avenger's true derivation. In fact, Belloc Lowndes has validated for us and her readers the duality of the Ripper and Avenger. In a diary entry dated March 9, 1923, Belloc Lowndes wrote that, "The story of *The Lodger* was written by me as a short story after I heard a man telling a woman at a dinner party that his mother had a butler and a cook who married and kept lodgers. They were convinced that Jack the Ripper had spent a night under their roof" (Susan Lowndes 97).

SOCIETY DEBUTANT
STABBED.

Murdered in Brother's Arm
at Coming-out Ball.

THIRD AVENGER
MURDER.

AVENGER TRIANGLE CL ir-haired Waitress Killed
at Charing Cross Station.

WORK OF A MANIAC.
Army Medical Corps and as yet no news has been
received

POLICE CLUES FAIL. AVENGER STILL AT
LARGE.

After a fortnight of terrifying
anxiety, yet another clue has failed
the Avenger is still at l...

Last night yet another murder
was discovered and again the

Newspaper clippings in Hitchcock's *The Lodger* show both the press' infatuation
with the murders and with Belloc Lowndes' rechristening the Ripper into the
Avenger.

The Avenger (Mr. Sleuth) maintains a powerful hold over Robert and
Ellen Bunting, from whom he has rented a room. In the guise of the killer
exploited in the tabloid press, the Avenger commands Robert's slavish servi-
tude even before the lodger comes knocking on their hostelry door one dark
evening. Despite the frightening circumstances of the poverty which has
reduced both husband and wife to inarticulate despair, teetering at the
precipice of financial disaster and having crossed over the edge to emotional
despair, the fortuitous arrival of the enigmatic Mr. Sleuth seemed providential at first. The arrival of their lodger with cash in hand to bail them out of
their troubles seemed nothing less than an act of God to Ellen Bunting. But
one of the opening scenes in *The Lodger* controverts this sense of hope for the
Buntings; the scene finds Robert in a fit of impulse, parting with a precious
penny for a copy of the *Evening Standard*. The newspapers had formerly been
one of Bunting's modest daily pleasures until financial want had snatched away
that tiny diversion. Now, with the mysterious Avenger's exploits chronicled
and exploited in the daily press, Bunting elects to take a guilty pleasure from
a copy of the *Evening Standard*. Instantly, however, he feels the weight of guilt
from his rash decision:

> A hot wave of unease, almost of remorse, swept over Bunting. Ellen would
> never have spent that penny on herself — he knew that well enough — and
> if it hadn't been so cold, so foggy, so — so drizzly, he would have gone out
> again through the gate and stood under the street lamp to take his plea-
> sure. He dreaded with a nervous dread the glance of Ellen's cold, reprov-
> ing light-blue eye. That glance would tell him that he had no business to
> waste a penny, and that well he knew it [11–12]!

Ellen Bunting's reaction is not a verbal one. Nonetheless, as written by
Belloc Lowndes, Ellen's emotional response keenly impresses the reader: "But
her hands trembled — they trembled with excitement, with self-pity, with
anger. A penny? It was dreadful — dreadful to have to worry about a penny!
But they had come to the point when one has to worry about pennies. Strange
that her husband didn't realize that."

Such was the power exerted by the Whitechapel killer in the Bunting
household that he could create wounding tensions between husband and wife.
In fact, the gnawing poverty at the root of the Buntings' difficulties threatened
to soon rival the poverty which had turned uncomfortable numbers of women
onto the streets of London's East End to sell themselves for a handful of pennies. Despite the Avenger's interpretation, life on the streets of Whitechapel
was less about sin than it was about appalling endemic privation. As Ripperologist Martin Fido pointed out in a 1995 Arts and Entertainment Network
cable channel documentary, "Jack the Ripper," London's East End was "an area
where at any time almost any woman might have to prostitute herself as the
only way to feed her children. I've talked to person after person from the East
End today who have said, yes, they always reckoned Grandma had to go out
on the streets when time was bad and nobody thought any of the worse of her
for it."

But Steinbrunner and Penzler correctly argue that Belloc Lowndes'
strength as a novelist lies not so much in social commentary as in her characterization; they note that, "Her major ability was character development [and]
she was overwhelmingly concerned about the relationships between her male
and female characters, with particular emphasis on sexual matters" which,
they are quick to add, were "discreetly handled" (252). *The Lodger* is then Mrs.
Bunting's story far more than it is the story of her husband, Robert, or of the
Whitechapel killer himself for that matter. Ellen Bunting becomes the reluc-
tant key to the Ripper's continued freedom, and as Ellen's suspicions incre-
mentally increase until unease makes way for apprehension, which in turn is
shoved aside by stark fear, Ellen is held to be part of the explanation for the
murderer's success.

The fortuitous arrival of the lodger, Mr. Sleuth, instantly provides the
Buntings with relief from their own financial hard times. The agonizing jour-
ney of awareness which Ellen travels as she comes to terms with the real identity of her boarder, in a sense, places Ellen in the same class as the women of

the Whitechapel district who were at that very moment selling their honor in order to survive. For Ellen does not go to the police with her suspicions; in fact, having been made aware that the police will be out in force on a given evening plotting to trap the Avenger, Ellen attempts, by oblique reference, to warn Mr. Sleuth of the danger waiting out on the streets.

By the time of her warning, Ellen Bunting has developed an attachment to her lodger not so far afield from psychological transference, or the emotional ties a patient sometimes develops for a physician who has affected a marked improvement in the patient's life. Ellen comes to find in her lodger elements of gentleness and trust which she is loathe to violate with first her suspicions or later her certainties. In the end, when the lodger has disappeared as abruptly as he appeared, neither of the Buntings is prepared to reveal the secret of his identity — not to the police, nor even to Bunting's beloved newspapers.

Belloc Lowndes' *The Lodger* proved popular with the reading public although critics were much less quick to endorse the novel. As she recalled some ten years after publication, "When *The Lodger* was published, I did not receive a single favorable review. When it came to sending a quotation for an advertisement for the American edition, I was not able to find even one sentence of tepid approval. Then, to my surprise, when *The Lodger* had been out two or three years reviewers began to rebuke me for not writing another *Lodger*" (Susan Lowndes 97–98).

Sensing that an audience was building for *The Lodger*, English playwright Horace Annesley Vachell adapted Belloc Lowndes' novel for the stage. Originally produced under the title *Who Is He?* at London's Haymarket Theatre, the play starred Henry Ainley as the mysterious lodger. Vachell, however, transformed Belloc Lowndes' searching character study into an undistinguished comedy which fared adversely with audiences. After its London closure, the play, with changes in cast and title, transferred to New York's Maxine Elliott Theatre, where it opened on January 8, 1917, with Lionel Atwill in the title role. Running in New York under the title of *The Lodger*, Vachell's version of Belloc Lowndes' work garnered some slight attention in the form of a mildly approving review in the *New York Times* and then folded after 56 performances.[1]

As tepid as the response had been to Vachell's adaptation of *The Lodger*, its appearance on stage nonetheless harbingered the many efforts that would follow. Mercifully, later versions would essentially eschew the ill-advised humor for a more fundamentally serious approach to the Ripper phenomenon. In this sense, its first legitimate dramatization was for the silent screen. Alfred Hitchcock chose, for his third directorial effort, to re-work *The Lodger*, and his film would represent the first of several screen versions of the celebrated novel.

---

[1]*For a review of the New York premiere and a history of this obscure and nearly forgotten play, see* "The Lodger *Proves Highly Amusing" in the* New York Times, *January 9, 1917, page 14.*

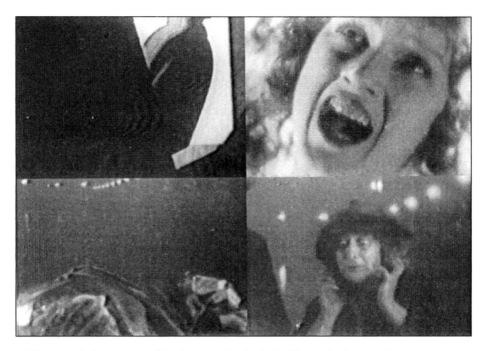

The screen's first victim of the Avenger, i.e., Jack the Ripper, in the opening sequence to Hitchcock's *The Lodger* (1926), beginning with E. McKnight Kauffer's title design and continuing though extreme closeup of victim, followed by body in street, and ending with horrified witness.

Released in 1926 under the formal title of *The Lodger: A Story of the London Fog*, the film represents Hitchcock's first screen immersion in the suspense genre, and a viewing of the film today reveals certain defining truths of the Ripper legacy. Although Hitchcock chose to remove his lodger from the Victorian past and bring his character forward to the present, certain social and historical truths were adhered to faithfully. William Rothman, in *Hitchcock: The Murderous Gaze*, notes Hitchcock's perception of the public's reaction to the Avenger killings. Rothman writes that:

> In one of the most remarkable sequences of the film, Hitchcock dissolves from a radio announcer reading the story of the murder to one solitary listener after another: a man who rolls his eyes, an angry woman who yowls like a cat, a man who listens taut with excitement, a woman so aroused that she runs her tongue sensually over her lips. Each listener appears less an individual than a representative of the London public [10].

Hitchcock is able to depict the London public's perverse fascination with the Avenger through powerful visual images. Marie Belloc Lowndes implied the

Ivor Novello's "out of the fog" appearance in Hitchcock's *The Lodger*. Note the ubiquitous hat, cape, and bag.

same self-absorbed reaction through the unforgettable spectacle of Robert Bunting squandering a precious penny in order to satiate his appetite for news of the Avenger. Both Belloc Lowndes and Hitchcock intuitively understood that the public's craving for word of the Avenger was as great as the Avenger's seeming thirst for blood. Ultimately, the story of Jack the Ripper is as much the story of society's passion to voyeuristically follow in the Ripper's footsteps.

Belloc Lowndes and Hitchcock, each in their own way, contributed to the Ripper's mystical aura. But Hitchcock's insistence on the ultimate innocence of his lodger, a favorite Hitchcock theme, contravenes the theme of Belloc Lowndes, who slowly built the case against Mr. Sleuth until there was no room left for denial. Hitchcock prefers to explore a skein of false suspicions which ensnarl Jonathan Drew (Ivor Novello), i.e., Mr. Sleuth, after he takes up residence in the Bunting household. Although a departure from the original novel, Hitchcock's inquiry into mistaken identities and mob vengeance was fairly rooted in the historical record of the Ripper murders. Early in the Ripper inquiry, suspicion fell upon a local figure, John Pizer, commonly referred to as "Leather Apron." Pizer was later conclusively cleared of the Ripper

Ivor Novello strikes a "Nosferatu stare" (c.f. German filmmaker F. W. Murnau's expressionistic film *Nosferatu*) to elicit suspicion from the audience in Hitchcock's *The Lodger.*

murders; however, false accusations vented in sensational press accounts of the day apparently were never fully overcome. A significant segment of the public apparently continued to believe in the guilt of Leather Apron (Begg 253). As the hysteria intensified in Whitechapel, any man spied carrying a Gladstone bag or similar satchel fell immediately under suspicion. More than one man so encumbered was reportedly forced to flee for his very life from an aroused mob.

Generally overlooked is the fact that Hitchcock returned to *The Lodger* in the summer of 1940. Then working in America, Hitchcock was approached by CBS executives to participate in a series of experimental radio dramas. The concept, sheltered under the umbrella title of *Forecast* over an eight week period, offered audiences 14 studiously varied program ideas. Hitchcock was asked to present his specialty — the suspense drama — which he directed on July 22, 1940. Electing to present *The Lodger*, Hitchcock fell heir to the talents of Herbert Marshall who performed the curiously dual roles of announcer and the mysterious Mr. Sleuth, a device destined to be repeated in additional radio adaptations.

The shadowy figure of Jack the Ripper was ideal for radio as Hitchcock must have understood, and as countless directors would later realize. But the horrific episodic murders perpetrated by the Ripper pushed the limits of radio's "theatre of the mind." Convention, public taste and the unwillingness of radio networks to offend the sensibilities of the nuclear family gathered around large console sets meant that Jack the Ripper would have to undergo an assiduous re-editing of the facts of history. But Belloc Lowndes herself had started the process a generation before with the conversion of the Ripper to the Avenger and a blurring of the killer's motives. "I am down on whores," the Ripper allegedly noted in a letter dated September 25, 1888, but Mrs. Belloc Lowndes' Avenger was down on young women whose fall from grace was less complete but nonetheless just as fatal. "He 'ave got a down on the drink," as a cabman summarized the Avenger's motives. Women who frequented public houses left themselves open to interpretation, and the Avenger acted on his own interpretation. But radio's interpretation would require considerable circumspection where the Ripper's motives were concerned if directors and playwrights expected to escape the blue pencils of the censors of the "continuity acceptance departments." Words like prostitute, whore, sex and harlot simply had no place on the radio; but since these terms represented the Ripper's reason for existence, changes in motive were decreed before such presentations would be allowed out over the air waves. Hitchcock wryly caused the victims to be described as "pretty, blonde" and "light-hearted," and such descriptions obviously begged the question of the victims' social status in life but certainly met radio's need to sanitize the Ripper's real nature.

Hitchcock's *Lodger* was effective radio. Marshall, as narrator and lead character, dominated the play, tugging at listener's emotions from two compelling directions, creating suspicion as the enigmatic Mr. Sleuth while interpreting and insinuating the worst as the omniscient third person observer of events, something that would find its ultimate effect in Robert Bloch's "Yours Truly, Jack the Ripper" (Chapter III).

More or less following Belloc Lowndes' story line, Hitchcock strategically breaks off adherence to the novelist's plot at the climax and reverts to the theme of his own screen version of *The Lodger* by reprising the lodger as an innocent man falsely accused. Fearing that their daughter, Daisy, is in immediate danger of becoming the Avenger's next victim, the Buntings burst unceremoniously into Mr. Sleuth's room. At this point, in a masterful yet stylistic departure from standard radio form, Hitchcock is heard from the director's booth ordering "cut." This stops the scene and the forward movement of the play, depriving the listening audience of the expected conclusion. Hitchcock then explains to a perturbed cast and crew that Mr. Sleuth's room is empty since he had left that afternoon not to be heard from again. Furthermore, Hitchcock wryly states that Daisy had merely gone out for a walk and was perfectly safe. Hitchcock's audience had once again been skillfully led to a conclusion of guilt which was ultimately unjustified. But Hitchcock's own ironic manner, reaching its pinnacle in his television series, would make the ending all too revealing: the Avenger/Ripper simply got away with it.

In 1932, Maurice Elvey's *The Phantom Fiend* retold the story of *The Lodger* from Hitchcock's perspective with the added benefit of sound. Ivor Novello once again starred as the "innocent," but outside of some atmospheric shots of foggy London streets there is little to recommend the film.

Belloc Lowndes' clever story underwent its next major screen re-interpretation through the auspices of Hollywood. In January 1944, 20th Century–Fox released John Brahm's *The Lodger* featuring Laird Cregar in the title role with Merle Oberon, George Sanders, Sara Allgood and Sir Cedric Hardwicke. Scriptwriter Barré Lyndon scrapped the illusion of the Avenger altogether; here, the lodger *was* Jack the Ripper in name as well as in fact. But for whatever creative reasons, Cregar's lodger became Mr. Slade rather than Mr. Sleuth; the Buntings become the Burtons; and the Bunting's daughter, Daisy, became their more worldly niece, Kitty Langley. In addition, Lyndon changed focus, like Hitchcock before him, from Ellen Bunting to the lodger, and this is what makes the film so memorable and effective. It is Cregar's characterization of the brooding lodger that strikes us; his 300 pound frame along with his rather plain features suggested a personality out of kilter with the rest of the universe. This is particularly apparent in Mr. Slade's ruminations about the river; here, he laments that he sometimes goes down to the Thames where the water will "wash against your hands as you look down into ... [the] deep water [that] is dark, and restful, and full of peace." Even more frightening are his ruminations about beautiful women, whom he sees as evil. He states that "it's one thing if a woman is beautiful merely for herself, but when she exhibits the loveliness of her body upon the stage as a lure...." He later tells Kitty that "you wouldn't think that anyone could hate a thing and love it, too," concluding that he knows "that there is evil in beauty." Later, when as the Ripper he confronts her, he malevolently tells her that "I have never known such beauty as yours, nor such evil in such beauty! Men will not look at you again as they did tonight!" Gregory William Mank, in his horror movie book *Hollywood Cauldron*, asserts that Cregar's performance was motivated by Cregar's own sexual torment. Mank writes, "That there was a strange garnish of sexual aberration in some of his performances was not surprising; a gay man himself, he was torn between acknowledging his sexual preference and hiding it" (245). Maybe, but such an assessment — almost excuse — for an actor's talent denies the actor's rightful claim to genius. Personal problems or not, Cregar's performance remains unforgettable.

The Ripper's escape at the conclusion of the movie conforms to Belloc Lowndes' original tale. In a particularly poignant scene, the stoic Inspector Warwick (George Sanders) sees the river as sweeping a city clean, but Kitty, herself an intended victim of the Ripper, philosophizes about her assailant in

Top and bottom: Laird Cregar's domineering presence as Mr. Slade is accented by low angles and chiaroscuro lighting in John Brahm's atmospheric *The Lodger* (1944).

the context of the river; she laments that the river "carries things out to sea, and they sink in deep water," a reference to Slade's own demented personality finally at peace. Unlike Mr. Sleuth in Belloc Lowndes' novel, Mr. Slade here arouses our sympathy if only because of Cregar's masterful performance. Slade is presented as not just a maniacal misogynist hell-bent on murdering actresses; Lyndon and director John Brahm turn Slade into a pathetic, introverted outcast, who is struggling against not just the world but with himself for no apparent reason other than that he seems to be so destined. For instance, Slade accepts the room from Mrs. Burton by sighing that it is "a refuge," and he entreats her to leave the Bible in his room because his "problems [are] of life and death." Here he is depicted as a lonely, melancholy figure who murmurs about late walks and empty streets, and one who prefers to be known as a lodger, not a guest. But a moment later Lyndon depicts the lodger as maniacal: Mrs. Burton returns to the room to find the paintings of the dancers all turned toward the wall. Slade rages that "wherever you went in this room the eyes of those women seemed to follow you about!"

Twentieth Century–Fox, in its 1953 distribution of *The Lodger* titled *Man in the Attic*, virtually cannibalized Lyndon's original script to the point of giving him co-screenplay credit with Robert Presnell, Jr. Director Hugo Fregonese elicited an exceptional performance from Jack Palance in the role of Slade, but the film lacks the intense psychological potency of the 1944 version, despite Freudian ruminations about Slade's mother, who was an actress and a domineering spirit in this variation. Both Palance and Cregar are large men with somewhat brutish features, but whereas Cregar elicited a dark and deep melancholy to his portrayal of Slade — reflective of the river — Palance remains merely aloof and reticent in his portrayal. But this reticence is strangely appealing to Lily Bonner (Constance Smith, who also played the Ripper's intended victim in *Room to Let*), changed from Kitty who had changed from Daisy, who refuses to believe that Slade, despite his suspicious actions, could possibly be the Ripper. In this variation, when Slade succumbs to the dark waters of the Thames, as he inevitably must, there is no ambiguity and no room for serious doubt: the Ripper is dead. What is also missing is the magic of Lyndon's poetry; the final verdict is left to representatives of the relentless police force — not Lily — to summarize Slade's fate. The officer remarks that "it's too dark and it's too deep; we'll never get him now," at which point Inspector Warwick reassures the officer that it is "not so dark and not so deep where he's going."

It is worth noting here that *Man in the Attic*, like Lyndon's 1944 endeavor, drew upon the scientific principle of fingerprinting in an effort to discover the Ripper's identity. Various critics have faulted the films, particularly the original 1944 version, for this obvious anachronism. In speaking of the film, Tom Cullen states that, "This film contains a howler, incidentally, in that fingerprints are used to trap the killer; M. Bertillon's methods had not been adapted by Scotland Yard in 1888" (240). True enough, but in fairness to Lyndon, Belloc

Lowndes' novel was the original source of this temporal anomaly. As Detective Joe Chandler is conducting Daisy and her father on a tour of Scotland Yard's famed Black Museum, Chandler pauses in the entrance of a half-open door and says:

> Look in there, that's the Finger-Print Room. We've records here of over two hundred thousand men's and women's fingertips! I expect you know, Mr. Bunting, as how, once we've got the print of a man's five finger-tips, well, he's done for — if he ever does anything else, that is [7].

Appropriate here is a look at an obscure British film produced in 1950 by Exclusive Films Ltd., the corporate predecessor to the celebrated Hammer Films. Godfrey Grayson's *Room to Let*, adapted from a BBC radio play by noted mystery novelist Margery Allingham, shares many characteristics with Belloc Lowndes' book. The setting is London, a few years after the Ripper killings, and an elderly invalid named Mrs. Musgrave (Christine Silver) and her daughter, Molly (Constance Smith), find it necessary to let one of the rooms in their home to a suitable boarder in order to make ends meet. Dr. Fell (Valentine Dyall), a tall gaunt gentleman in cloak and top hat, makes application for the room and is gratefully accepted by Mrs. Musgrave even though Dr. Fell proves to be a strange fellow. Unlike other works in which the lodger merely keeps strange hours and stranger habits, Dr. Fell moves quickly and inexplicably to control the household. He dominates both women to such a degree that their wills are slowly given over to him; even the assertive Molly is unable to void his psychological stranglehold on the household. At one point, when Molly threatens to call the police, Fell merely states rhetorically, "Police calling on the house to arrest the lodger? Curious, isn't it, that I should be the lodger?" The psychological horror, manifested by Grayson's frequent use of extremely low angles in framing Dr. Fell, slowly builds as Fell inexorably extends his power over the Musgrave household to the point at which he gives approval and disapproval to Molly's suitors. Dr. Fell's madness becomes morally certain when journalist Curly Minter (Jimmy Hanley), Molly's true love, believes that Fell escaped from a mental institution during a fire even though no one from the institution will verify a missing patient. Dr. Fell's other identity, that of Jack the Ripper, becomes obvious when he shows Mrs. Musgrave his cherished map of Whitechapel, and mutters that maps are "useful when you want to move about quickly." He then tells her that he intends to pick up where he had left off after the Miller's Court murder in 1888, and at this point Grayson heightens the desperation of Mrs. Musgrave by having her alone in a house with Jack the Ripper. At the moment of truth, however, Curly and Sergeant Cranbourne (Reginald Dyson) break into the house to find Mrs. Musgrave alive on the floor near her overturned wheelchair. They are then forced to break into Fell's room through a window where they find him dead, a bullet through the heart.

Frame sequence from the trailer for Hugo Fregonese's *Man in the Attic* (1953), a remake of Brahm's *The Lodger*, summarizes Mr. Slade's (Jack Palance) inner turmoil by first describing Lily (Constance Smith, as "notorious" and then noting that Slade both "loved her and hated her!"

Grayson's *Room to Let* is told in flashback by an elderly Curly to his journalist friends, Harding (Aubrey Dexter) and James Jasper, or J. J. (J. Anthony la Penna). Curly explains the locked-room death of Dr. Fell as a puzzle: the door was both locked and bolted from the inside and no gun was ever found; the only conclusion is suicide. J. J., however, explains to Harding what he believes to be the truth. Sounding very much like Sherlock Holmes, J. J. asserts that Mrs. Musgrave shot the Ripper in self-defense, and that she locked the door and then slid the key under the door into the room. J. J. continues, saying that Mrs. Musgrave descended the staircase ever so gently until her feeble hands gave out, and she crashed to the floor where she placed the gun inside a book box for posting to her sister. When Harding points to the bolt inside the room, J. J. explains that Curly was the first one into the room, and that he merely bolted the door himself to save the Musgraves from potential scrutiny by press and authorities. J. J. adds that Curly's gentility is ever fixed since he eschewed the scoop of the century for the love of a woman.

Viewed from a certain perspective, *Room to Let* might easily be taken as a sequel to Belloc Lowndes' *The Lodger*; indeed, Dr. Fell's admission that he is

Frame sequence from *Man in the Attic* shows Fregonese's intense cutting that manifested Mr. Slade's growing hatred for Lily. Fregonese cuts with growing pace among three elements: 1) Lily's sensual dance, 2) the lecherous joy of the ogling men in the audience and 3) Slade's growing hostility toward Lily.

"the lodger" smacks of an in-joke either by Allingham or screenwriters John Gilling and Grayson. As a sequel, *Room to Let* explains what might have befallen the Whitechapel killer after he fled the Bunting household in 1888. The consistency of character is, indeed, worth noting: the propensity for positioning himself in financially embarrassed families and the desire to kill certainly parallels major motifs of *The Lodger*. Moreover, Dr. Fell's overconcern for the welfare of Molly echoes Mr. Slade's own anxiety toward Kitty in Brahm's *The Lodger*. The explanation for Dr. Fell's need to kill, however, is much less obvious than the religious fanaticism ascribed to Mr. Sleuth or to Mr. Slade, but Dr. Fell's need to dominate women leads him to the act of murder as the final and inevitable step in controlling women.

Contextually, radio, like film and television, tended to focus upon the emotional storytelling aspects inherent in the Ripper saga rather than on any historical analysis, which seemed the province of books and magazine articles, although such works were not without a significant body of fictional narratives constructed from Ripper lore. But radio was a near perfect venue for Jack the Ripper and his various incarnations. From the start, the public had taken

Valentine Dyall as the sinister Dr. Fell in Godfrey Grayson's *Room to Let* (1950), a pastiche of Belloc Lowndes' *The Lodger* and a BBC radio play by mystery writer Margery Allingham.

to endowing this monster with personal touches, filling in the horrific details to meet some private emotional needs. Radio, by its very nature permitted — in fact encouraged — audiences to color details to personal taste, and in so doing radio was significantly contributing to the lengthy ongoing process which was radically transforming the original Ripper into an archetypal figure. The confluence of desire and means significantly accelerated the process.

On May 19, 1946, radio's *Hollywood Star Time*, a series that saw itself in the mold of *Lux Radio Theatre* and *The Screen Guild Players*, both being prestige radio offerings which produced versions of popular movies, presented a half-hour version of *The Lodger* based on the 20th Century–Fox production. Like its competition, *Hollywood Star Time* brought to the microphone top screen names to perform in lead roles. To assume the role of the mysterious lodger, director Robert L. Redd selected Vincent Price, whose association with horror roles had not yet been sealed. The opening narration skillfully and succinctly set the stage for the drama:

> This is the story of a scourge that broke upon the City of London in the year 1888. It is the story of a man who moved in the shadows, beyond the

flickering gaslights of that era and who wrote his name upon the scroll of
infamy with a knife, and his name was murder!

Within the constraints of a 30-minute aural production, *Hollywood Star Time*
attempted to adhere basically to the 20th Century–Fox outline, and certainly
the essential elements remained intact. The one key exception was the concluding moment at which the Ripper is dimly perceived swimming away
through cold dark waters to freedom after a revealing confrontation in Kitty's
dressing room. The *Hollywood Star Time* broadcast suggested, through Kitty's
final speech and an absence of any evidence to the contrary, that Price's Ripper had, indeed, drowned in the river. We are told by Kitty that, "The river
killed him, even at the last." She then reiterates, for the most part, Lyndon's
melancholic farewell: the river "carries things out to sea and they sink in deep,
dark water, in dark peaceful water forever." But the radio's cautious use of public air waves necessitated a sort of Victorian compromise all its own; indeed,
a plethora of station, network, and broadcasting codes in strict force at the time
of *Hollywood Star Time*'s presentation precluded the Ripper's escape. Justice
and inevitable retribution, an integral part of the National Association of
Broadcasters code, demanded a re-writing of the screenplay to fit such constraints. Accordingly, the addition of the key phrase that "the river killed him,
even at the last" sustained the broadcast standards, but it also subverted Kitty's
final sentiments, which were more ambiguous and, in the context of the
moment, made more sense.

The following year yet another version of *The Lodger* was presented, this
time on a short-lived yet expertly conceived and acted anthology series titled
Mystery in the Air. This rendering of *The Lodger* was broadcast on August 14,
1947, and featured radio veteran Agnes Moorehead as Ellen Bunting and series
host Peter Lorre as Mr. Sleuth. Free from respecting the 20th Century–Fox
account, *Mystery in the Air* tied its version much closer to the novel, and hence
the Ripper was once again vaguely disguised as the Avenger. The Buntings'
daughter, Daisy, was once more a secondary figure, all but inviting the attention of the Avenger. Moorehead's Ellen Bunting again served as the moral focal
point, struggling with her fears, suspicions, sympathies and misplaced loyal-
ties — just as Belloc Lowndes had conceived the character — and Lorre's Mr.
Sleuth was as intense as Cregar but yet at times overly hysterical in his religious fervor that "everything wicked and sinful should be purged from the
earth." Nonetheless, as closely as this rendering strived to adhere to the novel,
once again the demands of the broadcasters' codes necessitated a significant
change in denouement. While Ellen Bunting and her husband beat frantically
against a locked door, on the other side an insane and ranting Avenger pre-
pares to make Daisy his seventh and final victim. As he raises his knife to
strike, the Buntings succeed in forcing their way into the room. In the ensuing confrontation, the Avenger falls on his own knife, delivering his own

succinct epitaph which easily could have been that of Cregar's own melancholic figure: "It is burning in me like a fire. It purges me and consumes me. All sin and evil are falling away. Praise, praise and glory, for it is I who am the seventh. Yes, the vengeance is fulfilled."

Hitchcock's 1940 *Forecast* production of "The Lodger" led two years later to the premiere of *Suspense*, one of the longest running and most critically acclaimed mystery anthologies to appear on American radio. Defining itself as "radio's outstanding theatre of thrills," *Suspense* played for twenty years, consistently drawing upon the principles of fear and horror so skillfully articulated by Hitchcock in the pilot broadcast. Indeed, *Suspense* provided some of the most consistently frightening moments in radio drama including the often reprised "Sorry, Wrong Number," which was specifically written for the series.

On December 14, 1944, *Suspense* presented one of two adaptations of *The Lodger*. This time Robert Montgomery performed the twin assignments of narrator and lodger. The play was an essentially faithful translation of the novel, but the one significant dissimilarity was the final climactic moment when the Avenger holds Daisy at knife point, a scene that does not take place in the novel. In this instance, the Avenger dies not from his own hand, nor from the hand of the police or from the intervention of the Buntings rescuing their daughter, but rather the Avenger succumbs to an act of God. The Avenger's fanatical rage is more than matched by a raging storm which has newly descended over London. Miraculously, the Bunting house is struck by lightning, and the terrible shrieking screams of the dying Avenger ring in listeners' ears. This deus ex machina solution to the case, while perhaps lacking credibility, nonetheless offers the attraction of poetic justice: God punished the crimes committed in His name.

Four seasons later, on February 14, 1948, *Suspense* had shifted to an hour format, and again *The Lodger* was its subject. Coincidentally, Robert Montgomery was serving as host that season and found himself again playing the mysterious Mr. Sleuth. The radio adaptations, in both instances, were by veteran radio dramatist Robert Tallman, with the 1948 script essentially an expansion of Tallman's 1944 play. Another radio veteran, William N. Robson, directed the hour-long version and it featured Jeanette Nolan as Ellen Bunting and Peggy Webber as Daisy. The same convention was employed and the Avenger perished through God's wrath. Or did he? In both the 1944 and 1948 presentations, Montgomery in his role of host, closes with something of a teaser which once again demonstrates our reluctance to permanently say goodbye to the Ripper. Montgomery warns his audience that:

> There were those at Scotland Yard who were never quite sure that the charred remains of a man they removed from the ashes of the Bunting home were, indeed, those of the Avenger anymore than Mrs. Belloc Lowndes, who novelized the case, was ever quite convinced. And there are those who will tell you that the real Avenger, a tall man clad in an Inverness cape,

a man almost exactly like Mr. Sleuth, left England and came to America
to live in a town near your town.

One of the last substantive employments of Belloc Lowndes' narrative was
the 1960 opera by British composer Phyllis Tate which, together with Alan
Berg's *Lulu* (1936), forms the foundation upon which all musical adaptations
of the Ripper and his crimes are made. Tate's opera was first presented at London's Royal Academy of Music on July 14, 1960, and televised over the BBC in
1964. Faithful to the thrust of the original, the opera concentrates its tragic narrative more on the ambivalent relationship between the sympathetic Mrs.
Bunting and the deranged, yet surprisingly "good hearted," lodger than on the
murders. Following the tradition of tragedy, the crimes were all committed
offstage.

On the other hand, Berg's *Lulu* centered its narrative on a cabaret dancer
named Lulu and her various love affairs which led to her moral ruin; in the
end, she was reduced to a London prostitute who became a victim of Jack the
Ripper. Lulu was adapted from the plays *Erdgeist/Earth Spirit* (1893) and *Die
Büchse der Pandora/Pandora's Box* (1904) by Frank Wedekind, both of which
had been made into a film by G. W. Pabst in 1928, *Pandora's Box*.

Ironically, the most celebrated musical version of the Ripper and his
crimes actually bears little resemblance to the Victorian murderer and his
reign of terror. Kurt Weill and Bertold Brecht's *Die Dreigroschenoper/The
Threepenny Opera*, first presented at the Theater am Schiffbauerdamm in
Berlin on August 31, 1928, remains foremost in musical adaptations of the
Ripper story if only for the tremendous popularity of one of the play's songs,
"Mack the Knife." The song, which is heard in the prelude as an introduction
for the character MacHeath, recounts a string of Ripper-like murders and
warns that the perpetrator of the murders — MacHeath — is yet on the prowl.
The play itself, and its subsequent film versions including an expressionistic
interpretation by G. W. Pabst in 1931, deals more with Brechtian ideology than
murder. In this respect, the narrative offers the notion that the seedy political
maneuvering of underworld criminal organizations are analogous to the mundane operations of capitalist democracy; Brecht writes that the criminal mas-
termind MacHeath is a sign of capitalist greed in the sense of one who "takes
the greatest care that all the boldest or, at least, the most fear-inspiring deeds
of his subordinates are ascribed to himself." Such a view could be applied to
the oppressed economic and social conditions of Whitechapel itself, but it
remains the song "Mack the Knife," whose popularity soared after Marc
Blitzstein's Broadway revival of the play premiering on March 10, 1954, that
keeps the eponymous figure of the Whitechapel killer alive even if MacHeath
himself is more like Dr. Mabuse than Jack the Ripper.

A sampling of radio's attempts to approach the Ripper story from a documentary angle indicates that programs often indifferently researched renderings

The ever promiscuous Lulu (Louise Brooks) meets her fate at the hands of Jack the Ripper (Gustav Diessl) in G. W. Pabst's *Pandora's Box* (1928). In this sequence, Lulu enjoys a brief moment with the Ripper until a glistening knife enrages the Ripper into slaying Lulu. Afterward, Jack the Ripper becomes a shadowy figure as he slowly slips into the fog.

of the cases. One such documentary program was *Crime Classics*, an American syndicated program whose format was dramatizing actual crime cases. The series' fifty-first and final episode, broadcast June 30, 1954, was titled "Good Evening, My Name Is Jack the Ripper." As a document of Ripper history, it wavered between efforts at telling the Ripper's story through dramatizations of original newspaper accounts and fancifully conceived events in the final weeks of the life of Mary Jane Kelly, played by Betty Hartford as a fun-loving, soft-hearted — though larcenous — young woman. In a matter-of-fact manner, the play concludes with Mary Kelly's murder and the Ripper's successful escape. Though expertly produced and directed by Elliott Lewis, one of radio's foremost talents, the program unfortunately left audiences wondering where facts trailed off and fiction came into play. But the series becomes significant when one considers that by the 1950s the broadcast codes were slowly if unofficially being relaxed, and this in tandem with the cultivation of a new type of radio drama was leading to change.

The success of Jack Webb's *Dragnet* in 1949 had inaugurated the popular acceptance of what is known as "the police procedural," a fictional form which dramatizes authenticity. Particularly, what Webb had established was the heretical precedent that the criminal sometimes does, indeed, get away with his crimes. As a result, there was less of an imperative for poetic justice, and so the fictitious Thomas Hyland (Lou Merrill), narrator of *Crime Classics*, explains with a curious blend of historical accuracy, speculation, interpretation and wishful thinking that Mary Jane Kelly's death was the seventh and last Ripper killing as well as "the greatest unsolved crime in history." Hyland then adds that:

> The year was 1888 and it's generally considered that Jack the Ripper was a very young man. And it's thought that he ran away to America. So that spry old gentleman over there, carving so deftly the roast, spooning out the kidney pie; or that one there, whittling; or the one there, silver-haired, a fine surgeon by day. Well, I'm just pointing out the possibility, that's all.

Here, Hyland argues the dubious proposition that Emma Elizabeth Smith and Martha Tabram were the Ripper's first and second victims, respectively. Although not an uncommon argument, the more orthodox view today points to five victims, as previously noted, beginning with Polly Nichols, who was murdered on August 31, 1888, and ending with the November 9, 1888, savaging of Mary Jane Kelly. Morton Fine and David Friedkin, who dramatized "Good Evening, My Name Is Jack the Ripper," allege in the closing credits that the play was "adapted from the original newspaper accounts" of the Ripper case. Conceivably, they may have based their research on *The Harlot Killer*, edited by Allan Barnard and published to popular acclaim just the year before. In Barnard's introduction, he argues the case for inclusion of the Smith and Tabram murders as Ripper victims and provides certain reprinted newspaper accounts that would probably have represented the most easily obtained source material from which to work. But for the purposes of examining the treatment of Jack the Ripper in the media, it is less important to establish the actual number of Ripper victims than it is to inspect the recurring tendency to stretch the boundaries, as it were. By increasing the number of the Ripper's victims, by stretching his life span beyond all reasonable limits, by transporting the Ripper through time and space, our culture seems to be offering running commentary on the cosmic themes of moral guilt and innocence.

In like manner, the British radio drama *Unsolved Mysteries* combined history with speculation, and Jack the Ripper's lurid story naturally lent itself to the series. The end result, however, was a hopeless melange of obfuscation and an overly involved defense of clairvoyance as a worthwhile tool for police

Opposite: **Cover art for the seminal fact and fiction anthology *The Harlot Killer*, edited by Allan Barnard and published in 1953.**

DELL BOOK 797

The world's most
diabolical murderer...

25¢

the HARLOT
KILLER

Edited by
ALLAN
BARNARD

work. Essentially, the episode is predicated upon rumors of the active interest in the Ripper case by the Victorian clairvoyant and psychic Robert Lees. In order to reconcile its dubious conclusions with the facts, *Unsolved Mysteries* warns its listeners that "liberties of time, place and characters have been taken." The program then changes Robert Lees into James Wyss for the purposes of the narrative, with the basic elements of Lees' purported involvement in the Ripper case selectively retold. Lees' psychic impressions of the killer, his disbelief of police officials, his "encounter" with the Ripper aboard a London bus, and eventually his identification of the Ripper as a prominent physician with ties to the Royal Court are dramatized. Such detail is presented with finesse not unlike those presented in the modern television series *Unsolved Mysteries* with Robert Stack. Ultimately, the Ripper is distinguished only as "Dr. Blank" with not even the convention of a common pseudonym risked.

The Lees connection with the Ripper inquiry would be presented several more times over the years, although in more entertaining forms than what was embodied in the *Unsolved Mysteries* performance. For instance, the Lees account unquestionably forms the basis of "Jack the Ripper," an episode from an aborted 1958 television series titled *The Veil*, produced by Hal Roach Studios and hosted by Boris Karloff. Currently, four of the episodes have been strung together to form a telefilm titled *Jack the Ripper*, although only the final episode deals with the Ripper. In the episode, written by Michael Plant, a clairvoyant played by Niall MacGinness leads a Scotland Yard detective (Clifford Evans) to the door of a respected physician. Whether the physician was the Ripper was left undetermined, but considering that the doctor had been compelled to enter a mental institution and that the Ripper murders stopped thereafter, little doubt truly remained as to the identity of Jack the Ripper. Lees also appears, offering critical testimony to the solution, in Bob Clark's *Murder by Decree* (1978), and he figures prominently in David Wickes' telefilm *Jack the Ripper* (1988), both discussed later.

As late as 1967, the Ripper was yet another subject for a BBC radio documentary. "Smiler with the Knife: The Mystery of Jack the Ripper" (April 12, 1967) was a 45-minute chronicle of the Whitechapel killer's activities. Written and directed by Tony Van den Bergh, "Smiler with the Knife" advanced no theories of its own but essentially endeavored through dramatized vignettes to present a factual account of the key elements of the case. Interestingly, several popular theories about the Ripper's identity were briefly explored and quickly discarded, such as charges that the Ripper was really Dr. Thomas Neill Cream, Frederick Deeming and Severin Klosowski, who was also known by the name George Chapman. Theories alluding to the guilt of Montague John Druitt, "Jill the Ripper" and "Dr. Stanley," among others, were catalogued as "so many theories, so much mystery."

"Smiler with the Knife," while all too cavalier in its examination of major suspects, nonetheless offered a succinct enumeration of some of the more likely candidates. Thomas Neill Cream allegedly was in the midst of confessing to the Ripper murders when the hangman's rope cut the doctor off from further discourse. Cream had been convicted of poisoning four prostitutes during 1891 and 1892. The nature of his crimes suggested to many that Cream's alleged scaffold confession may indeed have been legitimate. The problem with that theory, however, is that Cream had been incarcerated in the United States during the period of the Ripper's killing spree.

Severin Klosowski (aka George Chapman) was a Polish barber and the prime suspect in the eyes of Inspector Frederick Abberline of the Metropolitan Police. Klosowski was hanged in 1903, the result of poisoning three wives. At the time of the Ripper murders Klosowski was living in London, never far from the scene of the crimes.

Montague John Druitt is perhaps one of the most plausible suspects of all. The candidate of several prominent Ripperologists, including Tom Cullen, Druitt was called to the bar in 1885 and had been dismissed from a teaching position just prior to his suicide in December 1888. An inquest into the circumstances surrounding Druitt's death was held two days after Druitt's body was fished from the Thames. The verdict was suicide while of unsound mind; allegations of sexual insanity hang heavily over the suspect.

The various works that incorporated Lees' supposed connection with the Ripper inquiry, as well as the above mentioned BBC documentary, were coincidental precursors to the startling 1970 claim by Dr. Thomas Stowell who ignited a firestorm of controversy by implying that Jack the Ripper was none other than Prince Albert Victor, Duke of Clarence and Avondale and heir to the British Throne (see Chapter I). What is so amazing about this is that Stowell himself, in one breath, backed away from his own words as he lay dying (Begg 453). Stowell's argument took on a dynamic of its own and has outlived the inventor. Books and articles have since been written linking the Ripper to the Royal Family. The 1973 BBC documentary, *Jack the Ripper*, as well as cinematic efforts *Murder by Decree* and Wickes' *Jack the Ripper* have been based upon what we suggest is in point of fact a variant of the Stowell theory, an argument propounded by Joseph Sickert. Sickert has argued that the Ripper murders were the work of Freemasons which included members of the British government in a misguided effort to conceal the claim that the Duke of Clarence had entered into an embarrassing marriage with a Roman Catholic woman from the lower classes, Annie Crook, whom Sickert claimed as his grandmother.

But what makes the Stowell and Sickert theories so significant to Ripper history is that their theories came along at a time when mistrust of government, in both the United States and Britain, was a pervasive way of life. The theories found favor because the charges of government conspiracy and cover-up in the Ripper case speak to the contemporary sense of suspicion about everything connected with government. In this regard, it is the elusive figure of Jack the Ripper that lends itself to everchanging artistic interpretations of alienation.

Without intending to do so, Marie Belloc Lowndes succeeded in defining an approach to the Ripper theme which would be employed by writers innumerable times over the ensuing years. While generally maintaining the Ripper in his historical context, writers had to constantly re-interpret the Whitechapel killer's motives in light of frequently changing popular conjecture. This rationalist approach requires believable explanations for the Ripper's irrational acts, and the explanations themselves may or may not stretch believability if viewed through the Victorian mind-set. From a contemporary vantage point, however, the reasons seem to make perfect sense. Radio's dilemma had always been the quandary of how to portray history's most celebrated sex killer in terms acceptable to a conservative listening audience, but by the 1960s, Jack the Ripper had found a continuing if sporadic cinematic fame built upon the cultural and political biases of the moment. The permissiveness of the 1960s allowed for a wider, less confining approach when it came to filling in many of the bloody details of the Ripper's accomplishments previously held back from sheltered audiences. The political turmoil, likewise so endemic to the decade of the 1960s, again fueled new interpretations of the Ripper's bloody killing spree, as we shall later note.

The first truly biographical dramatization of the Ripper and his crimes was appropriately titled simply *Jack the Ripper*. Released in the United States in February 1960 by the redoubtable showman Joseph E. Levine for Paramount Pictures, *Jack the Ripper* was a 1958 British film by the producer-director team of Robert S. Baker and Monty Berman, whose previous work included Henry Cass' gritty horror film *Blood of the Vampire* (1958) and Quentin Lawrence's science fiction film *The Crawling Eye* (1958).

Although Levine — whose promotion for Pietro Francisci's *Hercules* (1959) has become Hollywood legend — certainly appraised the profitability of exploiting such a figure as Jack the Ripper, he nonetheless denied any mercenary motive in securing the U.S. rights to the film. As reported by Bill Doll, publicity director for Levine's Embassy Pictures, Levine was actually interested in the quality of the film. Doll quotes Levine as saying that, "My sole thought upon acquiring the film was that here was the type of 'chiller' the British do so very well," adding that he was impressed by Baker and Berman's style, which Levine lauds: "With their acting company in fine fettle, Mr. Baker and Mr. Berman bring their camera to bear on a lengthy scene and let it grind away. There are none of the short 'takes' and obvious cuts which characterize so many hastily made movies. The mood is created and the actors are given full opportunity to sustain it" (Doll 149).

Opposite: **Lurid advertising art for Joseph E. Levine's American release of Robert S. Baker and Monty Berman's *Jack the Ripper* (1960).**

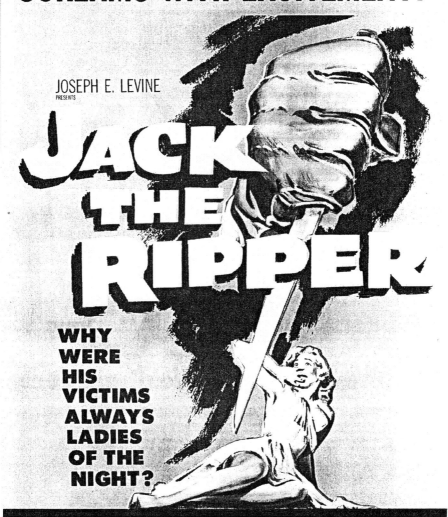

Levine's "slashing" title for Baker and Berman's *Jack the Ripper*.

Baker and Berman certainly demonstrate such stylish élan in a pre-credits sequence — itself inspired by Brahm's opening sequence in *The Lodger*— that it has been duplicated by those who followed, including Ray Milland for the "Yours Truly, Jack the Ripper" episode of the *Thriller* TV series; James Hill for *A Study in Terror*; Bob Clark for *Murder by Decree*, Nicholas Meyer for *Time After Time*, and Edwin Zbonek for the German film *The Monster of London City*. As the camera tracks across a fog-shrouded street, a title establishes "London 1888"; a young prostitute leaves a pub, encounters a street musician and his playful monkey, and then makes her way along the grim corridors of Whitechapel's narrow streets. Ultimately isolated, her footsteps reverberating in the darkness, she is confronted by a caped figure. Rendered faceless by the shadows, he mutters, "Are you Mary Clarke?" Before she can respond, a knife glistens in the gaslight and she becomes another victim of the Whitechapel murderer. The stylized credit design then "slashes" the title across the screen, punctuated by Jimmy McHugh and Pete Rugolo's intense score.

It should be noted that the British version of *Jack the Ripper* eschews Levine's overly self-indulgent exploitation; in a sense, the British version is presented as "just a movie," but Levine turns his presentation of the film into a carnival act. This is immediately sensed as the film opens: over the Paramount

Levine's carnival quality reaches its lurid climax as blood oozes through the floor-boards of an elevator car shot in color for Baker and Berman's otherwise black and white film biography of *Jack the Ripper*.

Pictures trademark, veteran radio announcer Paul Frees, like a barker, intones the following: "Ladies and gentlemen: You are about to see a masterpiece of mystery that has baffled even the experts. Try and match your wits against theirs. Watch every move. Listen to every word. Can you guess the identity of Jack the Ripper?" This is followed by that pre-credits sequence in which we are privy to the Ripper claiming his first victim. At this point the credits begin, and in Levine's version the title slashes across the screen by an animated knife accompanied by a new and jazzier musical score by Jimmy McHugh and Pete Rugolo. In the British version the title zooms out to full screen accompanied by a more traditional score by Stanley Black. In addition, the Ripper's fate is sealed at the bottom of an elevator shaft when he is crushed by the descending elevator, and for lurid detail there is a close shot of blood oozing through the floor boards of the elevator.

There is some controversy at this point relative to the exact Baker and Berman text. In the Levine version this bloody footage is in color resulting in an even more lurid effect, which is certainly in keeping with Levine's carnival act. But in the British version there was no color footage, and the issue would

Opening title sequence to the British version of Robert S. Baker and Monty Berman's *Jack the Ripper*.

be settled if not for comments by Andy Boot in his British horror film book *Fragments of Fear*, who derides the producers for ruining "the atmosphere and tension built up over the rest of the ninety minutes by adding the color scene" (75).[2] Whether Baker and Berman originally shot this brief scene in color remains in doubt, but the color effect nonetheless complements Levine's purpose.

Irrespective of Levine's motives, Baker and Berman, with the latter serving as photographer, imbued the extravagant qualities of Jimmy Sangster's narrative with a gritty yet expressionistic style. It is what David Pirie describe as a "fog-laden expressionism so inseparably associated with the Ripper in the English imagination" (Pirie 108). The crisp chiaroscuro photography turns the squalid East End into a shadow of London proper. That image, coupled with swirling fog, functions very similarly to the mountain and its swirling cold cloud in Baker and Berman's science fiction thriller *The Crawling Eye*, directed

---

[2]*Boot goes on to say that the "blood scene" had "censors in Memphis wildly declaiming that the film showed heads and hands amputated on screen." We were unable to substantiate any censorship of the film anywhere.*

by Quentin Lawrence from Sangster's screenplay. For Baker and Berman, the darkness and its fog evoke the misery of evil, whether that evil be a monster from outer space, a psychopath like the Ripper, or a social malignancy like Whitechapel. Just as the shadowy influence of the Trollenberg in *The Crawling Eye* turns men into crazed murderers, the shadowy influence of Whitechapel turns respectable men like Lord Sopwith (Bill Shine) and Mr. Blake (George Woodbridge) into lechers, and turns a respectable surgeon like Sir David Rogers (Ewen Solon) into a killer. More significant, the shadowy influence of places like Whitechapel transform people into obscene caricatures: women become sexual commodities and respectable citizens become mobs.

Baker and Berman's *Jack the Ripper* was ostensibly based on an original story by Peter Hammond and Colin Craig, but the crux of Sangster's script actually appropriates Leonard Matters' theory espoused in *The Mystery of Jack the Ripper*, which was originally published in 1929 but reissued with a new introduction in 1949 (Begg 322). Here, a deranged surgeon, Dr. Stanley, combs the squalid streets of Whitechapel in search of the prostitute who infected his deceased son with syphilis. Each victim is accosted by a caped figure who utters the name "Mary Jane Clarke" (i.e., Mary Kelly) before brutally killing her. The encounter, incidentally, is made all the more macabre by the eerie voice that mutters the name before each victim is dispatched in a suggested rather than literal depiction of the murders.

Sangster focuses the narrative on the Ripper's enigmatic search for Mary Clarke. The plot itself is centered on the plight of Inspector O'Neill (Eddie Byrne) of Scotland Yard and his American friend, Sam Lowry (Lee Patterson), in their fruitless search for Jack the Ripper. Since the knife wounds have been inflicted with precision, O'Neill and Lowry suspect members of the staff of a Whitechapel charity hospital run by the distinguished surgeon, Sir David Rogers. But the film is not a detective thriller in the "whodunit" tradition; instead, it is a quintessential suspense thriller, leaving the identity of the Ripper obscure until the climax, when his identity is revealed not by clever deduction but by simple divulgence. The secret is uncovered when the Ripper learns that a discharged patient named Kitty Knowles (Barbara Burke) is actually named Mary Clarke. The Ripper follows her to her flat where he reveals his identity as Sir David not only for Mary Clarke but for the audience as well. We then learn the significance of her name and his mad reasons for committing murder, which merely echo Matters' theory. To Sangster's credit, however, he offers enough red herrings, including an unsightly hunchback with the mundane name of Louis Benz (Endre Muller)—a hunchback figure carried over from Sangster's script for Cass' *Blood of the Vampire*—to preserve the identity of the Ripper until the moment of revelation. Also, to the film's credit there is no government corruption or cover-up; instead, Sir David's reign of terror is understood as wholly the work of a maddened individual, and the reason for his continued anonymity is played out by Sam O'Neill and Lowry in

Endre Muller as Louis Benz, the hunchbacked red herring in Baker and Berman's ***Jack the Ripper.***

a straightforward and simple manner: Lowry merely states that "we know [who he was] but we can't prove it."

Although successful financially, *Jack the Ripper* did not fare well with reviewers. Eugene Archer, in the *New York Times* (February 18, 1960), considered the film "incompetent, inadequate, and inept ... extravagant only in its amount of gore." A similar verdict was handed down by Paul V. Beckley, in the *New York Herald Tribune* (February 18, 1960), who complained that "theatrical effects take the place of plot as decor takes the place of mood."

The significance of *Jack the Ripper*, however, is that it marked something of a sea change in the exploitation of the Ripper as mass entertainment. Up to this point, Belloc Lowndes' lodger had proved the preferred method of telling the Ripper legend. After all, *The Lodger* had always reflected something of the Victorian tendency toward literary compromise. The artist's desire to tell an honest story was perpetually balanced against the Victorian decree that delicate religious and moral sensibilities be scrupulously respected. In this regard, *The Lodger* served as cover for the artistic exploitation of the Ripper's crimes while avoiding the responsibility of explicitly dealing with the sexual nature of those crimes. With Baker and Berman's *Jack the Ripper*, works of entertainment began

Jack the Ripper is revealed as Sir David Rogers (Ewen Solon) when he finds Mary Clarke (Barbara Burke) in Baker and Berman's *Jack the Ripper*.

to inch toward a more open and direct examination of the Ripper's hellish crimes. Appropriately, David Pirie discusses Baker and Berman under the heading of "Sadian," and Pirie claims that Baker and Berman "shot alternative versions for the continental market with more nudity and violence which resulted in an enthusiasm for their work in France and Belgium where the flavour of English decadence the films contained was much enjoyed" (108). On the other hand, Andy Boot correctly notes that Baker and Berman's English-speaking version of the film is "where the British approach works, [since] most people are aware of the ripper mutilations through folklore and history, and so the imagination can be far worse than anything Baker and Berman could squeeze past the censor" (74).

By the 1970s, the changing trends in the presentation and definition of cinematic horror made it inevitable that the Ripper would succumb to the mad slasher mentality captivating unthinking audiences (see Chapter III). This trend manifested itself in writer-director Jess Franco's *Jack the Ripper* (1976), a German film starring Klaus Kinski as the Ripper, who is now depicted as a sexually inhibited creature maddened by his relationship with his prostitute mother. According to Franco's script, the Ripper is an unnamed doctor (he is called simply "the doctor") who performs charitable work. He slays women as a result of some kind of internal rage seething below the charitable surface. Inspector Selby (Herbert Fux) searches for Jack the Ripper, but Selby is hopelessly ineffectual, receiving scorn from the community. Selby's girlfriend, a ballet dancer named Cynthia (Josephine Chaplin), decides to use herself as bait so that Selby may finally capture the Ripper and earn the respect that is due him. The Ripper kidnaps Cynthia and takes her to his botanical lair where he strips her, beats her and then rapes her. Before the Ripper can kill Cynthia, Selby breaks in the door causing the Ripper to flee to the upper level of his greenhouse. Selby asks Cynthia why she placed herself in jeopardy, and she answers insipidly that she did it because "I think I love you." Selby then orders the Ripper to come down, and in a most asinine and anticlimactic manner the Ripper merely obliges. Selby arrests the doctor as Jack the Ripper, but the doctor replies that, "You'll never prove it."

Franco's interpretation of the Ripper myth is nothing more than an excuse for presenting misogynistic horror complete with all the accoutrements of nudity, sexuality, gore and violence. Kinski's victims are beaten, raped and graphically mutilated on camera to an extent shunned by earlier Ripper films; close-ups of viscera during vivisection, including a detailed sequence in which the Ripper removes a victim's breasts, tend to objectify the female victims even more than the frequent nudity does. As such, the film is nothing more than a base exploitation feature, and the film's inattention to historical detail tends to reinforce the claim. Franco appropriates the Ripper's name and time period, but while Kinski's Ripper victims are women of the lowest class, they are not the Ripper's historical victims; they are showgirls at a tavern called Pike's Hole in London's Chelsea district, not Whitechapel. Kinski's victims, moreover, are dismembered and dumped into the Thames rather than left at the original scene of death for the next passerby to discover. But worse in a purely aesthetic sense is that there is little sympathy for the victims or for the Ripper's mental confusion; the women are simply sex commodities devoid of personality, and the Ripper is merely a killing machine. Even the very capable Kinski fails to imbue the Ripper with any personality. In one respect, however, the film is probably more faithful to the Ripper's motives than most films; Kinski's portrayal of a maddened, violent, depersonalized monster articulates the viciousness of the actual Ripper's deeds.

But what is so striking about Franco's film, the gore and sex notwithstanding, is that the squalor of London's East End as well as political implications are ignored. Nowhere in the film is Pike's Hole considered degenerate. The dark alleys are clean and appealing rather than soiled and forbidding. Moreover, the prostitutes and the sex trade are not presented as decadent, squalid, or even undesirable; they are presented as acceptable commerce, much like Franco's film itself. To underscore his point, the few characters who condemn the sex trade are depicted as old-fashioned intellectual dwarfs or

Blood spatters on the doctor's face as he removes his victim's breasts in Jess Franco's misogynistic horror film *Jack the Ripper* (1976).

oppressive moralists, made quite apparent by the homely dowager who objects to the prostitutes' discussion of menstruation during one of Selby's interrogations.

The overall effect of the film is unsettling as a result of all this. Rather than articulating the decadence of Whitechapel or eliciting compassion for the victims, as do most Ripper films in some variation, Franco's *Jack the Ripper* does just the opposite. In fact, the film venerates the Ripper. There is a certain delight to the carnage as Franco's camera, told from the Ripper's point of view, focuses on every detail of rape and murder. Franco seems to delight in this misogyny, and through vicarious means he and his audience become Jack the Ripper. The audience enjoys the carnage for no reason other than to enjoy the brutality before it.

What is ultimately most unsettling about Franco's film is the unhappy realization that an expanding segment of our society has come to accept this level of bestiality and human carnage as perfectly acceptable entertainment. Franco's *Jack the Ripper* is telling us truths about society's heightened threshold for perversity that warrant sober reflection.

If Franco's *Jack the Ripper* excreted an excess of psychosexual debasement and ignored history, then David Wickes' $9.5 million miniseries *Jack the Ripper* (1988) provided a hodgepodge of conspiratorial theories and an overindulgence of dubious historical characterizations. Produced to commemorate the Ripper's centenary, the film is ostensibly based on careful research and interviews with Ripper experts, but it fails to redeem itself as the serious drama it purports to be. Nonetheless, the film, as written by Derek Marlowe and Wickes, does take its lead from Sickert's theory. Wickes was responsible for a BBC documentary in 1973 titled *Jack the Ripper*, which introduced for the first time the allegations of Joseph Sickert. Sickert, as already mentioned, argued that the Ripper killings had been a plot on the part of the Queen's physician, Sir William Gull, and several highly placed Freemasons motivated to hide the embarrassing marriage of Prince Albert Victor to Annie Crook, a young Catholic woman who registered on the social scale barely above the Whitechapel prostitutes. Needless to say, the Sickert hypothesis was highly controversial, and it has since been examined and rejected by most serious students of the Ripper killings. Nonetheless, like the Stowell inspired theory that the Duke of Clarence was actually Jack the Ripper, Sickert's contention has taken root in the public mind. Sickert's explanation, whether by accident or design, was providentially timed to take advantage of the spreading public cynicism on both sides of the Atlantic that began taking hold in the 1960s as political scandals and dissent brought into question the legitimacy of governmental authority.

In *Jack the Ripper*, David Wickes again predicated his answer to the Ripper's identity upon Joseph Sickert's questionable evidence. It is unfortunate that in the process of preparing audiences for the premiere of *Jack the Ripper* the mistaken impression was instilled in many viewers that the film was somehow *the* definitive answer to the century old Ripper puzzle, thereby again giving credence to Sickert's theory. The scrolling prologue at the beginning of the film accentuates Wickes' averred "scholarly" approach; as the film opens, we are treated to the text and a soothing voice-over that states:

> For over 100 years the murders in Whitechapel committed by Jack the Ripper have baffled the world. What you are about to see is a dramatization of those events. Our story is based on extensive research, including a review of the official files by special permission of the Home Office and interviews with leading criminologists and Scotland Yard Officials.

Despite claims of extensive research, the film represents a rather eccentric historical interpretation, but the quality of acting and the high production values that enhance the picture add to the impression of the film's historical legitimacy. A close American equivalent is Oliver Stone's convoluted answer to the Kennedy assassination in his film *JFK* (1991).

Speaking reservedly of Wickes' effort, Ripper expert Donald Rumbelow, commenting for a 1995 Arts and Entertainment Network biography of Jack the Ripper, demurred. Rumbelow rightly states that:

> The films blur the issue. I've been astonished at the number of people, for
> instance, [who] look at the Michael Caine film, *Jack the Ripper*, and say
> "Oh, the mystery is solved." It's not. The whole thing, 99% of it, is fiction.
> But for a lot of people that's the solution to the case; so, therefore, if they
> do come across evidence, if they do come across documentation they're
> not going to put it forward because they think the mystery has been
> solved. It hasn't and that's one of the things we need to sort of get over.
> We are still looking for the identity of Jack the Ripper.

What is important here is that none of this would matter much if Wickes'
Jack the Ripper were permitted to stand or fall on its dramatic merits alone as
previous works in the Ripper canon had been allowed to do. The growing
trend of film and television is to assume the role of arbiters of historical truth
and relevancy as played out through the so-called "docu-drama." In this case,
Wickes centers his film on the struggling Frederick Abberline, an iconoclastic Metropolitan inspector whom the film names as the officer in overall charge
of the Whitechapel case, never mind that this is not accurate (Begg 8). What
matters here is that Wickes has a mouthpiece for his own interpretation of the
truth, and as such Abberline becomes the modern stereotypical doubter of
authority on a self-righteous mission for justice. Abberline shouts at one point,
"I hate politicians," thereby, undoubtedly, receiving the cheering accolades of
viewers who share that sentiment.

Interestingly, Wickes does stop short of a full restatement of the Sickert
theory. Sir William Gull, while culpable, is deemed to have acted out of personal madness rather than as part of a broader plot to conceal a scandalous
royal marriage. Political cover-up and suppression of evidence becomes integral to the plot, however, as Gull's guilt is kept from the public because of his
close relationship with the Royal Family. But in lieu of a full-blown recitation
of the Sickert plot line, Wickes chose to insert a lengthy sub-plot involving
the American actor, Richard Mansfield. The Mansfield redherring functions
as an intriguing, even clever roman à clef and it is historically accurate that
Mansfield was appearing at the Lyceum in the dual role of Dr. Jekyll and Mr.
Hyde during the time of the Ripper murders. Connection often has been made
between Stevenson's *Dr. Jekyll and Mr. Hyde* and Jack the Ripper, as noted.
Moreover, the hypothesis that Mansfield the actor might have conceivably
suffered from such a similar schizophrenic personality, leading to the Ripper's
murderous crime spree, has elements of entertaining melodrama, as Edwin
Zbonek recognized in *The Monster of London City*, based on a novel by Bryan
Edgar Wallace. Nonetheless, as previously underscored, no serious basis seems
to exist to support the contention that Mansfield had ever been a valid suspect
or had ever known any of the victims.

The quarrel with Wickes' approach to *Jack the Ripper* is not the degree or
nature of dramatic license employed by the filmmaker; every creative individual, from Sophocles through Shakespeare to Oliver Stone, has shunned

historical accuracy when that accuracy fails to conform to dramatic effect. The quarrel is with the public presumption of a film's historical credibility which is often manufactured by the artist through the means of the modern docudrama. Dramatic effect is no longer *dramatic effect* but historical accuracy; films that were once just films — presentations, not representations, of history — now masquerade as historical documents. Audiences are either willing to accept, or are unable or ill-prepared to challenge, the ideas that are conveyed as fact or truth through such films. As a result, history gives way to propaganda in a manner it never has before.

Wickes concludes his film with the same device used to open the film, a scrolling text accompanied by a soothing voice-over summation that draws strength, like the prologue, from its attempt at being objective:

> In the strange case of Jack the Ripper, there was no trial and no signed confession. In 1888, neither fingerprinting nor bloodtyping was in use and no conclusive forensic documentary or eye-witness testimony was available. Thus, positive proof of the Ripper's identity is not available. We have come to our conclusions after careful study and painstaking deduction. Other researchers, criminologists and writers may take a different view. We believe our conclusions to be true.

Again, Wickes gives the impression that his film has been a scholarly inquiry, but of particular and amusing note are the extensive credits which run at the film's completion that summarily abrogate any impression of scholarship. Recognition is extended in virtually all directions, including a bow to the boom operator, gaffer, property buyer, prosthetic makeup artists, stunt arranger and production accountant. Nowhere in that long list is acknowledgment given by name to any of the "leading criminologists" or "Scotland Yard officials" who we were assured in the prologue had been consulted. Such lack of attribution may be of little consequence in ordinary filmmaking, but it is a dubious omission for any work that presents itself as a serious piece of historical research.

III

BROTHER TO THE DARKNESS

In recent years, primarily because of the commercial success of works by such writers as Stephen King, Peter Straub and Clive Barker, and because of an ever increasing deterministic methodology rooted in psychological, social, cultural and ideological thematic analyses, what is now referred to as the "horror genre" has gained if not legitimacy at least passing recognition as a bonafide pedigree of fiction.[1] But prior to this acknowledgment of what was otherwise considered a tired old formula plot, the horror story was ignored by literary critics, and as a result it was pretty much relegated to the "pulp mills" of the 1930s where journeyman writers ground out 30,000 word novels at two cents a word on a weekly basis. Extensions of the Victorian "penny dreadfuls," as the English called them, the pulp magazines were printed on cheap paper (hence, pulp) which reflected, for the elite at least, the quality of the magazines' content as well.

One such magazine specializing in horror was *Weird Tales*, which began publication in 1923 and lasted for 37 years even though, according to Peter Haining, the magazine never turned a profit (10). At the magazine's peak, it was the literary home of H. P. Lovecraft, a writer who remains for the most part the sovereign of American horror fiction. He is so known, despite writing tales of the supernatural that are particularly short on style but long on imagination. Only because of his output and the creation of his celebrated *Cthulhu Mythos*, a series of stories detailing a whole schematic of monstrous "Great Old Ones" whose object is to regain possession of the earth from humans. Because of a modern interest in Lovecraft and because of the magazine's uniqueness among pulps, *Weird Tales* itself has received homage from

---

[1]*Stephen King's novels are studied as closely — and frequently revered as much — as those of Poe and Hawthorne. As if to drive the point home that King's works are serious literature, King's likeness now joins the likenesses of Poe, Hawthorne, Melville and Hemingway on the walls of Barnes and Noble bookstores.*

modern horror specialists like King, Straub and Barker, and, if for no other reason, the magazine remains a cultural artifact for twentieth century popular culture critics.

One of the magazine's premier contributors was Robert Bloch, himself a disciple of Lovecraft, whose renown rests singularly on Alfred Hitchcock's production of Bloch's novel *Psycho*. First published in 1959, it was based loosely on the infamous Ed Gein case about murder and cannibalism in Wisconsin in 1957. Bloch wrote in his autobiography that he based his "story on the *situation* rather than on any person, living or dead, involved in the Gein affair; indeed, I knew very little of the details concerning that case and virtually nothing about Gein himself at the time. It was only some years later, when doing my essay on Gein for *The Quality of Murder* [edited by Anthony Boucher], that I discovered how closely the imaginary character I'd created resembled the real Ed Gein both in overt act and apparent motivation" (228). But one of Bloch's short stories — one of many by the prolific Bloch — remains a benchmark for tales about Jack the Ripper. Bloch, like J. F. Brewer years before him (*The Curse Upon Mitre Square*), transforms Jack the Ripper from a common murderer into a supernatural demon.

At this point it needs to be noted that a subclassification of supernatural Ripper fiction is what we call the "waxwork motif." In such tales — which owe their inspiration certainly to the Ripper's representation in Madame Tussaud's celebrated waxworks in London — Jack the Ripper is an exhibit in a "chamber of horrors" inside a wax museum. According to the narrative structure of these tales, the wax figure becomes ambulatory as night falls and then embarks on yet another reign of terror.

German filmmaker Paul Leni's *Das Wachsfigurenkabinett/Waxworks* (1924) is the precursor of such stories. His stylish anthology presents the lives of various characters on exhibit in a carnival waxworks, and the final sequence depicted a nightmare in which the dreamer and his betrothed are pursued by the Ripper — here called "Spring-heeled Jack" — through an expressionistic maze. The waxworks motif was also evident in an episode of Rod Serling's *The Twilight Zone* titled "The New Exhibit," broadcast April 4, 1963. In this 60-minute episode written by Jerry Sohl, with screen credit given to Charles Beaumont (see Appendix C), and directed by John Brahm (who had directed the 1944 version of *The Lodger*), the murderous activity of the Ripper (David Bond) is actually the invention of the deranged mind of murderer Martin Senescu (Martin Balsam), the proprietor of a private wax museum. Similarly, the narrative of Georg Fenady's *Terror in the Wax Museum*, theatrically released by Cinerama Releasing in 1973, suggests that the wax figure of Jack the Ripper (Don Herbert), is possessed by an evil force. Specifically, the Ripper is blamed for the murder of Claude Duprée (John Carradine), the owner of the wax museum. In Andrew Fenady's screen story adapted by Jameson Brewer, however, the murders are actually committed by pub owner Tim Fowley (Louis Hayward) while masquerading as the person-ages of the exhibits.

Bloch's short story "Yours Truly, Jack the Ripper," first published in the July 1943 edition of *Weird Tales*, set the mold for the many works that take Jack the Ripper from the realm of crime fiction (i.e., from the realm of history) to the realm of supernatural horror, and it is in such tales that the truest mythic representation of Jack the Ripper is unveiled. Here the Ripper emerges as not just a criminal harassing London, as depicted in Belloc Lowndes' *The Lodger*, but rather as an absolute malevolent presence loose in the civilized world. As such, and because of Bloch's theme, the Ripper has become a major figure in the literary genre of horror. The Ripper's name may be absent but his pres-ence is nonetheless sensed in the spate of slasher films whose narratives may or may not be rooted in the supernatural but whose renderings are always hor-rifying, both aesthetically and morally. Hence, Jack the Ripper is now barely distinguishable from such other demonic figures in literature as Dracula and Mr. Hyde.

In "Yours Truly, Jack the Ripper," Bloch fashions a first person narrative about a distinguished Briton named Sir Guy Hollis who arrives in modern Chicago in pursuit of Jack the Ripper, whom he believes is still alive. Accord-ing to Sir Guy's implausible theory, Jack the Ripper was a sorcerer whose killings and mutilations were actually sacrifices to "Hecate and the dark gods" who grant "boons of eternal youth." Sir Guy's theory proves correct when Sir Guy himself becomes yet another victim. Afterward, the narrator, John Car-mody (with whom we have felt sympathy throughout the course of events), confides that Sir Guy — indeed, we — should address him as "Jack" not John.

To fully understand the effectiveness of Bloch's story, both as horror story and Ripper story, we need to make ourselves familiar with the critical patterns inherent in the horror story. It would be tempting at this juncture to subvert the literary elite by integrating the various new methodologies of popular crit-icism in an attempt to elevate horror stories into a sort of pantheon of liter-ary forms. But justifying the stories' esteem by analyzing their qualities according to their cultural effects, namely their psychological and ideological effects, is a tendency that is all too frequent in contemporary analyses of pop-ular culture. This is the attitude taken by Tom Milne and Paul Willemen in *The Encyclopedia of Horror Movies*, edited by Phil Hardy, which is indicative of the critical attitude of many current journals, magazines and reviews. In an evaluation of Bob Clark's *Murder by Decree*, the writers argue that

> the script doesn't have the courage of its convictions and fudges the issue [of government cover-up] in a lengthy scene in which Holmes directly confronts and accuses the leaders of government but then lets them off the hook, becoming part of the cover-up himself.... If the film-makers had been able to muster more political courage their movie could have been a very powerful masterpiece [331].

But if we value a work as such, we deny a story to be just that, a story; what we do is ignore its inherent value — and thus cheapen the work — by assigning value germane to the work's relevance to cultural themes, as transient as those themes are. According to such thinking, a work is good only because it meets a prescribed social agenda. In this regard, a work like David Wickes' *Jack the Ripper* is seen as possessing superior value because of its social relevance; that in addition to denouncing Victorian hypocrisy the telefilm affirms the claims made by such outspoken critics as filmmaker Oliver Stone about insidious government conspiracies. In this frame, a work like Bloch's "Yours Truly, Jack the Ripper" would possess lesser value because it makes absolutely no overt commentary whatever about social ills, psychological difficulties or ideological perceptions.

For our purposes, we return to a simpler aesthetic methodology for analyzing the horror story: inherent in the horror story is, to use the label that Patrick Lucanio applies in *Them or Us*, the story's "alternate world" appeal and its singleness of *effect*. It is necessary at this point to differentiate the two terms "horror" and "gothic." The latter is preferred to designate the traditional supernatural stories featuring the Ripper, since today the term horror conveys a much different meaning from that in the past, and it is problematic to our cause to use the term.

To use the word horror to describe such films as those in the slasher series as well as Jess Franco's *Jack the Ripper* is proper since the intention of such films, primarily through their gruesome imagery, is to elicit from the viewer a repulsion which might be said to define horror even as the actual effect if a sort of demented ecstasy among audiences — which is itself horrifying. Sheer common sense, all too frequently missing in discussions about such films, also tells us that a steady diet of such images cannot be healthy. Professors Daniel Linz and Edward Donnerstein concluded in a *World Health* article that their "studies do not prove that men who watched sexually violent films will commit rape as a result, [but] they *do* show that these men will find rape and violence against women more acceptable" (27).

David Toolan asserts in "Voyeurs of Savage Fury" that, "When ... we are inured, overdosed with shocks so that we no longer feel violated when a woman is raped, a panhandler has his eyes gouged out or his skull bashed in, all in living color, then art and special effects are collaborating with the enemy of the human spirit" (460). Toolan makes a salient argument here when he notes the symbiosis between art and special effects, a distinction that leads to our own differentiation between the horrific and the gothic.

The value of much of modern film is found in form alone. Content has transfigured itself commensurate with advances in technology; as technology has altered the means of artistic production, the content of artistic production has been altered as well. By appreciating the use of *suggestion* and *understatement* found in the classic narrative, content which was once suggested is now plainly apparent, made distinct by these immediate advances in technology. The depiction of violent acts which are so profuse in modern cinema (and not just in slasher films) could not have been made possible without the development of amazing prosthetic — i.e., technological — makeup effects engineered within the past twenty years. Gruesome detail, the result of those violent acts, is proudly and pervasively paraded, as in Jess Franco's *Jack the Ripper*. Even a cursory sampling of these images reveals that such depictions are not intended as images of aversion or sorrow; they are as images of celebration or, worse, images of want if only by their detail and quantity. The critical response is seldom one of disgust or repulsion, nor is the critical response one in which the critic interprets questions of inhumanity implicit within such images. Rather, the response is an analysis of how well the effect was *effected*, or a wholesale disregard — perhaps disinterest — for the effect. The former is certainly true with respect to violent video games in which positive critical responses are concomitant to lifelike depictions of vicious mayhem which in turn aids in marketing the games.

But the technological changes that allowed for more "graphic realism" — particularly as that realism related to violence — has wholly displaced creative suggestion with a bland literalness to the point that there is no distinction among images of a monster's rampage, wartime battle scenes, or traffic fatalities. As a result, form alone designates content — horror — and by extension form designates that which is considered aesthetically "good."

The demands of such depictions are so pervasive that they have created their own set of expectations that must be met. Hardly a movie thriller is released without an R rating which invariably signals (signifies in semiotic parlance) to audiences that the film is "rough," meaning that the film will contain amoral violence, nudity, profanity and sex depicted in what many reviewers have described as a "realistic and raw" manner (and, in a particularly mulish sense of critical response, "mature"). The pervasiveness of such minute detail of carnage engendered the slasher films, and like pornography the narratives of the slasher films are structured around a set number of visual situations. Instead of sex acts, however, the slasher film centers its narrative around graphic mutilations all effected by superior technology separated by obtuse plot contrivances. The graphic sequences create their own audiences, and the audiences demand that their expectations be met. This attitude is not limited to the exploitation filmmakers; indeed, this evidently drives mainstream filmmakers as well. *Newsweek* reported in its April 1, 1991, issue that director Jonathan Demme decided a scene in *The Silence of the Lambs* (1991) was "so tame — a long shot that pulled away from any detail — that the audience was cheated" (52).

If this were not enough, critical reaction invariably involves if not outright adoration of the special effects sequences — even to the point of raising makeup artists to celebrity status — at least a first amendment defense of its gruesome presence, a fiat that has consequently made legitimate that which was prized in ancient Rome but at one not-too-distant time scorned by modern civilization. Martin Scorsese, whose films are notorious for their violent and horrific detail, remarked in *Newsweek* that, "Maybe we need bloodletting like the ancient Romans — as ritual — but not real like the Roman circus" (51). The question remains, however, that with technology blurring the line between reality and fantasy, where do Scorsese's rituals stop and the actual events begin?

With technology leading the way through its triumvirate of film–television–rock music all controlled by the synergistic empires and through its solemnization of the mass or democratic media, the line between high culture and popular culture is blurred — if not outright eliminated — to make distinctions between the two a notion of the past. In this context T. S. Eliot is "high brow" and elitist, but Stephen King is populist and "relevant." Popular entertainment — forged by technology — has become the dominant form of creative expression in the Western world if only through economic and cultural peremptoriness. As a consequence, our evolution of political and social systems are no longer the province of great books by great thinkers but the province of the ever mass-induced media by capricious and self-indulgent "artists" who savor their own self-made celebrity status.

We need to define "horror" in its proper context to see correctly the value of Bloch's story. To distinguish such a story from slasher films and Stephen King works, "Yours Truly, Jack the Ripper" and stories like it are referred to as "gothic" if only for clarity. Thus, the gothic story is defined accordingly: it includes the "supernatural" in its narrative. The supernatural is rightly characterized by media historian Denis Gifford as a work in which an "element of fantasy is essential ... [i.e.,] the impossible rather than the improbable" (13). But Glenn St. John Barclay, in *An Anatomy of Horror*, dislikes the use of "supernatural," since "anything that can be experienced in any form at all must exist in nature, and therefore, deserves to be categorized as natural" (127). He prefers "occult" since "paranormal phenomena" (also an unsatisfactory term) are "certainly 'hidden' from us in the sense that they cannot be analyzed experimentally or theorized about rigorously the way that normal physical phenomena can. This is of course what makes them paranormal" (127). Preferring simply "supernatural," however, we are in agreement with Barclay's definition that such elements cannot be analyzed experimentally.

The gothic story is sketched by its reliance upon the exotic to convey its meaning, and this is to say that both its characters and its milieu are part of that alternate world alluded to earlier. Characters and settings are estranged from the actual world, and hence they function primarily as symbols rather than representations of actual things. Each reduced to moral absolutes of good and evil, stereotypical characters play out the conflict before a landscape that, as Elizabeth MacAndrew rightly notes in *The Gothic Tradition in Fiction*, comes from the world of art and imagination whose primary function is to "convey mood, tone, and emotions" (47–48); For example, a setting is not Chicago per se but what a travel brochure tells us about Chicago and what we imagine Chicago to be like.

As noted earlier, the qualities of the gothic story merge to form a singleness of effect, horror. Horror in this regard does not refer to repulsion but to the very real emotion of fear; moreover, this horror is elicited not necessarily by shock, and certainly not by disgust and repulsion, but through milieu. Lovecraft himself, in his spirited analysis of horror titled *Supernatural Horror in Literature*, writes that "the oldest and strongest emotion of mankind is fear ... [and] men with minds sensitive to heredity impulse will always tremble at the thought of the hidden and fathomless worlds of strange life which may pulsate in the gulfs beyond the stars, or press hideously upon our own globe in unholy dimensions which only the dead and the moonstruck can glimpse" (12, 14). The artist creates a fearful ambience which frequently finds form in the exotic and alternate worlds depicted. Hence, the gothic story elicits trepidation, and formally it uses *suggestion* and *understatement* to summon the human factor of fear in both an emotional and intellectual sense. It is suggestion and understatement, not explicit detail, that create the proper aesthetic value of the horror story, a point that is well made by critics who continually analyze and praise Henry James's *The Turn of the Screw* (1898) as well as the unequaled works of 1940s RKO Radio Pictures filmmaker Val Lewton.

What the gothic story does best is to use suggestion as well as understatement to "objectify fear" by giving fear a specific form; hence, the horror tale gives form to our fears in everything from alien monsters in science fiction works to Jack the Ripper in gothic works. John Cawelti, in *Adventure, Mystery, and Romance*, notes that "the key characteristic of the type is the representation of some alien being or state and the underlying moral fantasy is our dream that the unknowable can be known and related to in some meaningful fashion" (49). The effect may be to arouse fear, but the tale's overall consequence is to purge us of "the fear of fear" by making our dread malleable. Hence the horror story is very much like comedy, as Cawelti asserts, he argues that comedy often sets up situations that are dangerous or disturbing, such as the frantic Mack Sennett chases of the silent era, but through the bungling of the hero we discover that the dread that had gripped us was far less potent than we had thought (49). Likewise, the gothic story sets up situations in which fear is pervasive, such as a spectre prowling the dark fog-shrouded streets of old London, but through the courage of the hero we discover that the dead of night is far less intimidating that we had thought.

This long analysis of horror fiction is necessary in order to see just how Bloch's story serves as excellent proof that horror need not be basted in explicit gore to be effective. Indeed, Bloch's tale not only elicits dread, primarily through atmosphere, but it purges dread through its celebrated ironic ending. As a gothic horror tale, it has few rivals, despite its modern setting.

Structurally, "Yours Truly, Jack the Ripper" follows a simple four-part design marked distinctly by four changes of setting. Bloch opens his story in the office of John Carmody, a psychiatrist, where Sir Guy relates a succinct history of the Jack the Ripper crimes before telling Carmody that he believes the Ripper is loose in Chicago. Carmody objects to such a claim, arguing that a man of 85 years couldn't possibly be murdering young women in Chicago. At this point Sir Guy offers his theory, asserting that Jack the Ripper has never grown older. Admitting that his theory is a crazy one, he states a maxim that could easily elicit agreement from any modern Ripperologist: "All the theories about the Ripper are crazy. The idea that he was a doctor. Or a maniac. Or a woman. The reasons advanced for such beliefs are flimsy enough. There's nothing to go by. So why would my notion be any worse?" Carmody replies that even doctors and maniacs grow old, but Sir Guy will not be dissuaded by mere logic; he then advances his theory in detail:

> What about *sorcerers*? ... Necromancers. Wizards. Practicers of Black Magic? ... I studied everything. After awhile I began to study the dates of the murders. The pattern those dates formed. The rhythm. The solar, lunar, stellar rhythm. The sidereal aspect. The astrological significance.... Suppose Jack the Ripper didn't murder for murder's sake alone? Suppose he wanted to make — a sacrifice? ... It is said that if you offer blood to the dark gods that they grant boons. Yes, if a blood offering is made at the proper time — when the moon and the stars are right — and with the proper ceremonies — they grant boons. Boons of youth. Eternal youth.[2]

At this juncture, Lovecraft's influence on Bloch is evident. Bloch never truly identifies the "dark gods," although in an especially ironic yet subtle clue to the Ripper's identity, Carmody surveys his "neighbors and began to *wonder*.... How many of them were playing a part, concealing something? How many would worship Hecate and grant that horrid goddess the dark boon of blood?" Sir Guy states later that, "a mad beast is loose on this world! An ageless, eternal beast, sacrificing to Hecate and the dark gods!" But Bloch never specifically delineates this Hecate as the mythic "Terrible Mother" who devours men other than to make reference to a goddess. In other works, however, Bloch is quite explicit with respect to the mythology, such as the ample treatment of Egyptian mythology in "The Opener of the Way" (1936). In "Yours Truly, Jack the Ripper" Bloch merely drops the name Hecate, leaving us essentially with the generic dark gods as the true power for the Ripper's existence. As such, the dark gods' influence is not unlike the direct "Cthulhian" influence in Bloch's Lovecraftian works like "The Shambler from the Stars" (*Weird Tales,* September 1935). The theme of a pact with dark gods is pervasive in the Bloch canon, reaching its zenith in his Hugo award-winning story "The Hell-Bound Train"

---

[2]*All references to Bloch's "Yours Truly, Jack the Ripper" are from* The Harlot Killer *(New York: Dell, 1953), an anthology of Ripper fiction edited by Allan Barnard.*

ROBERT BLOCH
Author
"PSYCHO", "YOURS TRULY.
JACK THE RIPPER"

Robert Bloch, in a frame enlargement from the ABC television series *Secrets of the Unknown*, discusses the "brother of darkness."

published in the September 1958 edition of *The Magazine of Fantasy and Science Fiction*. As a supernatural element, it is easy to conclude that the dark gods remain pretty much Lovecraftian, if only by circumstance. But what is important is that the Ripper seems to be an extension of the dark gods. Amazingly, even Carmody balks at any kind of explanation for his existence; he is simply matter-of-fact, existing without explanation. Carmody, like those Lovecraftian researchers ever decoding the sacred writings of Cthulhu, has somehow discovered the secrets of eternity by making a pact with the dark gods, or perhaps with Hecate herself.

It is significant at this point in the story that Carmody, also like those Lovecraftian researchers, is no simple man but rather a man of letters, a member of the "so-called intelligentsia." As a psychiatrist, Carmody is sought out by Sir Guy because Carmody is the ideal man for his purpose. Sir Guy tells Carmody that, "You number among your acquaintances many writers, painters, poets. The so-called intelligentsia. The Bohemians. The lunatic fringe from the near north side" which seems to draw the Ripper. It is at this point that Bloch begins making an estranged, alternate world out of mundane trappings. In fact, Bloch turns the mundane into the bizarre by ever transfiguring his milieu, moving slowly from a Chicago office through the "lunatic fringe from the near north side" and a ginmill "off South Clark Street" to culminate in a dark alley whose fog resembles "London fog" in the month of November — "the place and the time of the Ripper murders," Sir Guy notes.

Accordingly, the characters grow ever more eccentric — ever more estranged from the norm — concomitantly to the settings. From the office of a respectable psychiatrist, Bloch takes us to the studio of Lester Baston — described by Carmody as "a real screwball" — where we meet the "lunatic fringe." It is here that Sir Guy gets a "monocle-full," as Carmody quips, of the members of the intelligentsia. Bloch writes that Sir Guy

> saw LaVerne Gonnister, the poetess, hit Hymie Kralik in the eye. He saw Hymie sit down on the floor and cry until Dick Pool accidentally stepped on his stomach as he walked through to the dining-room for a drink. He heard Nadia Vilinoff the commercial artist tell Johnny Odcutt that she thought his tattooing was in dreadful taste, and he saw Barclay Melton crawl under the dining-room table with Johnny Odcutt's wife.

Here Bloch plays up the stereotypes with purpose; he describes a world in which the elite eschew the social norm with self-indulgent resolve, and such a description may be stereotypical but it nonetheless illustrates the often hostile view of the intelligentsia by what is otherwise described as the common folk. But even more discerning is that Bloch depicts the group as itself eccentric. In fact, the group *accepts* Sir Guy's theory, but the members of this lunatic fringe accept the theory solely for its eccentricity and not for any inherent value — much like the manner in which our modern popular culture critics radically accept "cult films," particularly those of Edward D. Wood, Jr. Baston, always referring to Sir Guy as "the Walrus," states that Sir Guy "isn't kidding" about his search for the Ripper, but then just as quickly slaps Sir Guy on the back, telling the group that:

> Our English cousin is really on the trail of the fabulous Jack the Ripper. You all remember Jack the Ripper, I presume? Quite a cutup in the old days, as I recall. Really had some ripping good times when he went out on a tear.

We are then reminded that, "The tension was gone, the mood shattered, and the whole thing was beginning to degenerate into a trivial party joke."

Bloch next takes us to the "colored neighborhood off South Clark Street" where Sir Guy wants to wander because he has a hunch. Sir Guy states that:

> There's the same geographical conformation in these streets as in those courts where the Ripper roamed and slew. That's where we'll find him, John. Not in the bright lights of the Bohemian neighborhood, but down here in the darkness. The darkness where he waits and crouches.

Carmody and Sir Guy eventually find refuge in a dive where they order drinks until Sir Guy becomes, in Bloch's words, "*in vino veritas*," or drunk. Bloch has now taken us deeper into his alternate world; for, this neighborhood is a particularly tough neighborhood inhabited by unsavory characters. Bloch's descriptions of the neighborhood are perhaps true in that, "Some of these Negro places resent white customers," but Bloch's description of the bartender as a "black giant with prognathous jaw and ape-like torso" is racist. In that particularly innocent era of the 1940s, however, when racist attitudes were the norm — shared by even the elite — the inclusion of the black neighborhood signified exoticism; after all, racial divides create mystery which all too often gets transformed into suspicion and ultimately into hatred. But here the gin-mill, the dive, the exotic bartender create for us Bloch's world of "darkness and shadow" to which Sir Guy is convinced the Ripper will be drawn. "He's bound to come," Sir Guy says because "he'll be drawn here." Sir Guy lectures that:

> This is what I've been looking for. A *genus loci*. An evil spot that attracts evil. Always, when he slays, it's in the slums. You see, that must be one of his weaknesses. He has a fascination for squalor. Besides, the women he needs for sacrifice are more easily found in the dives and stewpots of a great city.

Here Sir Guy is simply correct; the Ripper is at home in such squalor since he feeds on the depravity of humanity.

Time through cliché has taken its toll on Bloch's surprise ending, but anyone reading the story soon discovers just how transparent the ending is anyway. This is not Bloch's deficiency as a writer, but it is evidence of a proficient writer of horror stories. The ending is actually the story's strength in that it does not rest so much on the ending as surprise, the sudden revelation that the narrator, with whom we have had sympathy, is the killer, but rather on the admission itself. By using a first person point of view, Bloch clearly establishes that the Ripper is not an objective evil (an omnipotent force "out there") but a subjective one, an omnipotent force that lives within us all. Bloch demonstrates this by allowing the Ripper to take us into his confidence; moreover, Bloch mirrors the ubiquitous "I" of the narrative to reflect back to us. After all, we become the Ripper. It is not Carmody who whispers "Never mind the 'John,' just call me — 'Jack'" as much as it is the reader who whispers the words and raises the knife. We indeed read it, we say it, we acknowledge it: We *are* Jack the Ripper.

Bloch himself writes that his story "has continued to lead a charmed life in print, and on radio and television ... [to the point that] over the years Jack and I have become blood brothers" (196). Charmed life indeed; by Bloch's own estimation the story has seen well over 50 "revivals" in its 50-plus years of existence. In part this is due to Bloch's heavy use of dialogue and his four simple settings; such a structure made the transition from pulp magazine to radio drama desirable. Those dark and sinister miasmatic alleys of nineteenth century Whitechapel and the uncountable other venues where Ripper-like murders have been conceived and executed just lend themselves admirably to the mental and emotional images that radio listeners create for themselves. Hence, just as the eerie, fog-laden byways of *The Lodger* found a receptive home in the imaginative minds of radio listeners, the frightening dens of Chicago's south side of "Yours Truly, Jack the Ripper" found a similar retreat.

According to Bloch, the first dramatization of "Yours Truly, Jack the Ripper" was broadcast January 7, 1944, on the CBS variety series *The Kate Smith Show*. Bloch wrote in the "Eyrie" (letters to the editor) section of *Weird Tales* (July 1945) that, "For many years I've had certain pet ideas about doing a radio 'horror show' of my own ... the closest I came to realizing my ambition in the past was when Laird Cregar did 'Yours Truly, Jack the Ripper' over the Kate Smith hour in '44" (Haining 199). We have taken the date of the broadcast from Sam Moskowitz's insightful study of Bloch in *Seekers of Tomorrow: Masters of Modern Science Fiction* (346).

Laird Cregar, who was currently starring as Mr. Slade in John Brahm's *The Lodger* (officially released by 20th Century–Fox on the very date of the broadcast), portrayed Carmody in the 15-minute sketch in which Carmody narrates the story; amazingly, the sketch ends with Carmody's admission that he is, indeed, Jack the Ripper. As innocuous as the ending sounds in our modern era, it nonetheless seems to run contrary to radio's standards that were outlined in the previous chapter. In context, the ending mitigates radio's fear of unjust compensation; the ultimate revelation of Carmody's true identity as Jack the Ripper serves only to validate what had been to that point perceived as Sir Guy's insane obsession. The concluding words of Carmody that we "Never mind the 'John,' just call me ... 'Jack'," remain the concluding words of the radio adaptation but with an emphasis on the *revelation*, not the Ripper's impending murder of Sir Guy. The audience is free to imagine that the Ripper is about to kill and escape into the fog; in fact, as the drama ends there are no creative sound effects employed to nudge the listener along to any conclusion. We do not hear the Ripper's knife plunging into Sir Guy's body, nor do we hear a lifeless body falling to ground. The faint of heart are at perfect liberty to invent an ending in which the police arrive and frighten off the Ripper. It is fair to conclude here that based on the logic of radio, Carmody's words may lead *in medias res* just as well as to denouement.

It needs to be noted at this point that the recording used for review was a single 15-minute sketch with no introduction or closing. The performance was acted by only two individuals playing Carmody and Sir Guy. It is not possible to detect Cregar's voice in the performance, however, nor to discern the context in which the sketch was included in the Kate Smith variety series.

Bloch adapted his story for his own series, *Stay Tuned for Terror*, a syndicated drama produced and directed by John Neblett. The production history remains obscure; apparently there are no recordings available of this series. Bloch writes that he now had the opportunity to knock "on the lid of my coffin in the shape of an assignment to adapt my own stories for *Stay Tuned for Terror*. This series of 15-minute programs is being transcribed at CBS studios in Chicago. A remarkable radio voice has been found in Craig Dennis, the narrator, and he is supported by a large and versatile cast. Original organ scores are used in each show, and the production is supervised by Johnnie Neblett of 'So the Story Goes' fame" (Haining 199–200). The program may have been also titled *Weird Tales* since Bloch notes that the magazine "has generously permitted the use of its name, and I trust that the program will prove worthy of this distinction" (Haining 200). Also, a full page advertisement in the magazine indicated that "*Weird Tales* is on the air .... in *Stay Tuned for Terror*."

A year later on March 6, 1945, "Yours Truly, Jack the Ripper" was dramatized on the NBC series *Mollé Mystery Theatre* (Moskowitz 347) and the production was later incorporated in the syndicated anthology series *Mystery Playhouse*. Host Peter Lorre introduced the *Mystery Playhouse* repeat by noting appropriately that "there is the element of the supernatural in the story that will amaze you; for it seems that the spirit world has given the black heart of Jack the Ripper the power of everlasting life." The 30-minute adaptation essentially follows Bloch's structure, but a few changes were made. Carmody is given a nurse named Miss Cannister, and the Bohemian, brusque artist Lester Baston is now a more subdued Les Banton, a newspaper reporter. Bloch's ending remains intact, but radio's decorum is preserved by an epilogue assuring us that Carmody will face justice. Following the murder of Sir Guy, Carmody is arrested, and Miss Cannister tells Banton that Carmody believes that "the gods won't let him be executed." Moreover, she insists that Carmody "actually believes that he is Jack the Ripper" which convinces her that Carmody is insane. This worries Banton because he tells her that the "law doesn't execute the insane — it allows them to live." Miss Cannister expresses fear at the revelation that Carmody just might be the Ripper, but Banton interrupts her gasp, saying cautiously, "Who knows?"

The story's best known dramatization, however, was written for the NBC television series *Thriller* by playwright and screenwriter Barré Lyndon, who had written the script for Brahm's *The Lodger*. Produced by Hubbell Robinson Productions for Revue Studios (now Universal Television), Bloch's succinct narrative necessitated a broader purview considering the hour format for the series. Accordingly, Lyndon embellished the story with an irrelevant romance between painter Hymie Kralik (Adam Williams), an otherwise insignificant character in the original story, and his model Arlene (Nancy Valentine), who becomes the Ripper's fifth victim. Lyndon added a third major character, police detective Captain Pete Jago (Edmon Ryan), who replaces Carmody as the voice of skepticism.

Directed by actor Ray Milland, "Yours Truly, Jack the Ripper" was broadcast April 11, 1961. Unlike the short story, Lyndon's dramatization opened in the Ripper's own gaslight era. A young woman leaves a pub and hastens through the dense fog to her flat in Whitechapel. In spite of police protection the Ripper gains entry into her flat and makes her his final victim — a nod to the Ripper's last victim, Mary Jane Kelly, found mutilated in her flat. Milland then cuts to a bit of dark humor as a street singer, played by J. Pat O'Malley, warns us in song (composed by Jerry Goldsmith) to beware of "yours truly, Jack the Ripper." At this point, series host Boris Karloff offers a brief mono-logue recounting the Ripper murders — mistakenly reporting, that the police gave the Ripper his name — in the context of Bloch's theory about supernat-ural evil. The setting then changes to an unnamed contemporary American city where Sir Guy Hollis (John Williams), identified in the episode as a Scot-land Yard pathologist, astonishes police by predicting not only the number of victims of a vicious serial killer but the exact time of each murder. When Sir Guy contends that the murderer is the actual Jack the Ripper — who would be at least 90 years old — Captain Jago considers Sir Guy a crackpot. Sir Guy, however, is defended by John Carmody (Donald Woods), a police psychiatrist, and together they seek the Ripper in the city's artistic community.

The value of Lyndon's adaptation to Ripper lore is that Lyndon admirably amplified the otherwise loose connection in Bloch's original between the artis-tic ("so-called intelligentsia") and the Ripper himself. Lyndon — foreshadow-ing the modern fashionable view of creative expression — cleverly expanded the artistic community to include the sordid side of expression. A sleazy strip joint — which featured a prominent stripper named "Miss Beverly Hills" in her television debut — actually comes to represent the Ripper's raison d'être in the sense that both "art" and perversity in this instance satiate his hunger for per-manence and infuse his being with an aberrant vitality. At one point, Sir Guy notes that the Ripper is inherently drawn to such places, and he describes Miss Beverly Hills as "exactly the sort of woman who attracts the Ripper." Director Milland imbues the strip joint milieu with an energy that fires the Ripper into committing his ultimate act, that of destroying the very force that threatens to restrain him — Sir Guy. In a juxtaposition of scenes, a nervous Carmody (surrounded by plainclothes police awaiting the Ripper's appearance) leaves the table, ventures backstage to purportedly check on the safety of Miss Bev-erly Hills, and then returns to the table to hear Sir Guy describe the Ripper as a "figure of evil, a vampire who fattens not on blood but life itself, a ghoul nourished by death." But Sir Guy's descriptions and the debauched atmosphere of the strip joint serve only to fill Carmody with confidence; in spite of a swarm of police officers stationed around the strip joint, Carmody suggests that he and Sir Guy venture into a fog-shrouded alley where Carmody reveals his true self and succeeds in eliminating Sir Guy.

One of the episode's most effective attributes is the casting of Donald Woods as Carmody. Though most unassuming, Woods is a consummate actor with a certain commonplace presence about him, in this case endowing the Ripper with that special "everyman" characteristic so crucial to Bloch's effect. Had someone like horror icon Vincent Price, or even a veteran brute like Charles Bronson, portrayed Carmody the effect would not have been as effectual. The image of the "common man" walking into the fog after murdering Sir Guy in cold blood is a striking one if only for its incongruity. But the casting visually articulated Bloch's theme that the Ripper, indeed, lives in us all.

Bloch's original script for the NBC television series *Star Trek* titled "Wolf in the Fold," broadcast on December 22, 1967, forces us to face the prospect that the future is not a hiding place where our own inadequacies will be smoothed away. People may change in meager and superficial ways, he asserts, but certain primordial instincts will live on through eternity and beyond, a notion that echoes the monstrous presence in Guy de Maupassant's "The Horla." The setting here is the peaceful planet of Argelius II, where the tranquillity is shattered by a series of grisly murders allegedly committed by Engineer Scott (James Doohan) of the *Enterprise*. In an effort to discern the truth, the inquiry into the murders is moved aboard the Enterprise where the investigation reveals that a timeless force of inhumanity, once known on earth as Jack the Ripper and since cloaked under other names on other planets throughout the galaxy, is loose. It is "a hunger that never dies," as one survivor describes the evil force, adding that it is "strong, overpowering; an ancient terror ... [that] has a name — boratis, kesla, redjac ... devouring all life." The force itself boasts that it has "existed from the dawn of time" and that it "shall live beyond its end." As the inquiry unfolds, Captain James T. Kirk (William Shatner) is left to voice the obvious and unflattering conclusion that "when man moved out into the galaxy that thing must have moved with him." Eventually the force is beamed into space where its consciousness will live indefinitely but where it will be unable to manifest itself. Even then, Bloch maintains, the force is slated to become a lingering — if momentarily impotent — evil.

As further validation of his theory, Bloch transferred the specter of the Ripper into the future in "A Toy for Juliette," a story specially commissioned for Harlan Ellison's original speculative fiction anthology, *Dangerous Visions* (1967). Here, the Ripper has been plucked from the streets of Whitechapel to a city of the distant future where he becomes a sexual toy for a spoiled and wanton woman named Juliette. What Bloch is articulating, in this iconoclastic collection of science fiction stories edited by Harlan Ellison, is the Ripper's unique talents seem all the more necessary in a futuristic world where violence and unrestrained sexual energy are commonplace.

The same cannot be said, however, for Bloch's final treatise on the subject, *The Night of the Ripper* (1984), a work that as a whole betrays the power and distinction of its predecessor, "Yours Truly, Jack the Ripper." Rumbelow best summarizes the work by noting that it "mentions the usual suspects and

The spirit of "an ancient terror ... [that] has a name — boratis, kesla, redjac" possesses Hengist (John Fiedler) in "Wolf in the Fold," Robert Bloch's original script for the NBC television series *Star Trek*.

practically everyone else — or so it seems — who was living at the time," and then adds that, "What the book lacks in suspense it makes up for with nastiness by spicing the beginning of each chapter with totally gratuitous examples of sadism culled from all ages and countries. None of these have any relevance whatsoever to the book" (237). In his autobiography, Bloch countered such criticism by asserting that his intent was to show that "throughout history crimes far worse than Jack's had been committed in the name of patriotism, religion, local custom or tradition." He then wondered how those critics who assailed his work as "gratuitous gore" would react to "the unexpurgated accounts in such respectable sources as Will and Ariel Durant's *The Story of Civilization*." He concludes by stating that, "One man's sleaze is another man's scholarship" (286).

Unfortunately, Rumbelow's assessment is more exact than Bloch's weak defense of his book. Simply put, *The Night of the Ripper* reads as a potboiler of the laziest kind. There is nothing new or unique in the book; incredibly, nearly every character, plot twist, theme and situation is borrowed from other works. The gambit of an American working with a Scotland Yard inspector, and the American's girlfriend threatened by the Ripper, echoes Baker and

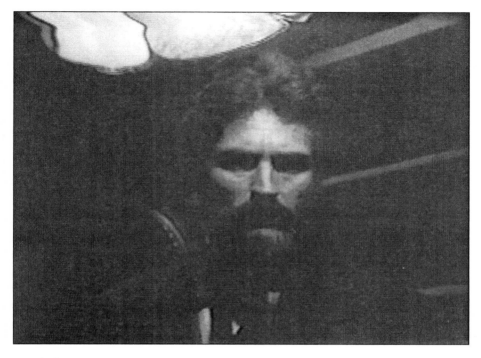

Jack the Ripper (Mickey Gilbert) is alive in modern-day Chicago in "The Ripper" episode of the ABC television series *Kolchak: The Night Stalker.*

Berman's *Jack the Ripper.* Myriad notables appearing every few pages from John Merrick (the "Elephant Man") and George Bernard Shaw to Sir Arthur Conan Doyle and Oscar Wilde, echo Nicholas Meyer's Sherlock Holmes pastiches *The Seven Percent Solution* and *The West End Horror* (Chapter VI) among other similar works. The ruse of a flaming finale in which most of the evidence is destroyed echoes James Hill's 1965 film *A Study in Terror.* Destroying evidence not destroyed by the flames capitalizes on the then new and popular conspiracy theories. This book isn't classic Bloch; there are no supernatural spirits, no "hunger that never dies," no horror of the imagination. What is left is merely a pastiche of *Psycho* with Jack the Ripper as a flamboyant villain instead of the urbane Norman Bates. *The Night of the Ripper* stands as a prominent slasher volume reflective of its own age and as a feeble monument to the master of Jack the Ripper lore.

Nonetheless, Bloch's original transcending specter of Jack the Ripper has been the stimulus for imitation, particularly in television. It was the focus of the premiere episode of the ABC series *The Night Stalker* (later titled *Kolchak: The Night Stalker*) broadcast September 13, 1974. In this episode written by Rudolph Borchert, reporter Carl Kolchak (Darren McGavin) spars with a

The transfer of London Bridge from London to Lake Havasu, Arizona, brings with it the spirit of Jack the Ripper that manifests itself in Roger Eddington (Paul Rossilli) in the TV movie *Bridge Across Time* (1985).

police captain named Warren (Ken Lynch) before overcoming the supernatural reappearance of Jack the Ripper (Mickey Gilbert) in modern day Chicago, which is an apparent nod to Bloch's "Yours Truly, Jack the Ripper." Here, however, no one is possessed by the Ripper's spirit. Jack the Ripper is simply alive and, amazingly, endowed with incredible, superhuman powers: he is impervious to bullets and he can leap tall buildings. There is no explanation for these powers and his apparent longevity, nor for the Ripper's vulnerability to electricity — which Kolchak himself effects by leading the Ripper to an electrified pond. Like Carmody in Bloch's story, the Ripper merely exists without explanation.

In a second example, the transcending specter of Jack the Ripper was haunting the community of Lake Havasu, Arizona, in a made-for-television movie titled *Bridge Across Time* (later reissued as *Arizona Ripper* and also available on videocassette as *Terror at London Bridge*) broadcast November 22, 1985, on NBC. The premise of William F. Nolan's script rested with the assumption that when London Bridge was purchased and transported to the Arizona desert the spirit of Jack the Ripper was somehow transported as well.

Nolan's narrative ignores much of the Ripper history, but it nonetheless echoes J. F. Brewer's idea about a curse on the Ripper's crime scene. To this end, Nolan fabricates a Ripper letter in which the Ripper threatens that the "stone has told me there will be more" victims. The "stone" is a single block of the bridge, and the bridge, or at least that single stone, becomes a supernatural agent all its own. Indeed, the Ripper reappears — slouch hat and cape intact — after tourist Ann Williamson (Barbara Bingham) accidentally cuts herself and bleeds on the stone. The supernatural quality is affirmed by Mr. Latting (David Fox-Brenton), who is depicted as a religious fanatic, when he asserts that there is a "curse on London Bridge." In fact, he is so sure of the bridge's evil that he even attempts to dynamite it in order to "scourge [it] by fire and brimstone." But whatever magic the stone has is never revealed. Only what the Ripper remarks to his intended victim Angie (Stepfanie Kramer) when he says that the stone will receive her blood, thus enabling him to return to his own century, is revealed. The Ripper's plan, however, is thwarted by Don Gregory (David Hasselhoff)— another rebellious "with-it" detective who has a preference for wearing his shirts unbuttoned and for screaming at his superiors — who shoots the Ripper, sending him and the stone into the lake.

In yet a third example, the psychic spirit of Jack the Ripper possessed a patient named Adam (Robert Foxworth) in "With Affection, Jack the Ripper," an episode written by Don Ingalls of the ABC series *The Sixth Sense* (October 14, 1972), a short-lived drama about the investigations of Dr. Michael Rhodes (Gary Collins), a researcher into psychic phenomena. In the Ripper episode (reviewed here in a 30-minute abridgement for the syndicated version of Rod Serling's *Night Gallery*), a young researcher named Elizabeth (Patty Duke) succeeds in getting Adam to psychically receive and then play nineteenth century melodies on a harpsichord, but unbeknownst to her the paranormal musical talent is emanating from Jack the Ripper. As a result, whenever Adam takes a walk in the park he reverts to the savagery of the Ripper. Director Robert Day cleverly blends the modern milieu with that of the fog-shrouded streets of London in 1888, allowing Adam and the victims to move seamlessly in and out of the different settings. Rhodes has "clairvoyant impressions" of the crimes, and he aids the police in seeking out the murderer. Later, Adam cryptically explains to Rhodes that "I was here [in the park] and then somebody else was here and I couldn't remember what he did when I was me." Rhodes agrees to help Adam by telling the police that "two strong forces [are] at work in Adam; one, his love for Elizabeth; the other, a psychic force — a murderous hate for women." When Adam escapes apprehension, however, Elizabeth offers herself as bait, and Adam-as-Ripper is subdued by the police. Rhodes then assures Elizabeth that Adam will receive the help he needs in exorcizing the Ripper's psychic hold on him. Rhodes' ability to "witness" the crimes seems to validate Robert Lees' psychic interest in the Ripper murders, but more to the point here is that the Ripper's "psychic presence" is never explained. As in

Title card for the Hammer production of a story by Edward Spencer Shew.

the Kolchak episode, the Ripper's presence merely exists, and the program seems to say that the Ripper's spirit can be apparently summoned by inadvertent psychic power.

The longevity of the Ripper's spirit is also a psychological matter in Peter Sasdy's modernist *Hands of the Ripper* (1971), a pretentious Hammer production which Tom Milne and Paul Willeman describe as "arguably the last masterpiece produced by Hammer" (234). In this instance, Dr. John Pritchard (Eric Porter), a disciple of Freud who seeks reasons for mankind's continued viciousness, believes that the Ripper's daughter, Anna (Angharad Rees), suffers from a newly discovered disease called schizophrenia, which he believes was brought on by repressed childhood memories. To accent Pritchard's claim Sasdy begins his film with a pre-credits sequence which shows just that: Jack the Ripper returns home and stabs his wife to death within a milieu of glimmering lights while his young daughter watches. In a rather poignant yet ironic scene following the carnage, the monstrous Ripper takes his young child from her bed and embraces her, revealing what appears to be genuine love for the child. In the film, when the adult Anna sees a glimmering reflection and feels an embrace she becomes the Ripper. The question that screenwriter L. W. Davidson raises is a simple one: Is Anna a schizophrenic killer or is she actu-

A brief ironic moment of tenderness between Jack the Ripper and his young daughter in Peter Sasdy's *Hands of the Ripper* (1971).

ally possessed by the spirit of Jack the Ripper? In an interesting turn in characterization, the scientific mind as represented by protagonist Pritchard steadfastly denies any supernatural activity, and is proved wrong; the intuitive mind as represented by the lecherous politician Dysart (Derek Godfrey) accepts that Anna is possessed by the evil spirit of the Ripper, and is proved correct. Dysart's belief is confirmed when psychic Madame Bullard (Margaret Rawlings) senses violence in the presence of Anna, and reveals that she is indeed the daughter of the infamous Jack the Ripper, telling Pritchard that "the violence of that man is still in this girl." A glimmering reflection off the psychic's spectacles coupled with her sympathetic gesture then causes Anna to kill Madame Bullard before the horrified eyes of Pritchard. Fearing that his theories have failed Anna as well as his progressive social agenda, Pritchard assents to Dysart's more reactionary theories about crime, and a despondent Pritchard apologizes to Anna before kissing her. Of course, at this moment the Ripper's spirit erupts possessing Anna, and she assaults Pritchard. Pritchard finally sanctions Dysart's belief that the Ripper's spirit does indeed possess Anna, and in a rather uneventful climax inside St. Paul's Cathedral Anna falls to her death next to the dying Pritchard.

Sasdy's film has a documentary quality to it; indeed, Sasdy savors Victorian detail, and he often resorts to the handheld camera for an extemporaneous look. However, as Alan Frank has rightly observed, the film is "strangely lifeless" (70); neither the case for schizophrenia nor the case for possession is really portrayed to any extent in the narrative. The notion that the Ripper's spirit possesses Anna seems to exist by default since Pritchard's psychological ruminations go nowhere. This leaves the film with little except its unobtrusive style, and here much of the film's effect relies on the depictions of the gory murders, particularly the gruesome slashing of Pritchard's maid, Dolly (Marjie Lawrence), and the stabbing of a prostitute named Long Liz (Lynda Baron), which may be a coincidence or an inside reference since one of the Ripper's actual victims was Elizabeth Stride, known by the nickname "Long Liz."

The film's significance to Ripper lore rests in its resultant theme: The Ripper's essence — what Bloch describes in "Wolf in the Fold" as "a hunger that never dies"— consumes innocence, for the Ripper's influence is pervasive in the film, corrupting or consuming everyone. Anna is an innocent who is trapped by opposing influences. She is not only a victim of the Ripper's supernatural influence, which causes her to kill, but she is also a victim of Pritchard's scientific rationalism, which suppresses any illusion of Anna being restored to spiritual health. Pritchard, as well, becomes a victim of the Ripper's influence by overtly eschewing any moral principle. He purposely withholds important information about the murders even to the extent of harboring Anna when he discovers that she is the murderer. Much like other movie mad scientists, he sees no moral imperative to prevent other murders if his own experiments with Anna will lead to what he believes will be a better world. But even more pronounced are Sasdy's visual signs: gestures of love — the kiss and the embrace — are corrupted into rituals of raising the evil specter of the Ripper. The Ripper's presence is indeed a puissant evil; it is a malevolence that not only corrupts innocence but love as well.

The psychological issue is again raised in a theatrical feature with the ambiguous title of *Jack's Back* (1988). As written and directed by Rowdy Herrington, the film — which a cynic could easily subtitle *James Dean Meets Jack the Ripper*— relates the centennial observance of the Ripper murders which inspires a madman to recreate each murder in gruesome detail exactly 100 years to the day of the original events. Herrington weaves a "wrong man" narrative by having John Wesford (James Spader), an idealistic medical student serving his time in a clinic for the indigent, identified as the Ripper during what is perceived by witnesses as an escape. In actuality Wesford was pursuing a fellow student named Jack Pendler (Rex Ryon) whom he thought was the Ripper. When Wesford catches up with Jack, they struggle and Jack garrotes Wesford and then makes it look like Wesford hanged himself. Wesford's twin brother, Rick (Spader), "sees" the whole incident in a vision as well as feels his brother's death throes. The police are convinced, however, that John was the

Ripper and that he hanged himself because he was recognized leaving the home of the last victim. Rick, a brooding rebel clad in leather jacket, then embarks on a quest with the aid of a sympathetic detective (Jim Haynie), a suspicious psychiatrist (Robert Picardo) and John's girlfriend (Cynthia Gibb) to clear his brother and bring the real Ripper to justice. His visions eventually lead him to Dr. Sidney Tannerson (Rod Loomis), the moralistic director of the clinic.

In essence, *Jack's Back* has nothing to do with Jack the Ripper other than appropriating the name and the crimes. Unlike the works discussed previously, the psychological issue is actually limited to Rick's ability to "see" the crimes, and as such there is no supernatural quality relevant to Jack the Ripper himself. There is no spirit — supernatural, psychological, or otherwise — possessing Tannerson, nor explanation for Tannerson's crime spree other than implied moralistic perversion vis-à-vis Mr. Sleuth and Mr. Slade. Consequently, despite its title and reference to the Ripper's centenary, the film is nothing more than a rather tame slasher film.

Finally, the specter of Jack the Ripper was used by *The CBS Radio Mystery Theatre*, one of the most heralded attempts to resurrect dramatic radio in the 1970s, for an episode not unlike Bloch's "Wolf in the Fold." Writer George Lowther offered a tale of the Ripper's wandering immortal spirit in "The Strange Case of Lucas Lauder," broadcast on February 28, 1975. A prisoner named Guy Richards, soon to be executed for a series of brutal killings, calls warden Lucas Lauder (Robert Lansing) to his cell to offer a strange confession. According to the prisoner, he is possessed by the evil spirit of Jack the Ripper which passes from host to host over the generations, using each host to the Ripper's murderous benefit. Upon the death of each host the spirit transfers to a new host, and Richards startles Lauder by saying that the warden has been selected as the Ripper's new incarnation. In an interesting twist, Richards tells Lauder that he can escape the Ripper's grip by finding a love that is as strong as the Ripper's hate. Lauder scoffs at the story, but he later begins to experience powerful, hateful desires which he is barely able to overcome. By the time Richards is executed, Lauder comes to believe that the Ripper's murderous soul has possessed him — even to the point that Lauder seriously contemplates his wife's murder. But Lauder is stopped, and his sanity returns, when in a moment of reflection Lauder realizes that the Ripper's spirit has been repulsed by his wife's unyielding and unconditional love.

In total, what makes the singular story "Yours Truly, Jack the Ripper" so vital to the Ripper's myth of Jack the Ripper is that Robert Bloch cleverly blended history with fiction. The appeal of Bloch's tale relies more on its ability to elucidate the mystery of the Ripper (i.e., the vicious crimes and his eerie anonymity,) in terms of the motif of the traditional horror story, namely that evil is a metaphysical reality than on storytelling alone. The result is that the figure of Jack the Ripper transcends history to become that eponymous figure so aptly described by Rumbelow. The Ripper is no longer just a criminal, but a hateful monster possessed by supernatural evil. For the Ripper, in Bloch's view, the maxim *ars longa, vita brevis* (what Longfellow translated subjectively as "Art is long, Time is fleeting") takes on a new meaning: Jack the Ripper has transcended life to become art. Sir Guy says as much in Lyndon's television adaptation of the story when he tells Carmody that Jack the Ripper is drawn to art because "art is limitless, and it would give him an interest in living." But the Ripper's art is art that is expressed in its most depraved form. Certainly, the connection between the ageless fascination with "art eternal" and the Ripper takes on an even greater significance when one considers that creative expression alone, as noted, has kept the Ripper alive in the public mind for well over 100 years.

Moreover, Bloch's periodic resurrection of Jack the Ripper has provided a subtle but important difference in approach from many of the other attempts at capturing the Ripper's evil presence. Whereas other depictions of the Ripper focus upon the crimes and the question of "who" the Ripper may have been, like Belloc Lowndes' *The Lodger* and Baker and Berman's *Jack the Ripper*, Bloch has posed the more philosophical question of "what" Jack the Ripper may represent. In an interview for the ABC television project *Secrets and Mysteries* in 1987, Bloch observed that Jack the Ripper "with that knife ... penetrated the deepest secrets of our own being," and accordingly Bloch reached the inescapable conclusion that Jack the Ripper is in all of us. Bloch's conclusion that the Ripper is the dark side of our human nature — a "brother to the darkness" — helps to explain our own morbid fascination with this mysterious killer. But such an explanation is at once both unsettling and reassuring. It is reassuring in the sense that we have used and will undoubtedly continue to use Jack the Ripper as a catharsis for the primal urges all of us feel, and the bestial urges that most of us have the civilized understanding to suppress. If Jack the Ripper provides for us, as he did for Victorian London, an empathetic means of purging our own bile then his lingering presence is not without merit.

On a frightening note is the discomfiting verity that indeed a correlation now exists between unrestrained sexual expression and the Ripper — as investigated by Lyndon's adaptation of Bloch's story — which has resulted in a revitalized viciousness that corresponds uncomfortably to the urbane viciousness of modern serial killers like Ted Bundy and John Wayne Gacy. Such a notion is best illustrated in Nicholas Meyer's *Time After Time* (1979), a cleverly contrived film about H. G. Wells (Malcolm McDowell) pursuing, by means of his time machine, Jack the Ripper (David Warner) into modern San Francisco where pornographic films, sex shows and brazen prostitution fascinate, delight and inspire the Ripper. In Meyer's intelligent narrative, Wells envisions a future where mankind has overcome his primal instincts for war, greed and lust. Hence, the thought of the Ripper unrestrained in a utopian world so horrifies Wells that he feels morally compelled to follow the Ripper into the future and apprehend him. But the future which Wells uncovers is disquieting to say the least; the future belongs much more to Jack the Ripper than it does to Wells. The Ripper says as much to Wells after he tries to convince the Ripper — and perhaps himself — that neither of them belong in the future. The Ripper then demonstrates just how wrong Wells is via the television. Surfing from channel to channel, from riots to assassinations, from massacres to the violent excesses of rock music, the Ripper comes to a chilling conclusion: "We don't belong here? On the contrary, Herbert; I belong here completely and utterly. I'm home!"

In somewhat the same vein — the Ripper as time traveler — the ABC television network inaugurated *Time Cop* on September 22, 1997, utilizing a variant of the Ripper saga. Based upon a successful motion picture of the same title, *Time Cop* was succinctly if unbelievably described in its weekly opening signature:

> FEMININE VOICE: The year ... 2007. Time travel is a reality. It has fallen into criminal hands. With history itself at risk, the United States has formed the Time Enforcement Commission, a secret agency responsible for policing the temporal stream. An elite team of agents track unlawful travelers across time — their mission: protect the past, preserve the future. These agents are known as timecops.

The premiere episode of the series, "A Rip in Time," written by Alfred Gough and Miles Millar from a story by Gough, Millar and Art Monterastelli, clearly hoped to capitalize on the continuing sensational appeal attached to the Ripper theme. The teleplay, however, quickly dispensed with any serious pretext of historical accuracy or contextual logic.[3]

In a pre-credits segment imitative of virtually all other Ripper presentations; a Victorian cobblestone street is seen, bathed in nighttime but with only the dim flare of a gas lamp to light the eerie environment. Shortly, a brassy streetwalker appears as we hear the coming and going of a hansom cab. Once the streetwalker is seen, the stage is set.

At the bottom of the screen, viewers are alerted to the time and place: 1888 — London, England — November 7. A London prostitute, one Catharine Eddowes, is approached by a caped figure whose sinister intentions are apparent to the audience and quite quickly to Eddowes. The streetwalker is young, physically appealing and well dressed in a flashy and vulgar sort of way. This is not the actual Catharine Eddowes of history but rather the usual media variation designed to elicit a maximum emotional — and prurient — reaction from the audience. The attack on Eddowes begins and it appears that the Rip-

---

[3]An interesting footnote to "A Rip in Time" is the cameo appearance of H. G. Wells, serving to drive home the obvious point that the teleplay, with its pursuit of Jack through time, was derivative of Time After Time, *though far less effective.*

per will claim his fourth victim as decreed by history. Suddenly, from behind, the Ripper is seized and expertly dispatched by means of a snapped neck. Another taller dark figure then presents himself to a cowering Eddowes who mouths an hysterical thanks to her savior. "You've just killed Jack the Ripper," she tells him. It is at this point that we discover Eddowes' champion is no savior but a demented figure of evil. The man tells the prostitute that he hasn't killed Jack the Ripper; instead, he intones, "No Catharine, I just became him." At this point Catharine Eddowes dies at the stranger's hands.

The fact that the November 7, 1888, date was bogus and that the Ripper actually claimed Catharine Eddowes some five weeks prior — on September 30, 1888 — seems to have gone unnoticed by Time Enforcement Commission's chief historian, Easter (Kurt Fuller). Easter's assignment with the Time Enforcement Commission is to pinpoint the temporal anomalies as they take place in order that Enforcement personnel can correct the errors. Easter, however, does note that the body of Sir William Gull, "noted Harley Street physician," was found some ten feet from Catharine Eddowes. Since Easter's previous research confirmed to his own satisfaction that Gull was, indeed, Jack the Ripper, the obvious conclusion is that someone from the future assumed the Ripper's identity with plans to continue Jack's work on a grander scale.

The assignment to track down the assumptive Ripper falls to Logan, a young hotshot Timecop. Logan, by personality and temperament, is the stereotypical "free spirit" who acts to satisfy his own set of values and ethics rather than following the guidelines and directives of the organization which has bequeathed him authority to act in the first place.

The Ripper is eventually identified as Ian Pascoe, a criminal genius on a personal quest to make a name for himself as the greatest criminal of all time. The illogic of Pascoe choosing the identity of Jack the Ripper as the means of achieving his ambition seems manifest. The world would still only recognize "Jack the Ripper," the original product of an unintentional collaboration between William Gull and the tabloid press. A demented personality as deeply committed to personal recognition as Pascoe would hardly seek to buttress the reputation of someone else.

Logan finally confronts the Ripper and prevents another murder. In the ensuing confrontation Pascoe manages to escape apprehension just as the historical Ripper managed to elude his pursuers. Indeed, Pascoe would continue to pop up occasionally during the series to plague Logan.

The metaphysical ability of Jack the Ripper to conquer time was also demonstrated in a broadcast of the syndicated television series *Babylon 5*, essentially the serialized story of the intergalactic confrontation between the forces of light and shadow. "Comes the Inquisitor," a teleplay by J. Michael Straczynski with contributions by Harlan Ellison, was broadcast in late October (approximately the 25th, depending upon the viewing market) 1995, and what is so interesting is that the Ripper makes a short but critical appearance.

The story tells how the Vorlans, who have joined the fray against the Shadows, are demanding proof of the strength and commitment of their allies. To this end the Vorlans have arranged to test the physical and emotional resolve of Delenn (Mira Furlan) and Captain Sheridan (Bruce Boxleitner). To conduct the test, the Vorlans have selected an enigmatic figure they had scooped up from Victorian England. This special inquisitor, Sebastian (Wayne Alexander), subjects Delenn and Sheridan to tremendous physical and psychological pain. Delenn's willingness to sacrifice herself in order to save Sheridan satisfies Sebastian and the Vorlans and the test is concluded. Only at the end does Sebastian identify himself as the Ripper.

This chapter began with a look at the Ripper as Robert Bloch portrayed him, a sorcerer apprenticed to the dark gods, capable of immortality as long as he could keep the blood flowing. In this fashion and with the public's help, Jack has triumphed over time. As a creature of our own darkest fantasies, the Ripper would inevitably appear on the offbeat ABC television series *Fantasy Island*. Running during the late 1970s and early 1980s, the premise of the series was always built around the arrival of a small private plane to the island resort operated by the enigmatic Mr. Roarke (Ricardo Montalban). Two or three passengers would emerge from the plane to be welcomed by Roarke. Each guest had paid the sum of $50,000 for the privilege of visiting Roarke's personal paradise and having their fantasy brought to life. Endowed with the powers of a sorcerer, Roarke would inevitably fulfill his guests' wishes.

On November 29, 1980, *Fantasy Island* presented "With Affection, Jack the Ripper"/"Gigolo." The Ripper segment focused on the obsession of a young female criminologist in pursuing and identifying Jack the Ripper. Roarke grants the young woman's fantasy, however, the age-old theme of the hunter becoming the hunted comes into play when the Ripper targets the young criminologist as his next victim.

The *Fantasy Island* episode, written by Don Ingalls and Ron Friedman, rather deftly offered a reverse twist on several Ripper themes which had become staples of the Ripper canon by 1980. Rather than representing Jack as a dark force capable of spanning time, Ingalls and Friedman offer the Ripper as a passive historical figure being acted upon by Roarke's extraordinary powers. Instead of the Ripper coming forward into the future to plague humankind in our venue, we are drawn back into Victorian London of Jack's day. In perhaps the most honest text to come along yet, we make the tacit admission that pursuing the Ripper is our fantasy. Most theme renderings of the Ripper — whether it has been "Yours Truly, Jack the Ripper;" *Time Cop's* "A Rip in Time," *Star Trek's* "Wolf in the Fold" or *Time After Time* — have shown the Ripper appearing as an uninvited agent to stalk us against our will. In reality, as *Fantasy Island* so keenly demonstrated, we are the stalkers as we chase Jack across the ages.

IV

RIPPER REDUX

Jack the Ripper continues to haunt the world by wearing many disguises, but none is more pervasive than the face of the serial killer who strikes with brutal suddenness and seemingly without cause in our media-filled world. Thus it is the serial killers, real monsters like Ted Bundy and Randall Woodfield and fictional predators like Freddy Krueger and Leatherface, who have become not only an extension of the Ripper but also a staple of popular entertainment as well. Inevitably there is the tendency to compare the serial killer's deeds with the Ripper's own handiwork. More often the Ripper's name is merely appropriated as a means of suggesting the heinousness of the crimes scrawled in blood across motion picture and television screens. If one were to include the alarming number of "spatter" films which rose to dubious prominence in the late twentieth century, the Ripper canon would swell into the several hundreds.

A brief case in point here is an Italian film titled *Blade of the Ripper* for English-language audiences. Considered in the context of late twentieth century Western culture, the film functions as an example of our continuing fascination with the stalker pursuing his terrified prey. The film clearly owes its dramatic genesis to the original Whitechapel killer, but *Blade of the Ripper*, as well as scores of other such debasing pictures, has shifted emphasis from the suspense of the crimes to the horror and barbarism of the acts; the film allows us to wallow in the murderer's vicious sexual attack. Tight close-ups of clothing being ripped away, naked breasts being pawed and a glistening knife penetrating flesh are paraded like scenes in an industrial training film. Worse, however, is that close shots reveal the victim's agony from the point of view of the assailant; the film's point of view is always that of the murderer. There is no empathy for the victim nor is there any sense of repulsion — a sense that the attack and the carnage are just too abominable for our eyes. The sequences are so finely honed and crafted that they function as celebrations for another conquest by a murderer. Consequently a film like *Blade of the Ripper* has nothing to recommend it except an overabundance of depravity, and as noted, Jack the Ripper has provided a convenient measure with which we have been able to gauge our emotional health as a civilized society.

It is disquieting to realize that we have come to a point at which the catharsis provided by Jack the Ripper is insufficient to satiate our blood lusts; we now demand from our entertainment greater and greater depictions of violence and ever escalating acts of ferocious sexuality. To this end we commonly use various identities of Jack the Ripper perhaps only because the original Whitechapel murderer has become quaint and old-fashioned; he is hardly up to the task of meeting our elevated need for figurative blood sacrifices in order to sustain our emotional existence. By contrast, in previous decades we employed variants of the Ripper personality for precisely the opposite reason. For many years, Jack the Ripper connoted images of violence and sexuality too strong to be allowed to stand on their own; his viciousness was so abhorrent that we dared not to look upon the gorgon's face. As such, dramatic works designed to capitalize on the natural suspense and allure of the Ripper theme either diluted the details of the Ripper killings or invented Ripper clones in order to avoid those same inconvenient details.

Even without consideration of the spatter films, any examination of these "Ripper rip-offs" can only hope to discuss a representative sample since no definitive list is possible or even worthwhile. By probing the structure and content of a few subjectively selected works constructed from elements of the Ripper legend, we can see the extent to which Jack the Ripper has permeated our culture, often without our conscious realization.

The name *Jack the Ripper* has proven to be an inspired choice beyond all reasonable expectations for the Whitechapel murderer. The name quickly came to represent in the collective mind not just a single murderous thug but rather a primordial way of life — a human predator devouring human prey. Dramatists in their quest to replicate the Ripper generally have not strayed far from the core of the Ripper's success, a predator at liberty among the weak and vulnerable, and writers have tended to endow their fiends with routinely descriptive names thereby forsaking the imaginatively subjective which invested Jack the Ripper with his immortal authority. Such appellations as *The Slasher, The Creeper, The Lonely One*, and even *Nick the Knife* pursued unassuming victims on a recurring basis, and radio early on learned that it could readily tamper not only with the Ripper's name but with the motif itself. It was simply easy to extract the elements of suspense inherent in the Ripper case by substituting a thinly veiled persona for the Ripper, and by altering the details to avoid directly confronting the embarrassing sexual overtones implicit in the original Ripper killings.

For instance, during its summer run in 1938, the celebrated radio program *The Shadow* offered an intriguing variant of the Ripper theme in an episode titled "The Creeper." The Shadow, played by Orson Welles, is called upon to investigate the recent disappearance of several beautiful and wealthy young women from an exclusive section of town. The Shadow trails the mysterious Creeper through a labyrinth of dark, abandoned subterranean water conduits which function very much like Whitechapel alleyways. The Creeper, however, is not "down on whores" as was the Ripper, but rather he is a demented and lonely killer who has gathered together his victims for the purpose of companionship until the avenging Shadow inevitably frees the surviving victims and disposes of the fiend.

A far more suitable Ripper surrogate was heard on the March 29, 1946, episode of *Mollé Mystery Theatre*. In this episode titled "The Creeper," which was based on a story by Joseph Ruscoll, we open *in medias res* with the disclosure that a mysterious killer dubbed "The Creeper" is loose, and that to date he has killed three women — all redheads. The dramatic suspense is unveiled as the Creeper's next victim appears to be Dorothy Grant, police officer Steve Grant's "less than moral" wife. Dorothy recognizes that each of the killer's victims had experienced problems with door locks prior to being murdered and that she has just such a malfunctioning lock. Frantically, Mrs. Grant summons a locksmith to make the necessary repairs, but only too late does she discover that the locksmith was the Creeper. Her dying gasps as the Creeper squeezes the air from her throat and the unmistakable thud of a body falling to the hardwood floor underscore the certainty that Dorothy Grant has become the Creeper's fourth victim. But, in keeping with the general reluctance of radio to allow crime to go unpunished, a postscript is added: the audience is permitted to listen in as a journalist reports that a bellboy in Dorothy Grant's building alerted police officers who gave chase and killed the Creeper. Justice is served swiftly and righteously on radio.

A more appropriate alias for Jack the Ripper is certainly "The Slasher." It, too, was inveighed many times on radio, and nowhere is such an appellation made more apparent than in the classic radio horror-thriller *Inner Sanctum*. The episode was an original drama by Milton Lewis titled "The Song of the Slasher," broadcast April 24, 1945. Lewis, who also wrote for such popular series as *The Thin Man* and *This Is Nora Drake*, focused his play on Dan Miller, an undercover police detective, who moves himself and his wife to an apartment along the waterfront, the center of the Slasher's murderous activities. Miller is convinced that he has identified the Slasher, and he is so certain of his suspect that Miller smugly carries out an ancillary plot — the murder of his wife and the framing of the Slasher for the deed. Everything seems to be going according to plan except that Dan Miller makes the mistake of misidentifying the Slasher. Miller's entire plan falls apart and he is convicted of his wife's murder.

Yet another Slasher appeared on the NBC drama *Nightbeat*, an early 1950s series which starred veteran radio actor Frank Lovejoy as Randy Stone, a reporter who was always on the lookout for a good human interest story for his employer, the *Chicago Star*. There was a poetic quality to Stone's melancholy stories about struggle and loss in the Windy City. Just such a story unfolded on the broadcast of November 10, 1950, in which we hear Stone pay tribute to the night, and yet remind us that it is also the night that breeds evil:

> You ever notice how, when the sun goes down, the whole earth starts a new reaction? The flowers close with the shop doors, the sunshine leaves town with the busses and the birds settle down like the dust covers on department store counters. At night perfume replaces the flowers, neon takes up the task of the sun and the birds take flight in the hearts of the people looking for love and the good tomorrow. Someone said night is the mantle that covers the weary and the cave of excitement for the adventuresome. They forgot to add that the night is also a mask for the evil.

Stone, on his beat, stumbles across the fourteenth victim of a fiend everyone has begun calling the Slasher. Stone describes the victim as "a woman ... lying on the sidewalk with a frightened look in her eyes; the shoulder of her dress was ripped open and there was a red stain growing on her side." Stone's suspicions quickly focus on an itinerant artist named Rick Bennett, whose portrait signature includes a scar drawn on a beautiful woman's face. We learn that Bennett is obsessed with finding a woman named Selma, a nightclub performer with whom he had once had a relationship. When Stone tracks down Selma, and the reporter hears Selma's story of Bennett's relentless pursuit, it seems apparent that the Slasher has been identified. In a final twist of perverse fate, Stone discovers that although Bennett had been searching for Selma with murder in mind, Bennett proves not to be the Slasher; he is incapable of carrying out his murderous intentions. In the end Stone has not captured the Slasher, but he has uncovered one more human interest story, which is what the reporter had been after all along.

Deftly used, the image of a Ripper-like creature overwhelming our senses with undiluted and uncensored passions is as poetically powerful in its own way as the more conventional images employed by the versifier. Ray Bradbury, who has long been noted for the poetic power of his short stories, employed such imagery to weave a yarn of a nocturnal killer called "The Lonely One" in his short story "The Whole Town's Sleeping," published in the September 1950 issue of *McCall's*, and included as a chapter in Bradbury's novel *Dandelion Wine* (1957). Radio was able to recognize the potential inherent in Bradbury's Ripper when the story appeared twice on CBS radio's classic *Suspense* anthology, on June 14, 1955, and August 31, 1958. In both instances the radio play generously pulled narration and dialogue from Bradbury's original story, and Anthony Ellis' adaptation prudently effected few substantive changes.

Both presentations of "The Whole Town's Sleeping" wisely employed the talents of William Conrad as narrator. Conrad's deep commanding voice delivered Bradbury's imagery with cool unhurried authority, which remained in unchanging contrast with the rising hysteria of the Lonely One's prey, Miss Lavinia Nebbs, played initially by Jeanette Nolan and much more effectively by Agnes Moorehead in the later production.

On a warm summer evening, Lavinia Nebbs plans an outing with her friends Francine and Helen to the Majestic theatre to take in the newest Robert Mitchum picture. A killer called "The Lonely One" has been dispatching vulnerable women for the past several weeks, but Lavinia is not afraid. Her courageous resolve apparently never falters, not after Lavinia and Francine discover the body of their friend, Eliza Ramsell; not after learning that a mysterious stranger had been asking after Lavinia in the drugstore; and not even after her two friends point out that Lavinia must return home alone in the dark through a forbidding ravine. But this stalwart courage slowly begins to disintegrate when the darkness and the sounds of the night activate her imagination. She now fears that she is being followed, and she hurries home to lock herself indoors, to reassure herself that she was being foolish and promise herself that she would not make such a mistake in the future.

Just when Lavinia and the audience seem convinced of the absurdity of Lavinia's fears, the narrator's voice intrudes, murmuring quietly, "She had just put her hand to the light switch when she heard it behind her in the blackness … just a movement." At this point, Lavinia as well as the audience hears the slow cadence of heavy footsteps coming from the darkness, followed by the Lonely One's demented, slavering whisper that sighs "beautiful." In this moment of revelation we understand that the Lonely One has conquered his loneliness.

But Ellis' adaptation is in accord with radio decorum; just as other writers had done before him, Ellis mitigates the ending by suggestion. No definitive sounds of death are allowed to imply the outcome of Lavinia's confrontation with the Lonely One. The sound department is not marshaled to produce the auditory signals of Lavinia's breath being choked from her throat, her body being ripped apart with a knife, nor sound of her lifeless body crumpling to the floor. Members of the audience are allowed to surmise an ending, be it the Lonely One's conquest or merely Lavinia's imagination. The radio script merely leaves an ending to the discretion of the listener.

In his novel *Dandelion Wine*, however, Bradbury allows Lavinia Nebbs to clearly escape the clutches of her pursuer. Unlike the radio broadcast, there is a next chapter, and it finds the reader privy to a discussion by three small boys lamenting the end to the excitement created by the Lonely One's reign of terror. One of the boys complains that, "After ten long years escaping, old Lavinia Nebbs up and stabbed him [the Lonely One] with a handy pair of sewing scissors. I wish she'd minded her own business." In many ways, this echoes Bradbury's own childhood since he has stated there was indeed a "Lonely One" and "that was *his* name. And he moved around at night in my home town when I was six years old and he frightened everyone and was never captured" (xiii). Such sentiments echo our own perceptions of Jack the Ripper as well. Should someone finally and unequivocally identify the Ripper, our interest in him and his exploits would vanish; we would all wish that someone had minded his or her own business.

For the *Ellery Queen* radio program, Anthony Boucher and Manfred B. Lee scripted "Nick the Knife," broadcast by CBS on August 1, 1945. This whodunit opens after 31 women have fallen victim to the murderous, knife-wielding attacks of a phantom killer who calls himself "Nick the Knife." Each of the victims is young and pretty, but after the attacks the victims are found horribly disfigured. Despite a massive deployment of police personnel, another attack takes place, but this time the victim is a homely girl, attacked inside the ornamental maze of a newly dedicated park. This time, however, the victim, Jane Stepply, uncharacteristically survives the attack. The police find three possible suspects inside the park, but the hysterical victim is unable to identify her assailant. Ellery and his colleagues map out a plan expected to reveal which of the three suspects is guilty, but the unexpected denouement comes after Ellery is forced to eliminate the original suspects from consideration. Once Ellery is compelled to cross off the initial suspects, and after ruling out the cop on the beat who discovered Jane Stepply wounded in the maze, only one viable suspect remained — Jane Stepply herself. Ellery notes that "it's not so strange ... [that] this homely woman brooding over unattractiveness became psychotic and began hunting and attacking girls who were pretty." Incidentally, this parody of the Ripper case also neatly utilized the "Jill the Ripper" conjecture which had come back into vogue with the recent publication of Edwin T. Woodhall's *Jack the Ripper: Or When London Walked in Terror* and William Stewart's *Jack the Ripper: A New Theory* (Chapter I).

As the 1950s drew to a close so too did radio drama. As a cultural force, radio drama virtually ceased to exist, but attempts have been made periodically to re-energize the medium. Radio veteran Himan Brown attempted such a rejuvenation with *The CBS Radio Mystery Theatre*, hosted by E. G. Marshall and broadcast in the 1970s. On at least two occasions the Ripper found himself resurrected on the series. The second episode, "The Strange Case of Lucas Lauder" written by George Lowther, was mentioned in Chapter III in the context of the Ripper and the supernatural. The first resurrection, also adapted by Lowther, was titled "The Lodger" (May 13, 1974), and although there was no internal recognition as such, Lowther's play was unquestionably inspired by Belloc Lowndes' *The Lodger*. Lowther's play, updated to the present and set in a large American city, focuses on the Ninth Street boarding house owned by Mrs. Nell Pearson (Kim Hunter), a widow. Because his victims have all been widows, Nell is very much intrigued by the killer whom the police and public have come to refer to as "The Ripper." Soon after the arrival of a new boarder, a newspaper reporter named Tony Adams, the Ripper draws his next victim from Nell Pearson's own household. It is immediately apparent that Nell had been the intended victim; Nell suspects her new boarder and reports her suspicions to the police. The police promise to send an undercover officer to take up residence in Nell's boarding house in order to shadow Tony Adams, and soon a prospective boarder named Lawrence Bowen appears and is quickly taken in by the landlady. Only when it is almost too late does Nell realize that, rather than being the police officer sent to protect her, Bowen is the Ripper who has come to kill her. Only the timely arrival of Tony Adams and the police forestalls the Ripper's next killing.

Interestingly, when Alfred Hitchcock took to the new medium of television, Belloc Lowndes' *The Lodger* never appeared on the director's docket as it had done in film and radio. But another Ripper inspired tale was broadcast on May 5, 1957, on Hitchcock's CBS series titled *Alfred Hitchcock Presents*. Screenwriter Francis Cockrell adapted Thomas Burke's "The Hands of Mr. Ottermole," the story of a series of murders committed by a strangler first published in 1930. Although Burke's killer had forsaken the knife for a pair of strong hands, his connection with the Ripper has always been self-evident. In fact, Allan Barnard included "The Hands of Mr. Ottermole," along with an abridgement of Belloc Lowndes' *The Lodger* and Robert Bloch's "Yours Truly, Jack the Ripper," in his anthologized homage to Jack the Ripper literature titled *The Harlot Killer* (1953).

What is effective about Burke's "The Hands of Mr. Ottermole" is that the point of view is not that of a typical narrator but rather that of an omniscient storyteller. The narrative takes the role of a second person expositor; he is one who not only narrates, but at times intrudes with passion into the narrative. To effect this style, Burke often shifts from past tense to present tense. For example, as the storyteller closes his long narrative about the impending murder of the strangler's first victim, Mr. Whybrow, he suddenly jumps in with, "And now you are at your gate. And now you have found your door key. And now you are in, and hanging up your hat and coat." Moments later, the storyteller warns Mr. Whybrow to, "Go away.... Go away from that door. Don't touch it. Get right away from it. Get out of the house...." The storyteller then closes the narrative by stating matter-of-factly that, "Mr. Whybrow opened the door." As such, the storyteller functions very much like a rambling consciousness that doesn't just relate events but interprets events.

Also of significance is that Burke's narrative is similar to Bloch's story. A strangler is loose in London, and the storyteller conveys that an "air of black magic" surrounds the murders. Burke exacerbates the eerie milieu by introducing two characters who have no identities as such, but rather are identified by mere labels: "the journalist" and "the sergeant." In context, the journalist becomes an irritation to the sergeant by arriving at the scenes of the crimes before the sergeant does, or so the journalist believes. Finally, the journalist concludes that the sergeant is the strangler, and at a crucial moment, the

Sergeant Ottermole (Theodore Bikel) seems unnerved by Mr. Summers' (Rhys Williams) theory about the strangler loose in London in Hitchcock's presentation of "The Hands of Mr. Ottermole," directed by Robert Stevens.

journalist says, "Now, man to man, tell me, Sergeant Ottermole, just *why* did you kill all those inoffensive people?" With a tincture of the supernatural, Mr. Ottermole explains that:

> Everybody knows that we can't control the workings of our minds. Don't they? Ideas come into our minds without asking. But everybody's supposed to be able to control his body. Why? Eh? We get our minds from lord-knows-where — from people who were dead hundreds of years before we were born. Mayn't we get our bodies in the same way? Our faces — our legs — our heads — they aren't completely ours. We don't make 'em. They come to us. And couldn't ideas come into our bodies like ideas come into our minds? Eh? Can't ideas live in nerve and muscle as well as in brain? Couldn't it be that parts of our bodies all of a sudden, like ideas come into ... into— he shot his arms out, showing the great white-gloved hands and hairy wrists; shot them out so swiftly to the journalist's throat that his eyes never saw them — into *my hands!*

Hitchcock's version, directed by Robert Stevens, follows Burke's narrative closely, and to Cockrell and Stevens' credit they manage to emulate cinematically Burke's style through a keen use of the subjective camera. In addition,

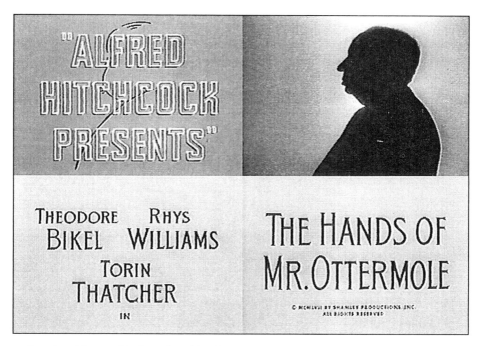

Opening titles to Alfred Hitchcock's television presentation of Thomas Burke's story "The Hands of Mr. Ottermole."

the use of the subjective angle places the audience in the role of the murderer. This is aptly illustrated in the opening sequence when Stevens, in one continuous take, follows Mr. Whybrow through the foggy corridors of London in 1919. At first we are merely following Whybrow until we hear someone whistling "Greensleeves" off camera, at which point we now suspect that we are a character in the drama as we approach Whybrow standing at his door. Our suspicions are proved correct when Whybrow turns and waves at the camera — *to us.* Whybrow enters his home, and Stevens cuts to an interior shot where idle chat fills the room; a moment later, however, a knock is heard and Whybrow answers the door. Stevens then cuts back to the subjective angle. Whybrow speaks directly to us, in a friendly manner, until he is stifled by the sudden appearance of two strong hands that throttle him.

Hitchcock's version remains of interest for two reasons. First, for a Hitchcock treatment and for a crime thriller, there is little effort to cast suspicions on an innocent character; indeed, there is absolutely no effort at even creating red herrings. Suspicion remains on the sergeant, played by Theodore Bikel, primarily because the sergeant repeatedly conveys painful guilt each time the strangler is mentioned. Stevens, however, understates this by never jumping to a close shot of Bikel, but always having him in the foreground where he remains at a distance from those who discuss, in a most stoic fashion, the strangler's actions. Ottermole, then, becomes the first and remains the only suspect in the drama, and through Bikel's melancholic performance Sergeant Ottermole also becomes a sympathetic character.

Secondly, Cockrell and Stevens see control, whether psychotic or supernatural, as the defining factor in the story. Even Hitchcock himself, in his wry opening monologue, carefully defers to a power outside his control when he tells us that "due to circumstances over which our sponsor has complete control" a commercial must displace his presence, which it does. In context, Hitchcock makes for an interesting choice of words. But nowhere is the notion of control more visually pronounced that during the murder of the flower woman. Here, Stevens again uses a subjective camera for the assault, but at the point of the murder the camera pans away from the victim to a close shot of a palmistry storefront where a mechanical hand is seen revolving in the window. Clearly, the message here is that a supernatural force, manifested by palmistry, serves as the controlling attitude. Cinematically, the murder itself is supplanted by the image of a mechanical hand, a hand that has no puissance independent of the mechanical control behind it. But more important, Stevens' use of the subjective angle controls the viewer, and the viewer becomes Mr. Ottermole himself; we simply have no control over what we are observing and, what we are doing within the narrative. Stevens, or the camera, television, or the media — however one wants to describe it — controls us. In "The Hands of Mr. Ottermole," we have no exit or alternative other than to *become* Ottermole — killing vicariously and in context. Like Ottermole, the "thing" that is outside our control takes on ideas all its own independent of our own control.

In Hitchcock's television version standards and practices demanded that Ottermole be apprehended. At the climactic moment the journalist is saved by a constable (Torin Thatcher), who states that he has trouble believing Ottermole could have committed the crimes. Nonetheless, the constable must arrest him, and at this point Stevens cuts to a close shot of the constable applying the handcuffs, apparently noting for us that the hands of Mr. Ottermole are under yet another type of control. As Ottermole is led away, the journalist ruminates on the reasons for Ottermole's depravity by repeating Ottermole's defense that "ideas come into my hands." A fellow journalist describes Ottermole as insane, and the journalist mutters unconvincingly "I suppose so" while looking into the distance for a rational explanation.[1]

On November 19, 1971, NBC television broadcast a made-for-television

---

[1]*If the student of Ripper lore believed he had heard such an explanation before, he had twelve years earlier on NBC radio's Mollé Mystery Theatre in a broadcast of Robert Bloch's "Yours Truly, Jack the Ripper." In the closing moments, the murderer claims that he is Jack the Ripper, but the survivors wonder if the man who is officially considered insane could actually have been Jack the Ripper himself (see Chapter III).*

Director Robert Stevens displaces Ottermole with the audience in the two murder sequences in Hitchcock's presentation of "The Hands of Mr. Ottermole." In this frame sequence, the flower woman turns to the camera and speaks casually as the camera gets ever so close. Suddenly, hands erupt into the frame and strangle the woman as the camera slowly pans to take in the window of a palmistry establishment with its rotating hand.

movie titled *Ellery Queen: Don't Look Behind You*, based on Ellery Queen's novel *Cat of Many Tails* as adapted by screenwriter Ted Leighton. Definite Ripper elements are at work in the novel, which Ellery Queen critic and biographer Francis M. Nevins, Jr., has claimed in *Royal Bloodline* "stands with *Calamity Town* at the pinnacle of his [Queen's] work" (142). The centerpiece of the Queen novel is "the Cat," a mysterious strangler who has the terrified attention of New York City one sweltering summer at the end of World War II. The crux of the story is the bizarre series of murders promulgated by a Ripper-like killer who goes about systematically murdering his victims in order of descending chronological age. Exhibiting a macabre sense of etiquette, the killer strangles his female victims with a length of pink rope, and his male victims with blue rope.

The translation of the story to television was not a successful one, casting errors and plot adjustments simply undermined the film. Nevins observed that the novel is deeply rooted in the late 1940s, and that modernizing the setting to 1970 "killed" the effect of the novel. Moreover, Nevins censured

Leighton and director Barry Shear for reducing Ellery Queen's rich character-
izations to what Nevins described as "cardboard," and for adding several senseless "suspense" sequences with no equivalents in the novel (79). Nevins,
however, reserves his shrillest disdain for the selection of Peter Lawford as
Ellery Queen, who played the part "as a mod Londonesque swinger, complete
with veddy accent and silver-streaked hair down to the eyebrows" (78). Lawford, who had from 1957 to 1959 played the witty and urbane Nick Charles
opposite Phyllis Kirk in the TV version of *The Thin Man*, unfortunately carried his Nick Charles persona over to his Ellery Queen role, and it was the
wrong approach. Further, because Lawford was much older than the Ellery
Queen of the novels, the pivotal role of his father, Inspector Richard Queen,
was altered to that of his uncle, played by Harry Morgan. All of these various
distractions and absurdities undercut the film's effectiveness and ensured that
the pilot would not harbinger a new series. Indeed, when four years later NBC
presented a fresh *Ellery Queen*, with a youthful Jim Hutton as Ellery and David
Wayne as his father, the new series seemed to go out of its way to avoid the
mistakes of 1971.

In this instance we are presented with an intriguing example of the Ripper mythos being affected by trendy and superficial cultural fads rather than
by questions of morality and what is right. Which is to be deplored more, the
pained self-righteousness of Sherlock Holmes in Bob Clark's *Murder by Decree*
or the smug dilettante's view of the world espoused by Lawford's mod Ellery
Queen, who finds in his personal Ripper cause for cerebral amusement?

A much more affecting film featuring a Ripper-like killer was John
Brahm's *Hangover Square* (1945), with Laird Cregar in the story as a demented
composer named George Harvey Bone who is driven to murdering women
whenever he is shaken by loud noises. Produced to capitalize on the success of
The Lodger released a year earlier, *Hangover Square* is similar to its predecessor. In addition to featuring both Cregar and George Sanders in major roles,
and to having been written by Barré Lyndon and produced by Robert Bassler
for 20th Century–Fox, both films are set in Victorian London where fog, Hansom cabs and gaslight are as much a part of life as breathing. Gregory Mank
summarizes the film's appeal in *Hollywood Cauldron* by articulating its narrative:

> The close-ups of Laird Cregar suffering a Jekyll/Hyde fit, his eyes heart-
> breakingly shining fear, bewilderment, and horror on a dark, Whitechapel
> street are memorable. Then there is the Guy Fawkes bonfire, where singing
> and dancing revelers place their dummies on a huge pyre, and Cregar car-
> ries the naked corpse of a strangled Linda Darnell to the top, cremating
> his dead lover to the eerie piccolos of Bernard Herrmann's demonic music.
> In the fiery, Wagnerian climax, George Sanders, the criminal psycholo-
> gist who finally trapped Cregar, rescues the madman's loyal love from the
> flames as Cregar pounds the final notes of the concerto he had composed
> while violently losing his sanity [325].

In Edgar G. Ulmer's *Bluebeard* (1944), a poster warning Parisians of a murderer in their midst reminds one of the numerous posters in the Ripper's Whitechapel.

Certainly two of the premier and more interesting of the Ripper redux works are Edgar G. Ulmer's *Bluebeard* (a low-budget programmer produced by PRC Pictures in 1944) and "Alias the Scarf" (an episode of the ABC television series *The Green Hornet*), both featuring John Carradine. In both works, the murders by "Bluebeard" and "The Scarf" clearly parallel those of Jack the Ripper. Moreover, in both instances art and creative expression are used as milieu for the killer's motive, if not for his own raison d'être.

Despite the title, Ulmer's *Bluebeard* (1944) has nothing to do with the historical "Bluebeard," Henri Landru, who murdered at least ten women in France in the 1920s. In fact, the film owes much more to Jack the Ripper than to any "lonely hearts" killer. The Ripper's influence is reflected by Ulmer in the film's first few sequences. We see the police retrieving the body of a woman from the Seine, and we next see officers hanging a poster — echoing the numerous posters hung in Whitechapel — that warns the public "A murderer is in your midst! A criminal who strangles young women!" Ulmer then offers two scenes in which men are concerned about unescorted women on the streets at dark before cutting to three young women who express fear about the dark. The women scurry into the streets where they encounter a tall figure in top hat and cape emerging from the Parisian fog. The man is recognized as Gaston Morel

Title card for Edgar G. Ulmer's "Ripper Redux" film.

(Carradine), the puppeteer who stages operas in the park performed by marionettes.

Morel is a combination of Mr. Slade and George Harvey Bone from Lyndon's adaptations of *The Lodger* and *Hangover Square*, respectively. Indeed, Morel, like Bone, is a mad artist, but Morel's murders are an attempt to eradicate his wanton model, Jeanette (Anne Sterling), from his mind. At the film's climax, Morel explains to the frightened Lucille (Jean Parker) that he thought by killing Jeanette he could stop her from "defiling the image" he had created of her. The image is both a perfect portrait he had painted of her, a portrait that was chosen to hang in the Louvre, as well as his own ideal of womanhood. In this respect Jeanette represents for Morel just what Kitty represented for Slade: a perfect woman whose outward beauty manifests her inward, moral beauty. But as Morel seeks Jeanette so that he can share the joy of "their" portrait together, he finds that Jeanette is not so pure after all; he discovers debauched men leaving her apartment, and he learns that she is a libertine who suddenly derides him for his portrait of her. Morel describes her as a "low,

Opposite: Gaston Morel (John Carradine) dressed in familiar Jack the Ripper attire comes out of the fog in Ulmer's *Bluebeard*.

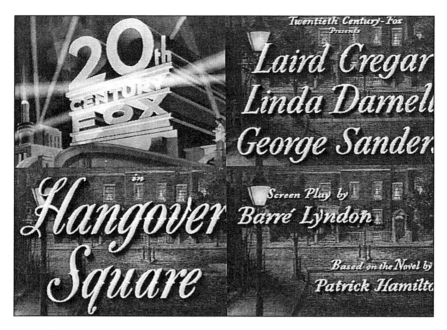

Main title to *Hangover Square*, Fox's follow up to the successful *The Lodger*, both scripted by Barré Lyndon.

coarse, loathsome creature" whose lifestyle mocks his paintings and thereby mocks his ideal. In his mind, the sacred muse that inspired him has now become a devil that corrupts him, and this devil needs to be eliminated. Morel explains how he lost control and strangled Jeanette: "I thought that would be the end of what she could do to me, but it wasn't. Every time I painted again, I painted Jeanette." Later, in a scene that echoes Slade's own torment, Morel laments that "every girl I painted turned out to be Jeanette, and I couldn't permit it, I couldn't stop myself. Every time I painted her — I had to kill her again. Finally, life came to mean nothing to me, not even my own."

Morel believes that Lucille, however, can purge him of Jeanette's specter. He warns Lucille that "anyone seeking to destroy our happiness is a menace — a menace that would have to be done away with." But Lucille exclaims that she is going to the police, at which point a desperate Morel stops her. While embracing Lucille he tells her that "you wouldn't do that to me! Not you, Lucille, I wouldn't let you turn against me, too." It is a somewhat tender scene as Morel entreats Lucille, but as he is embracing her, his autonomous hands — like those of Mr. Ottermole — are rising to her neck. Once those artist's hands reach her neck, Morel is genuinely surprised to see his hands throttling her. But Ulmer undercuts any sympathy for Morel by jumping directly to a close shot of one of Carradine's greatest assets as an actor, his flared eyes. Framed

In a tender moment, Morel (Carradine) explains how his beloved Jeannette became a "low, coarse, loathesome creature."

in stylish chiaroscuro lighting, Morel's eyes convey an evil presence so pervasive that those eyes could have belonged to Jack the Ripper himself.

Lucille is rescued by the entrance of Inspector Lefevre (Nils Asther) and members of the Sureté who chase Morel over the rooftops of Paris. Like Slade, Morel is unable to avoid capture; the police close in, and Morel falls into the river. As Morel disappears beneath the rippling waters of the Seine, we can almost hear Kitty again, saying that the river "carries things out to sea, and they sink in deep water."

Ulmer's *Bluebeard* is so stylish that it plays like a nightmare. Ulmer's expressionistic design — especially the flashback sequence with its distorted images and tilted angles — draws us into Morel's twisted mind, or what John Belton describes in *The Hollywood Professionals* as "the mystical power of a traumatic mental experience that has stunned the action of Ulmer's characters and made them prisoners of their own nightmares" (160). But the film also conveys the dichotomy between art object and observer as well. We attempt to remain objective and merely observe the object, and yet at the same time there is something about the object that penetrates deep into our soul. We remain fascinated by what we see, and the reason is most likely that the object

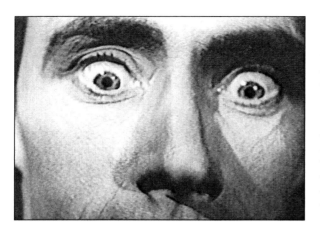

The flared, domineering eyes, one of Carradine's greatest assets as an actor, are maximized by director Ulmer to convey Morel's madness.

penetrates into the collective unconscious where that very object has been dormant since primordial times. As psychologist C. G. Jung asserts, art has the power to elicit our most primordial secrets. In this sense, we can say that just as Morel's artistic fetish perverts his relationship with women, Ulmer's stylish film distorts our own relationship with the horror that is enacted before us. For Morel is no monster possessed of archetypal evil (he is not a Dracula or a satanic fiend). Rather, Morel is clearly the inferior side of the individual, or what Jung described as *the shadow*, because our response to Morel is at once a sympathetic one as well as a fearful one. We see him as one whose twisted view of the world has alienated him from that world. This remains disturbing for us because as such he is symptomatic of us all; at any moment we, too, can become alienated. We could become like Morel, as pleasing and genteel as when we first see him on that Parisian street, as talented and gifted as when we see him perform the puppet opera, and as melancholy and strangely rational as when we see him destroy the things that mock him and his world. The film becomes a nightmare of our greatest inner fears: that we could become such a shadow figure. Like the mythic sense of Jack the Ripper, Morel is the horror that lives in us all.

John Carradine also starred in "Alias the Scarf," an episode broadcast on February 24, 1967, of the ABC television series *The Green Hornet*, a serious "super hero" program produced by William Dozier during the Batman craze of the 1960s. So significant is "Alias the Scarf" to Ripper lore that some Ripper historians have cited the episode as an example of an appearance of Jack the Ripper by name (Begg 161). This is not true, however. The derivation is so apparent that the episode is worth examining inasmuch as we are concerned here with some of the more representative clones of the Whitechapel killer.

Scriptwriter William L. Stuart and director Allen Reisner united to imply the guiding presence of Jack the Ripper in their tale that speaks not only about murder but, more important, about immortality. The program opens on familiar Ripper trappings: Fog and lamplight immediately define the ambience. In the next instance we are ushered into a familiar waxworks motif (complete with a menagerie of replicated criminals) known as "The Chamber of Evil." Museum guide James Rancourt (Carradine), who reportedly knows more about criminals than the police, leads a group of reporters on a tour of the Chamber of Evil. He introduces a "bluebeard" who murdered his wives, then a gangster who turned on his own men, and finally the waxen image of a serial killer known as the Scarf. He tells the group that the Scarf's identity remains unknown, and that for years, before the arrival of the Green Hornet effigy in the wax museum, the Scarf was the star attraction of the Chamber of Evil. Rancourt then describes, in a melancholy fashion, that the Scarf was "urbane, ruthless, contemptuous of the police; he killed by using a white scarf as a garrote; he was never captured, and then more than 20 years ago he simply vanished."

Soon after the museum closes for the night, the wax effigy of the Scarf seemingly comes to life and takes up his old habits of strangling people. The Scarf first murders Rancourt's partner, Peter Willman (Ian Wolfe). Then adjourning to a fog shrouded park, the Scarf kills a derelict on a park bench, frightens off a young woman, and attacks a man waiting at a bus stop. The Scarf's new killing spree catches the attention of the Green Hornet (Van Williams), who discovers in an old trunk at the museum a book manuscript about the Scarf written by Rancourt. The information in the manuscript leads the Green Hornet to Hazel Schmidt (Patricia Barry), who danced in burlesque under the name Vena Rose. She tells the Green Hornet that the Scarf's interest in her was solely platonic; she states that all he wanted to do was talk, and that she was a good listener. Vena tells the Green Hornet that one night the Scarf explained "he was going away because he was going to be immortal so people would never forget him all those years; that's what he wanted."

When Vena appears at the Chamber of Evil she is immediately noted by Rancourt, and while staring at the lifeless wax figure of the Scarf, Vena tells Rancourt that the Scarf isn't immortal after all; he's just a wax dummy. Rancourt demurs, saying that "you remembered and that's what's important. For a part of immortality is that one is remembered." Vena suddenly recognizes Rancourt as the shadowy figure she had once befriended as the Scarf, and in this moment of shared revelations we come to understand the Scarf's raison d'être. Inasmuch as the Scarf had no dark gods to petition for immortality (such as were available to John Carmody in "Yours Truly, Jack the Ripper") the Scarf is content to settle for a figurative — the artistic — rather than literal immortality. The murders were not political protests or manifestations of some sort of governmental cover-up; nor were the murders moral judgments or acts inspired by sexual madness or personal revenge. The murders perpetrated by the Scarf were, in the final analysis, a means of certifying the killer's greatness. He joins, as he says, "Attila the Hun, Jack the Ripper, Bluebeard, and Captain Kidd" in extending his presence beyond the grave. Rancourt's capture by the Green Hornet, which comes only seconds later, is truly anticlimactic.

The ubiquitous man in top hat and cape in the London fog in "Fog," an episode of *The Avengers*.

Similar in concept to "Alias the Scarf," in certain respects, was a 1969 episode titled "Fog" of the celebrated British television series *The Avengers* with Patrick Macnee and Linda Thorson as secret agents John Steed and Tara King. As written by Jeremy Burnham, the similarity is most pronounced in the suggestive imagery employed throughout both episodes to conjure up the Ripper's London in the context of the current day. Just as Marie Belloc Lowndes' Lodger was unquestionably Jack the Ripper, the Scarf in the case of the *Green Hornet* and the Gaslight Ghoul in the case of *The Avengers* were both clearly Jack.

Burnham's story begins with the standard imagery of fog, narrow dark streets, dim gaslight and footfalls on cobblestone to imply another time and another place. Viewers' attention is drawn initially to a discarded handbill which only underscores and validates the imagery for the audience. The handbill is headed by "Gaslight Ghoul" followed by an explanation that states:

> 100 Guineas reward for information leading to the arrest of the person known as the Gaslight Ghoul, perpetrator of may vile and grisly murders near Gunthrope Street London during the months of October & November 1888. He is tall, bearded and has been seen carrying a long carpet bag.

At this point viewers might easily suspect that they are in London of 1888, and nothing the audience has seen would seriously argue otherwise. It is only when the scene shifts to the arrival of a Disarmament Committee foreign delegation at a fog-bound railway platform that the true setting is established. Here, an inquisitive diplomat asks if a steam pipe had broken, and Steed assures the diplomat that it is only fog. "We still lead the world in that department," Steed tells the perplexed diplomat with pride. But even in this present-day setting, director John Hough leaves his audience with a sense of anachronism, that the present is out of place and it really is 1888, which is further stated by the sequence that follows. In the dense fog, one of the diplomats becomes separated from the others and is stalked by a tall lean figure which seems to fit perfectly the description of the Gaslight Ghoul mentioned in the handbill — right down to the detail of the long carpet bag. As the audience anticipates, the diplomat meets his end at the hands of the Gaslight Ghoul. The means of dispatch is the Ghoul's trademark sword stick, and his means of escape is apparently a hansom cab.

When the slain diplomat's body is discovered lying in Gunthrope Street, all the clues point to the Gaslight Ghoul despite the fact that the Ghoul would be over 100 years old. When Steed and Miss King visit the scene of the murder, they spot a man answering the description of the Gaslight Ghoul, but before they can apprehend the figure he escapes. The man carelessly leaves behind an item of his costume which leads Steed and Miss King to a theatrical costume shop which seems to specialize in Gaslight Ghoul outfits. Records at the shop indicate that the man is one C. Osgood, and when Steed and Miss King confront Osgood in his lodgings they learn that Osgood is a member of the Gaslight Ghoul Club, which was "formed to investigate the unsolved murders of the Gaslight Ghoul," as Osgood explains. When Miss King expresses the opinion that it is a bit late in the day to track down the Ghoul, Osgood assures Steed and Miss King that "the identity of the Ghoul has remained a source of constant fascination through the years."

Almost immediately upon the departure of Steed and Miss King, Osgood is killed, thereby eliminating a prime suspect, and Steed finds a warning that cautions the investigators not to interfere. Steed and Miss King, however, do elect to interfere. Armed with a forged diary purporting to recount an original hitherto unsuspected Gaslight Ghoul murder, Steed gains admittance and membership in the exclusive Gaslight Ghoul Club where each member is expected to attire himself in the garb of the Gaslight Ghoul. The club's president, Sir Geoffrey Armstrong (Nigel Green), explains that the club had been formed some eighty years ago, after the first Ghoul murder was committed. When it becomes clear that the police were getting nowhere, Sir Geoffrey further explains, a number of amateurs decided to pool their abilities and form a society to bring the Ghoul to justice. The present members, Armstrong points out, are merely carrying on where the original members left off. Steed

John Steed (Patrick Macnee) discusses Jack the Ripper theories with Sir Geoffrey Armstrong (Nigel Green), one of the "Gaslight Ghouls," in "Fog," an episode of the ABC television series *The Avengers.*

is also introduced to the society's secretary, Mark Travers (Guy Rolfe), and the club's own Black Museum of crime.

The impression that the Gaslight Ghoul Club harbors a group of harmless eccentrics is belied by Steed's conviction that one of the members has taken his assumed role of Gaslight Ghoul literally. For a time it appears that Sir Geoffrey is the most likely suspect, and being a respected surgeon with right wing politics (as a member of the Society Against the Disintegration of the British Empire) would make him appear to have reason to disrupt the work of the Disarmament Committee and it foreign delegates.

Soon another member of the committee is killed and the pace quickens. When Sir Geoffrey is attacked and critically wounded Steed must look elsewhere for another suspect. The search leads Steed back to the Gaslight Ghoul Club and to the Black Museum where Steed confronts Mark Travers in the guise of the Gaslight Ghoul. Travers, a dealer in armaments, is determined to protect his lucrative business by destroying the Disarmament Committee and its potential threat to the gun trade.

What both "Alias the Scarf" and "Fog" ably demonstrate is the power of

certain imagery to conjure up the shadowy Ripper from our collective unconscious without ever mentioning his name. Just as Marie Belloc Lowndes left
no doubt that her lodger was the Ripper, viewers of "Alias the Scarf" and "Fog"
understand completely that they are dealing with Jack the Ripper under the thin
cover of another name. Like a potent witch's brew, a writer or director merely
needs to add a soupçon of fog, a dram of yellow gaslight, a hint of echoing
footsteps, a modest dose of darkness, maybe a valise with a few optional ingre-
dients, and an audience is presented with a mental image which overrides all
pseudonyms. The result screams "Jack the Ripper" as loudly as the news vendors of Victoria's London once screamed the name. Call it clichéd or stereotyped, but the imagery works.

In 1972, a radically different approach was taken with Jack the Ripper
when Avco-Embassy Pictures released Peter Medak's *The Ruling Class*, a controversial satire that was met by mixed reviews and poor box office returns.[2]
The film features Peter O'Toole as Jack, the 14th Earl of Gurney, a certified
lunatic, who is released from incarceration upon the accidental death of his
eccentric father (Harry Andrews). Jack then inherits the family fortune, much
to the annoyance of the so-called sane members of the household. Upon his
return to the ancestral home Jack comes to believe, or at least proclaims, that
he is Jesus Christ. Garbed as a vagabond messiah, Jack remains convinced that
he is Christ until he encounters another lunatic named McKyle (Nigel Green)
who calls himself the "Electric Christ." Once this "new" Christ appears —
defining himself through supercharged ravings — Jack withdraws from his
messiah personality. Believing that he is Jack the Ripper, he accordingly pro-
ceeds to act out the role. In a nightmarish fantasy sequence Jack murders a
prostitute, but in fact Jack murders his aunt, Lady Claire (Coral Browne), and
later murders his own wife (Carolyn Seymour).

O'Toole once remarked that *The Ruling Class* was "a comedy with tragic
relief," but such a description fails to acknowledge the storm of controversy
which greeted the film upon its release, or the brutality of the film. Medak's
film is no genteel satire modestly pricking at selected pomposities, but rather
the film slashes with razor-like viciousness — in imitation of the Ripper himself — at a host of 1970s targets, primarily the British Aristocracy, organized
religion, manners and morals, and governance itself. In a particularly abra-
sive speech to the House of Lords, Jack — believing himself to be the Ripper —
offers an eloquent soliloquy in defense of perversity and hatred. If Jack's speech
was not unsettling enough, the standing ovation from the Earl's peers provides
a hellish commentary on the true leanings of "The Ruling Class."

However, the film reaches a crescendo of comic horror when the Earl's

[2]*Succinctly, the critical response is summarized by the* New York Times *(September 14, 1972), which
praised the film as "fantastic fun," and by* Newsweek *(September 25, 1972), which denounced the
film as "odious" (115). O'Toole was nominated for an Academy Award for his performance as Jack,
but he lost to Marlon Brando who played Don Corleone in Francis Ford Coppola's* The Godfather.

recently born son cries out, in ratification of his lineage, that "I am Jack!" The child's cry is as hair-raising as the Ripper's words to H. G. Wells in Nicholas Meyer's *Time after Time:* "I am Jack!" coupled with "I belong here completely and utterly. I'm home," speaks pointedly about the twentieth century. As such, both films make the case that the Ripper is as much a part of the twentieth century as the air we breath.

In the final analysis, Jack the Ripper was a murderous thug, and the world has always had a plentiful supply of such beasts. But as a symbol, the Ripper has been adopted and recreated to fill a certain role in our lives. Even his name was not his own but probably the product of an overactive and irresponsible reporter, and the world has long suffered a plentiful supply of these creatures as well. Immortality fascinates us. Most of us seek it in the conventional way by adopting a belief system that promises life after death. The Ripper has achieved immortality through other means, however. We are "the dark gods" of whom Bloch spoke in "Yours Truly, Jack the Ripper"; it is to us that the Ripper appeals for immortality, and we grant that immortality. All the Ripper is required to do is keep us entertained with his knife tricks on the stage of our choice.

V

APOCALYPSE:
SHERLOCK HOLMES AGAINST
JACK THE RIPPER

Arguably, the two foremost symbols of the Victorian age were Sherlock Holmes and Jack the Ripper. Whereas Holmes served as a reflection of the Victorian proclivity for order, patriotism, duty and faith in the process of scientific reason, the Ripper functioned as the direct opposite, representing the "other Victorians," as Steven Marcus called them, symptomatic of chaos, naked emotion, and self-absorption. In truth, Sherlock Holmes never met Jack the Ripper, at least insofar as the original canon of 56 short stories and 4 novels is concerned. Nonetheless Watson comments in "The Veiled Lodger" that Holmes' cases proved "a perfect quarry for the student, not only of crime, but of the social and *official* scandals of the late Victorian era" (emphasis added). Although ambiguity reigns here with respect to "official scandals," a case can be made that one of those official scandals was the result of an investigation into a "delicate and sensitive" matter, which easily could have been Stowell's claim itself.

Over the years a number of writers have attempted to place the great detective and Jack the Ripper in mortal combat, an encounter that for many Sherlockians far surpasses in eminence and significance that of Holmes and Moriarty at the Reichenbach Falls in Switzerland. Recently the number of these encounters has increased, reaching perhaps its most bizarre level in a particularly radical if not heretical novel titled *The Last Sherlock Holmes Story* (1978). Author Michael Dibdin postulates the gross suggestion that Holmes and the Ripper were one and the same; indeed, that Holmes and Moriarty were one and same. Holmes is depicted as a Jekyll and Hyde schizophrenic. Dibdin alters the "facts" at the Reichenbach Falls to reveal that it was not Holmes and Moriarty who struggled to the death at Meiringen, but rather a deranged Holmes believing that Moriarty had killed Watson and assumed his identity. Watson feels the moral imperative to destroy Holmes since Watson had discovered Holmes' secret. Confronting Holmes at the precipice, revolver in hand, Watson cries out that, "I tell you I know.... I watched you butcher Mary Kelly and I've read your unspeakable verses on the subject. The game is up! Try to understand! You are a homicidal maniac! A deranged killer!" After a brief struggle, Holmes regains his composure, telling Watson to "Never fear, old fellow.... You shall not be hurt. I shall not let him hurt you." Watson then writes that, "With these words he stepped backwards off the edge of the precipice. I crawled to the brink of that fearful abyss and looked over in time to see Holmes' body strike an outcrop of rock far below. Then I knew no more." Naturally, Watson discreetly destroys the evidence that proved that Sherlock Holmes was Jack the Ripper.

Most Sherlockian theorists and writers have taken a saner course in attempting to suggest that a duel between Holmes and the Ripper had taken place; a confrontation, moreover, that has been traditionally comported out of the public eye for reasons that are most often described as "delicate and sensitive," and hence wholly within the Victorian character. Although relatively few in number, authors use the confrontation for one or two reasons: they use it as a milieu for their political or social polemics, which is particularly true of Bob Clark's post–Watergate film *Murder by Decree* (1978); or, like the Ripperologists, they use the confrontation to postulate their own unique claims in a *literary* rather than historical sense for the identity of Jack the Ripper, such as the absurd claim by Dibdin.

As far as can be determined, the first to pit Sherlock Holmes against Jack the Ripper was a Spanish vignette titled "Jack el Destripador," whose only known existence is that which was "translated" by Anthony Boucher as a synopsis in 1945 for *Ellery Queen's Mystery Magazine*, and reprinted in Alan Barnard's *The Harlot Killer*.

Perhaps the first to make a complete and sensible case for Sherlock Holmes investigating the Ripper murders is noted Sherlockian scholar William S. Baring-Gould, who, in his seminal biography *Sherlock Holmes of Baker Street: A Life of the World's First Consulting Detective* (1962), startled Sherlockians by exposing a Scotland Yard detective as Jack the Ripper. In a particularly gifted device for structuring his biography, Baring-Gould uses a series of "interruptions" to his chronology to detail reportage from the *Times of London* about the Ripper murders. He ultimately relates how Holmes, disguised as a harlot, traps the Ripper off Cable street "at the entrance to a dirty court" only to have the Ripper gain the advantage in a struggle. But at a perilous moment, when the Ripper "advanced on the prostrate body of the unconscious detective," Holmes is rescued by Watson, who subdues the Ripper, revealing Jack the Ripper to be Inspector Athelney Jones, "the red-faced, burly, and plethoric" detective who investigated the murder of Bartholomew Sholto in

The Sign of Four. In a turnabout at the denouement, Watson relates to Holmes how he deduced that Jones was the Ripper by comparing information about Mary Jane Kelly related by Jones with information published in the *Times*. Watson tells Holmes that, "Unless Inspector Athelney Jones was himself the Ripper for whom he professed to be hunting, how then did he know — *a day before the* Times *was published* — that Mary Jane Kelly, shortly before her hideous death, was plump, rosy, *singing*?" (177). An elated Holmes takes the pipe from his mouth, and exclaims, "Extraordinary, my dear Watson." A proud Watson mutters in turn, "Elementary, my dear Holmes." Ultimately, Holmes tells Watson that "while you have all the facts in your journal, the public will never know of them. Scotland Yard can hardly admit that the Ripper who has terrorized the entire East End of London for so many months is one of its own men — an inspector, at that, and a rising one" (176). Unfortunately, Baring-Gould never allows Holmes, or Watson for that matter, to divulge Jones' motive for his reign of terror; he simply existed without explanation.

One of the more interesting and detailed analyses connecting Holmes with the Ripper investigation is offered by Michael Harrison, who first postulates his claim in *Clarence: Was He Jack the Ripper?* (1972), which was published in Great Britain as *The Life of the Duke of Clarence and Avondale 1864–1892.* Here, Harrison rather effectively dispels Stowell's notion that the Duke of Clarence could possibly have been the Ripper by demonstrating that the Prince was far removed from London during the crucial times of the Ripper killings. Harrison offers instead the name of J. K. (James Kenneth) Stephen, Clarence's tutor and alleged homosexual lover, as the Ripper. Harrison, a devoted Sherlockian as well as Ripperologist, takes his theory into the Holmesian canon in *The World of Sherlock Holmes* (1975), in which Harrison asserts that "The Adventure of the Norwood Builder" and Watson's enigmatic reference to "The Case of Bert Stevens, the Terrible Murderer" (one of the cases that Watson felt compelled by circumstances to withhold from the public), leads Harrison to the conclusion that Holmes himself proved Stephen's Ripper identity. Harrison notes the fundamental observation, understood by even the most casual Sherlockian researcher, that Watson "always made some alteration, great or small, in the names of the dramatis personae, in the locations of the adventures, and in even the dates involved" (130). Harrison is finally left to speculate that the similarities in the names "Bert Stevens" and "Jim Stephen" could not be coincidence; "the Terrible Murderer" Watson names as Bert Stevens, in Harrison's view, could be no other than J. K. Stephen — the Ripper (130).

But the two most conspicuous works on the subject are two British films, and it is regrettable that both James Hill's *A Study in Terror* (1965) and the aforementioned *Murder by Decree* use the Holmes/Ripper confrontation to expound, in varying degrees, controversial attitudes about government suspicions, arguably in response to suspicions set in motion by the political protests of the 1960s. As such, these themes are not without a certain amount of accuracy since elements of political strife coupled with government corruption are found in the original Ripper case. The squalor, poverty and depravity symbolized by life in Whitechapel and the East End were useful to the opportunistic radicals who were desiring to alter or completely topple the existing lines of authority. Genuine reform-minded souls, such as George Bernard Shaw, interpreted the Ripper's actions as something of a public service, intentionally or unintentionally underscoring the political neglect which had more or less created the wickedness to begin with. In a letter to *The Star* dated September 24, 1888, Shaw spoke for many of the radicals when he wrote in part that:

> Whilst we conventional Social Democrats were wasting our time on education, agitation and organization, some independent genius has taken the matter in hand, and by simply murdering and disemboweling four women, converted the proprietary press to an inept sort of communism. The moral is a pretty one, and the Insurrectionists, the Dynamitards, the Invincibles and the extreme left of the Anarchist party will not be slow to draw it.... . If the habits of Duchesses only admitted of their being decoyed into Whitechapel backyards, a single experiment in slaughterhouse anatomy on an aristocratic victim might fetch a round half million [for charity] and save the necessity of sacrificing four women of the people [Cullen 201].

Interestingly, Baring-Gould tells us that Holmes and Shaw shared enmity between them. Baring-Gould cites Shaw's biographer, Heskeath Pearson, who wrote that Shaw labeled Holmes "a drug addict without a single amiable trait." Baring-Gould claims that the rancor grew out of Shaw's caustic review of the art and skill of Pablo de Sarasate, a Spanish violin virtuoso whom Holmes admired greatly (185).

As progressive as Shaw's letter sounds, it is nearly impossible to conceive of the very British Sherlock Holmes siding with such anti-establishment views, although much of Holmes' political views are missing in the canon. Indeed, Watson notes, in *A Study in Scarlet*, that Holmes' knowledge of politics was "feeble" although Watson later recalled that Holmes' knowledge of politics was "zero" ("The Five Orange Pips"). We can infer, however, from internal evidence that Holmes' loyalty to the Crown was solid, if not by his patriotic "V. R." for Victoria Regina etched into the wall by bullet holes at 221 B Baker Street, then at least by his service to the government in three significant adventures. In "The Adventure of the Bruce-Partington Plans" set in 1895, Holmes recovers the Bruce-Partington submarine plans for which he was decorated by Queen Victoria herself, and for which he was given an emerald tiepin which piqued Watson's interest: "When I asked him if he had bought it, he answered that it was a present from a certain gracious lady in whose interests he had once been fortunate enough to carry out a small commission." Secondly, in "The

Adventure of the Second Stain," Holmes recovers an important state paper and earns the gratitude of a relieved Prime Minister and the Secretary for European Affairs. Thirdly, in "His Last Bow" set in 1914, Holmes' willingly comes out of retirement to expose and dispatch the dreaded German spy ring led by Von Bork at the onset of World War I. Such evidence leads one to conclude that Holmes' loyalty to the Empire remained inviolate throughout his active career and beyond.

James Hill's *A Study in Terror*, the first and better of the two Holmes/Ripper films, whose "story contains characters who are to some extent patterned after the real-life Douglas family (the Marquis of Queensbury and his son Lord Alfred)," according to Robert W. Pohle, Jr., and Douglas C. Hart in *Sherlock Holmes on the Screen* (216), nicely blends a seasoning of Holmes' political propensities with some historical accuracy as well as insights into the canon itself. The British co-production by Compton-Cameo-Tekli and Sir Nigel Films, the latter being the film production unit of the Doyle estate, featured John Neville as Sherlock Holmes and Donald Houston as Dr. Watson with an especially adroit performance by Robert Morley as the canonically corpulent as well as imposing Mycroft Holmes. Pohle and Hart write that Adrian Conan Doyle "not only had a hand in the script of this venture, but also contributed to its financing as trustee of his father's estate; in partnership with the American Henry E. Lester he had originally planned not only to film more combinations of Holmes-and-horror, but also to base a television series called *The Sir Arthur Conan Doyle Theatre* on his father's works..." (215). The precise identity of the American Lester is elusive; his name appears in the screen credits to Terence Fisher's *The Hound of the Baskervilles* (1959) as production supervisor for the Sir Arthur Conan Doyle estate, and he is identified as "technical advisor" in the credits to Irwin Allen's *The Lost World* (1960), based on Doyle's adventure novel.

The original story and screenplay were written by Donald and Derek Ford, but some sources assert that the script was adapted from an original treatment by Adrian Conan Doyle titled *Fog*. As noted, Pohle and Hart assert that Doyle "had a hand in the script," but executive producer Herman Cohen, in an interview with Jessica Lilley in *Scarlet Street* magazine, claims that he came up with the original idea. Cohen states that "I met Henry Lester, who was representing the Conan Doyle estate ... [and] Henry Lester had talked to a pair of independent producers [Tony Tenser and Michael Klinger] in London who were interested in making a Sherlock Holmes picture, but they didn't have the money. I got the idea of pitting Sherlock Holmes against Jack the Ripper, which Conan Doyle never wrote. He wrote *A Study in Scarlet*, but this was an original that we came up with: *A Study in Terror*" (75). Cohen's comments, however, are in conflict with his interview with Tom Weaver, in *Attack of the Monster Movie Makers: Interviews with 20 Genre Giants*. Cohen tells Weaver that "Donald and Derek Ford get screen credit for the writing but they

Jack the Ripper strikes in James Hill's *A Study in Terror* (1966).

didn't write it, although the idea of combining Holmes and Jack the Ripper was theirs" (Weaver 75). Cohen adds that "Donald and Derek Ford did the original story and screenplay, but then we brought in a top writer named Harry Craig to do the final screenplay with me" (75). Cohen expounds to Weaver that, "Michael Klinger and Tony Tenser had signed them [Donald and Derek Ford] for 'their' Sherlock Holmes movie, but they didn't execute their script properly and I didn't like it. I hired Harry Craig, a writer that Adrian Conan Doyle and Henry Lester liked very much" (75). With respect to Adrian Conan Doyle's involvement, Cohen told Weaver that Adrian Conan Doyle "just visited with his wife and friends for tea and lunch occasionally. But Henry Lester and I discussed many, many facets, and there were many things we wanted to do that he would say, 'Oh, no, *no*, Sherlock Holmes wouldn't *do* that!'" (75).

Cohen told Lilley that the film was originally titled *Fog* but that Bob Ferguson, head of advertising for Columbia Pictures, came up with the title, *A Study in Terror* (Lilley 75), which, at least sounds canonical. Cohen told Weaver that "Columbia insisted on *A Study in Terror*; [but] I hated it. They wanted it because Sir Arthur Conan Doyle had written a book called *A Study in Scarlet*, but I didn't like the word 'study' in there; I felt that the teenagers would think it would be like extra homework! Columbia fought me, and I had to go along with them in the end. My title was *Fog*, a nice, simple, one-word title" (Weaver 76).

The narrative, along with Alex Vetchinsky's production design, is characteristically Sherlockian. The plot is a pastiche of Conan Doyle right down to the Holmesian aphorisms and such canonical traits as Holmes describing himself as a "consulting detective" and his use of "baritsu," the Japanese method of self-defense. As Holmes searches for his pipe, Watson mutters his shock at the grisly murders occurring in Whitechapel. When Watson tells Holmes that a second body has been found, Holmes replies that the murder is, indeed, interesting. When Watson asks why, Holmes replies wryly, "because it is the second murder." Following the murder of Annie Chapman (played by Barbara Windsor with such verve as to give life to the word "tart") Holmes receives an anonymous package containing a box of surgical instruments from which a scalpel is missing. Holmes deduces that the box came from a pawn shop, and that it was sent to him by a woman; Holmes characteristically tells Watson that "a woman wishes to introduce me to these crimes, and I find that provocative." Holmes traces the box to the estate of the Duke of Shires (Barry Jones), and there he learns that the box of instruments once belonged to the Duke's eldest son, Michael Osbourne (John Cairney), whom the Duke has disowned for marrying a prostitute named Angela (Adrienne Corri). Holmes then learns that the Duke's younger son, Edward, known as Lord Carfax (John Fraser), had been paying blackmail to a Whitechapel thug named Max Steiner (Peter Carsten) in order to protect family honor. The murders are now eliciting political ramifications, prompting Mycroft Holmes, at the behest of the Prime Minister (Cecil Parker), to entreat the aid of his brother in solving the crimes so that the government shall be preserved; Sherlock, however, answers that he has little concern for politicians, and that he is on the case only for its challenge and nothing else. Implicated in the murders is Dr. Murray (Anthony Quayle), the administrator of a Whitechapel hostel, who seems to know more about Michael that anyone else in the case. Holmes entreats Dr. Murray to give him the truth, saying that "we are in Victoria's England, sir, not Caligula's Rome; at least consider his family and tell me what happened." Murray then confesses to Holmes that his mute, dimwitted assistant at the hostel is Michael Osbourne, whose mind snapped when the boy learned that his wife was a blackmailer involved with Steiner, and that Michael was indirectly involved in scarring Angela with acid. Holmes then confronts both Angela and Steiner at the Angel and Crown pub where Angela tells Holmes a different story. She tells him that Michael was a brute who had forced her back into prostitution, and thrown acid in her face when he learned that she was leaving him. Angela states he was responsible for the blackmail scheme against not his father but his brother, Lord Carfax, because he knew he would never get a shilling out of his father. As Holmes and Watson leave the pub, Watson remarks that Angela is a remarkable woman, but Holmes counters by saying that she has deep scars, preferring Murray's account of the incident. Holmes takes Michael back to the estate where father and son are reunited, then sets a trap for the killer in Angela's room. As the Ripper is about to attack Angela, Holmes exposes Jack the Ripper as Lord Carfax. During a struggle a lamp is hurled at Holmes, igniting the room into flame; Carfax, Angela and Steiner perish in the conflagration. Holmes explains to Watson that his investigation of the Osbourne family revealed a strain of insanity. Lord Carfax sought revenge on Angela for her treatment of Michael, but since Carfax could not recognize Angela he embarked on a mad systematic scheme of exterminating all prostitutes, thereby eventually destroying, in his crazed mind, Angela. Holmes tells Watson that no purpose shall be served if the truth is revealed publicly. He notes that not even Inspector Lestrade (Frank Finlay) knows the identity of the Ripper, and out of deference to the infirm Duke and the family's past suffering, the identity shall be known only to himself and to Watson.

The remarkable thing about the film is that the story presages Stowell's theory, published four years after the film's release, that Jack the Ripper was of royal blood. The ever-resourceful showman Cohen asserts, in his interview with Jessica Lilley, that "Queen Victoria sealed some secret documents on the case of Jack the Ripper, to be opened after a hundred years! It all points to a member of the royal family. That's why we did what we did. We didn't want to get too close to the royal family, but we made the Ripper an aristocrat." His proof is that he says he got to know several Scotland Yard inspectors, and that he was "one of the first Americans to be taken through Scotland Yard's Black Museum" as a result of his 1959 film *Horrors of the Black Museum*" (76–77).

Although Buckingham Palace is spared and political cover-ups are overlooked, the actors are handed dialogue that at times runs counter to the Holmes brothers' patriotic nature; but it nonetheless conveys, for Sherlock at least, the truly canonical intolerance for those with "less alert intelligences than his own" ("The Adventure of the Blue Carbuncle"). For instance, Mycroft is summoned to a meeting with the Prime Minister and the Home Secretary (Dudley Foster) to discuss the Ripper affair. When the Home Secretary is introduced, Mycroft wryly reminds him that "I knew your predecessor, sir. No doubt I shall soon be making the acquaintance of your successor, unless the police do a good deal better than they're doing at the moment." The Home Secretary answers that he has "every confidence in the police," but Mycroft retorts "that, sir, must be why there is none left in the House of Commons." The scene is full of acerbic wit and the cadence of Robert Morley's delivery adds to the charm of the moment.

In a second example, Mycroft entreats Sherlock to take up the Ripper case for the sake of the government, but Sherlock angrily denounces the government, saying that "any government which allows the poverty of Whitechapel deserves, as far as I'm concerned, riddance!" Sherlock then vows that he will not "become engaged in political maneuvers" to save the apparent ineffectual government. This is certainly Holmes at his individualistic best; he is slave to no one, not even the government. Furthermore, Mycroft is aghast when Lestrade bursts into the room, carrying the infamous "Dear Boss" letter. "Good heavens, Sherlock!" he shouts, "you're already involved." Sherlock characteristically responds with a caustic, "a case of detection, Mycroft, always means more to me than a politician's career."

The focus in *A Study in Terror*, however, is not so much on Holmes' dissatisfaction with inferiors as it is on his passive approval of radical efforts to shake up the status quo at the expense of public order. The film allows men like Dr. Murray to view the Ripper as attacking a corrupt system from the outside, and Holmes is viewed as a dissenting voice from inside the system — but he is *inside* the system, an important distinction especially when comparing the film to its remake, *Murder by Decree*. Dr. Murray, for example, has drawn a considerable crowd to hear his harangue against the government for its indifference to the despair of the East End. Murray is able to speak with a certain shrill moral authority based upon his charitable good works in offering food and medical help to the destitute of the district. He lectures that:

> Thanks to Jack the Ripper, thanks to this brutal killer, yes, thanks to him, the world is watching Whitechapel. And I'll tell you this, it's not the killings by a demented hand that the world finds horrible. No! It's the murder by poverty, the murder by misery, the murder by hunger in Whitechapel. Whitechapel, the cry of the starving, the moan of the sick. For years we've tried to get one paragraph into the newspapers to expose what's happening here. I've been myself to the editors, hat in hand. It's not news, they said. Well, now it is news. One man has made us news!

At first the crowd sides with Murray, applauding his condemnation of the government, but the moralistic Murray ultimately lays part of the blame closer to home, suggesting that Whitechapel is being punished for its licentiousness. The crowd then turns ugly and the police are required to disperse the mob. Holmes merely acquiesces to the events without comment.

If Shaw and the radicals of the 1880s were interpreting the Ripper's actions as reinforcing this end, then *A Study in Terror* was reinterpreting Holmes for 1960s audiences in much the same way. Audiences of *A Study in Terror* were treated to examples of anti-establishment rhetoric leveled by both Mycroft and Sherlock, leaving the viewer with the queasy sensation that the dialogue was sometimes designed as sycophantic succor for protest-prone young viewers who would be more at home in the coming years with such irreverent films as Dennis Hopper's *Easy Rider* (1969) and Robert Altman's *M*A*S*H* (1970). This attitude was made even more apparent by what Pohle and Hart describe as a "nameless Compton P. R. man" who stated that, "No longer is Holmes the old fuddy-duddy which the public tended to classify him as in the past, he's now way-out and with-it" (216). Moreover, executive producer Cohen feared that the title *A Study in Terror* wouldn't be effective for modern audiences; he said that he "didn't like [the title] because I don't believe people will be interested in a horror film with the word 'study' in it" (Lilley 75), effectively either showing contempt for his audience or, more likely, reading his youthful audience too well.

Such opinions were, indeed, amplified by the abysmal American advertising campaign that irresponsibly betrayed the film's dignity. Capitalizing on both the popular appeal of the James Bond movies and the television phenomenon of *Batman*—a curiosity that ingrained the euphemism "camp" into the national vocabulary—the promotional campaign did nothing but slander the value of the film. It denigrated John Neville's witty yet accurate performance by describing Holmes as being "James Bond in a cape" and as being the "original caped crusader" as well as "Batman with brains." Moreover, by displaying such coined words as "Aiee!" "Biff!" and "Pow!" on posters and in trailers to accent Holmes' encounter with the Ripper, the otherwise serious, well-crafted, and articulate narrative was reduced to drivel. To his credit, though, Cohen disavows any part in concocting that miserable advertising campaign. He told Weaver that, "The big hit on TV at that time was *Batman*, so the head of advertising, Robert Ferguson, wanted to sell *A Study in Terror* almost like a comedy. On one of the one-sheets, he had POW, BIFF, CRUNCH, BANG, and HERE COMES THE ORIGINAL CAPED CRUSADER—which I didn't like at *all*! I wanted to sell it as horror, and so we had a big fight about the advertising. We did our own campaign for the United Kingdom, France, Italy—Columbia had nothing to do with the picture there—and it was a much bigger hit over there than it was here" (76-77).

The film itself proves these sycophants wrong. True, an underlying subtext of radical politics easily abrogated for the 1960s audiences the film's overt and stylish melodrama, thereby making the film relevant for 1960s audiences. But the staid formulaic elements of Victorian melodrama, mocked by the advertising and its own subtext, actually comprise the film's strength, and these elements never deign to parody despite the proclamations of the advertising. This is certainly what A. H. Weiler, in a review in the *New York Times* (November 3, 1966), meant when he wrote that "the supersleuth and the superkiller are well met ... because a sense of humor and an unvarnished, old-fashioned melodrama raise the film several cuts above the normal chiller dreamed up these days." But perhaps Kevin Thomas, in the *Los Angeles Times* (January 25, 1967), said it best when he succinctly stated that the film possessed "art without artiness."

The value of *A Study in Terror* is its unabashed melodramatic code; for all its political underpinnings, director Hill never once falters in presenting not only polarized characters—Sherlock Holmes and Jack the Ripper—but a narrative pattern that generates, as James L. Smith writes in *Melodrama*, "a suspense so acute [that] it must be resolved at once" (24). The episodic structure

Sherlock Holmes (John Neville) struggles against the Ripper in James Hill's *A Study in Terror*. In the background is the body of one of the Ripper's victims.

leads ultimately to a climactic confrontation in which, as Smith continues, "even the scenery joins the conspiracy against virtue triumphant" (26). In the case of *A Study in Terror*, not only is Holmes pitted against Lord Carfax at the film's climax, but indeed he is pitted against the very scenery itself as it bursts into flame. Remaining loyal to the melodramatic code, Hill does not bother to explain any logical connection between the climax and the denouement; once Carfax perishes, the *deus ex machina* of Hill's camera merely dissolves from Holmes circled by flames to 221 B Baker Street, where Holmes explains wryly that he escaped the inferno. All of this is good melodrama in which virtue and evil are pitted against one another in an apocalyptic confrontation where virtue triumphs. Elitists and pedantic artists balk at such simplicity in creative expression, but, as Smith writes, "No one really believes that virtue is impregnable, but from time to time everyone needs to pretend that he does. The dream world of melodrama caters to that need. It posits ideals of courage, integrity, patriotism and moral excellence" (54). In this regard, *A Study in Terror* reflected its own Victorian roots; the film not only demonstrated that virtue would triumph but that even decency as well as the classicist notion of decorum would triumph. Holmes defeats two monsters here; he not only

defeats the monstrous Jack the Ripper, but his idealistic political views from within the system are at least made manifest. More important, Holmes also represents that crucial notion of decorum; he recognizes not just the social suffering but also individual suffering. He truly means that "no useful purpose will be served by disclosing" the Ripper's identity; it is not merely public knowledge for the sake of knowledge. Holmes remains the purest of Victorians when he reasons that, indeed, "the Osbourne family have suffered enough as it is. Lestrade has his three buckets of ash, but we will keep the name."

In a sense, *A Study in Terror* is a transitional film in both the Holmes canon and in the literature of Jack the Ripper. The film is restrained in its depiction of the carnage and horror which the Ripper visited upon London late in 1888, and this echoes earlier presentations of the 1940s and 1950s which had pulled their punches fearing to cross the perimeters of public acceptance. Horror, as previously stated, is subjective rather than literal, and perhaps such a notion is best summarized by the great detective himself when, in *A Study in Scarlet*, he declares that, "Where there is no imagination there is no horror." Curiously, *A Study in Terror* is much more willing to yield to a sort of political revisionism than it is to appreciably succumb to the laxness of the new morality coming into vogue with the 1960s. David Stuart Davies, in *Holmes of the Movies*, states that the British "X" certificate for adults only was "not for any horror content, but for the sexual elements implicit in the movie" (132). As a result, it all seems rather Byzantine; there is the necessary patina of madness required to make the explanation work as a device of fiction, and yet that patina is acceptable because it is good melodrama, good fiction and good Sherlock Holmes. For all of its drawbacks in styling Holmes to the dissident 1960s, *A Study in Terror* retains a certain charm consistent with entertaining, rather than inculcating, an audience.

In some respects, the novelization of *A Study in Terror*, by the American writing team of Manfred B. Lee and Frederic Dannay under their longtime pseudonym "Ellery Queen," represents a much more traditional approach to Sherlock Holmes and to Jack the Ripper. For some reason, however, Lee and Dannay changed some characters' names and locations. For instance, Max Steiner becomes Max Klein, and Edward Osbourne (Lord Carfax) becomes Richard Osbourne, who now has a 9-year-old daughter named Deborah (who, in her elder years, brings a mysterious manuscript to Ellery for his professional opinion).

Conspicuously absent in the novel is the acerbic anti-establishment rhetoric, leaving the reader with a Sherlock Holmes pastiche crafted by an established mystery writing team firmly grounded in the Holmes canon. For example, Lee and Dannay write that Watson's wife — never mentioned in the

Opposite: Cover art for Ellery Queen's original adaptation of Donald and Derek Ford's script for *A Study of Terror,* which reveals a different ending.

film — is away allowing him freedom to join Holmes in the investigation. They also write that Holmes sends the omnipresent Baker Street Irregulars to Whitechapel to find Joseph Beck's pawn shop, and that Holmes and Watson consult with Mycroft at the Diogenes Club rather than having Mycroft break his cycle and visit Baker street.

The novelization restores Holmes to the more traditional image of the stalwart Victorian detective, and the novel cleverly alternates between Holmes' investigation of the Ripper case and Ellery Queen's parallel investigation effected through a close examination of Watson's heretofore unpublished manuscript. The novelization offers a further bonus: a different solution to the Ripper's identity. The film ends with the revelation that Lord Carfax was the Ripper, and that he perished in the fire at the Angel and Crown tavern. But Ellery deduces from what Holmes "didn't say" that the Duke of Shires was the actual Ripper and that his son assumed the blame to preserve his father's honor. Ellery determines that Holmes knew the truth but silently acquiesced following Lord Carfax's sacrifice and the Duke of Shires' suicide. Ellery then reveals the truth to his client, "And Deborah's faith in her father has been vindicated after three-quarters of a century." Clearly, we have further evidence from Ellery Queen, no less, of Sherlock Holmes as the soul of Victorian decorum.

Bob Clark's *Murder by Decree* (1978) reworks the Fords' script to dangerous levels of plagiarism. Cohen reflected that, "Everybody asked, 'Are you gonna sue them? They stole your story! They stole your picture!' I was tied up in production at the time, and I just never saw the picture [*Murder by Decree*]; I only heard that it was very similar and that they stole an awful lot of things from *A Study in Terror*.... I don't have to tell you about people stealing ideas" (Lilley 109).

Nonetheless, *Murder by Decree* represents a much more cynical view of the Ripper case, and certainly a grittier portrayal than most earlier Ripper films. The Canadian and British production unabashedly advances a Holmes solution to the Ripper in emphatic terms of ideological polemics. Amazingly, for the reviewers of *Murder by Decree* in Phil Hardy's *The Encyclopedia of Horror Movies*, the movie isn't political enough. They write that, "If the film-makers had been able to muster more political courage their movie could have been a very powerful masterpiece" (331).

Frequently praised (Matthew E. Bunson, in *Encyclopedia Sherlockiana*, describes the film as "one of the finest of all Holmes films" [174] perhaps only because of its pretentiousness and big name cast) *Murder by Decree* appropriates as its narrative thrust the Sickert account of the Ripper slayings. John Hopkins' screenplay (based on *The Ripper File* by John Lloyd and Elwyn Jones, according to Bunson, but credited as an "original screenplay"), indulging itself at times in copious political recriminations and conspiracy theories, slices away at the established body politic in a frenzy rivaling the Ripper's flesh and blood mutilations. We are again confronted with a Sherlock Holmes in character styled to curry favor with an even more dissent-besotted audience. Historian David Cannadine, reviewing the historical accuracy of *Murder by Decree* as part of *Past Imperfect: History According to the Movies*, describes Holmes (Christopher Plummer) as being "more than in any of the original Conan Doyle stories ... on the side of the underdog and in a crusading mood against the British ruling establishment" (169). This observation, however, fails to negate interest in the film from Cannadine's viewpoint, which he concedes has a certain "power and integrity" based on Clark's grim but accurate portrait of the crime and poverty endemic to the East End of London of the 1880s. But even Cannadine draws back in professional horror at the extensive historical inaccuracies afflicting *Murder by Decree* and the plot absurdities rife during the film's 120-minute running time (169).

For all its praise, *Murder by Decree* opens immediately with the bane of all modern reviewers, cliché. Once again, audiences are treated to the murder of a prostitute by a shadowy figure. Here, Clark packs his heavy fog milieu with a suspenseful sense of horror yet to be played out — the murder of another *beautiful* prostitute thereby denying historical accuracy again — as well as drab images of the squalid conditions that could exist in a great and civilized city such as London. Moments later, he makes his social dichotomy even more obvious by jump-cutting to the opulence of the London Opera House where Clark underscores the rupturing social order between the haves and the have-nots. Clark's own ideological predilections are reflected in Holmes' own dissatisfaction with current social conditions. Holmes notes irritably that the performance of Donizetti's *Lucretia Borgia* has failed to begin on time, but Watson (James Mason) reminds him that they are awaiting the arrival of the Prince of Wales with his entourage, and, of course, the performance could not begin until the Prince's appearance. "He [the Prince] seems to take a delight in keeping his subjects waiting," Holmes grumbles, adding that "I suppose since, after all, he's only the Prince of Wales we should not expect the same degree of courtesy."

When the Prince does appear, his arrival sparks a minor demonstration between anti-monarchical elements occupying the cheapest seats in the uppermost reaches of the opera house, and pro-royalists ensconced in the desirable seats. Watson, ever the loyal servant of the Crown, is aghast. "Good God! Insulting the Prince," he laments, and when the hooligans rain down their contempt — much like the protesters of the 1960s — thereby threatening the evening with violence, Watson becomes the voice of the establishment by stating the refrain heard all too frequently during the radical 1960s, "more respect is wanted." Amazingly, Holmes is tolerant of the demonstration. He responds by saying that "if the Prince wants more respect he should conduct his affairs with more discretion." A somewhat disinterested Watson mutters that "it's a damned disgrace," but a smug Holmes replies, "On the contrary. I prefer bad

**Sherlock Holmes (Christopher Plummer) comforts an injured Inspector Foxbor-
ough (David Hemmings) after a fierce struggle with John Slade, i.e., Jack the Ripper, in Bob Clark's *Murder by Decree* (1978).**

manners in the theatre to acts of violence in the streets." Watson then initi-
ates a counter-demonstration by offering up the cry "God save his Royal High-
ness" which soon sweeps the theatre. Holmes sarcastically congratulates
Watson moments later, saying, "Well done, old fellow; you saved the day."

Such language seems wholly out of place for Holmes since it deflects itself
from Holmes' own proclivity for impatience with, to uncharacteristic scorn
for, the royal family. The rhetoric is simply too modern; the use of the understatement reveals its adolescent *ad hominem* attitude which, if not outside the
bounds of Victorian propriety, at least betrays an emotionally wrought figure
rather than one so attuned to the rational. This is simply not the language of
Sherlock Holmes of the canon, but it is certainly the language of Clark's
intended audience.

The film reaches a crescendo of rhetorical excess with the bitter confrontation between Holmes and the Prime Minister (Sir John Gielgud). After
Holmes has adduced the culpability of certain members of Her Majesty's government in a misguided effort to protect the Crown from perceived embar-
rassment, Holmes — in a scene of breast-beating despair and self-righteous
fury — threatens to expose the plot unless certain conditions are met by the

government. With a passionate conviction echoed only by chauvinistic moralists, he rebukes the Prime Minister and his cabinet by stating that:

> You used the prospect of a Catholic succession to justify a course of action the devil himself couldn't justify. These crimes are civil war, Prime Minister, and denial of the primal human right to live. In order to protect a social order, society turns and rends itself. The safe, secure, rich, and powerful ones tear the bodies of the poor, the weak, and the helpless. No, it was not the threat of a Catholic succession that prompted these heinous crimes. It was the mere threat of scandal; that the Prince's cavalier treatment of an innocent girl might trigger violence and result in a toppling of the Government — a threat that was very personal to every man in this room.

Hence, what Clark has done is turn the staid Victorian bohemian, who at best may be considered a royalist and at worst apolitical, into an opposition party radical whose previously mentioned breach with Shaw would by now be surely mended. Holmes is clearly political; he has become the hero for the disenfranchised and an enemy of a government that ignores social injustice. In so doing, however, Clark has reduced the Ripper to secondary status; Saucy Jack now functions more as a symptom of government oppression than a cosmic villain. As a result we really don't have much of a Ripper confrontation or Ripper story; indeed, Clark's climactic moments are reserved for that confrontation between Holmes and the government, and Jack the Ripper himself melds into the background as a sort of afterthought. His villainy is no match for the various ministers on trial in Holmes' court.

What Clark has accomplished, with class tensions so quickly and skillfully established as hovering near the boiling point, is a polemic that legitimizes the conspiracy theories of Joseph Sickert and Stephen Knight. While capitalizing on the sensational success of Knight's *Jack the Ripper: The Final Solution*, which outlined the Sickert account in best-selling detail, Clark charges the film with a certain aura of credibility when paraded before modern audiences. *Murder by Decree* becomes the precursor to those works, like *JFK*, which root themselves in conspiracy. Indeed, ours is now a culture saturated in conspiracy theories and Clark skillfully answers the question: How could Jack the Ripper kill repeatedly and successfully in an area as confined as Whitechapel when it seemed that the whole world was searching for him? Obviously, the only reliable answer is that he had to be aided and abetted by powerful forces, namely the government. Holmes says resolutely to the ministers, "The two men had official sanction. They acted in the interests of their country. And the life and death of their intended victim mattered little enough to anyone ... and not at all to them."

David Cannadine offers a salient observation in his analysis of the historical relevance of *Murder by Decree* when he compares the British fascination with Jack the Ripper to the American obsession with the Kennedy assassination (166). Today, he argues, both events are primarily interpreted not by debate but by popular media presentations, and in both cases the results are interpreted as conspiratorial acts. Bill Waddell, curator of Scotland Yard's Black Museum, commented in a 1987 British television documentary titled *The Black Museum* (filmed by Central Independent Television) that he is often asked about persistent rumors of an official cover-up in the Ripper case. His answer is always the same; he states that:

> It's often said that there's a set of records kept here [The Black Museum] and a set of records at the Home Office that tell us who it is. That's nonsense. At least, I've never seen them. I can certainly say, if they do exist, that we do not keep a set of records here at New Scotland Yard that tell us who Jack the Ripper was. We do not know. We never solved it.

The lone killer acting to fulfill some warped personal need for vengeance or sick satisfaction is a motif that is out of theatrical favor when it comes to explicating events of worldwide impact. In the last generation or so, the purveyance of conspiracy theories has evolved into an industry whose logic would undoubtedly confound the great detective himself.

As previously explored, the Ripper's crimes have been closely approximated untold times, and for Sherlock Holmes the case of the "finger murders" had definite Ripper elements. Roy William Neill's *The Woman in Green* (1945), one of the so-called "Baker Street Dozen" of Sherlock Holmes films released by Universal Pictures between 1942 and 1946, starred Basil Rathbone and Nigel Bruce as Hollywood's definitive Holmes and Watson (A famous "radio blooper" recalls how one announcer introduced Rathbone by stating, "with Sherlock Holmes as Basil Rathbone"). Each of the dozen films is stylishly directed (all but one, John Rawlins' *Sherlock Holmes and the Voice of Terror*, were directed by Neill), skillfully written and superbly acted not only by Rathbone and Bruce but by Mary Gordon as Mrs. Hudson, Dennis Hoey as the exasperated Inspector Lestrade and supporting casts composed of some of Hollywood's foremost character actors. When Universal Pictures acquired the screen rights to Sherlock Holmes from 20th Century–Fox, Holmes was updated into a contemporary figure presumably in an effort to join the war effort. The first three films in the series, *Sherlock Holmes and the Voice of Terror* (1942), *Sherlock Holmes and the Secret Weapon* (1942), and *Sherlock Holmes in Washington* (1943), dealt specifically with Nazi fifth columnists, with *Secret Weapon* revealing that Moriarty (Lionel Atwill) was in league with the Nazis. Naturally, some controversy among Sherlockians erupted over changing the settings, and Universal attempted to mitigate the damage by posting a title that read, "Sherlock Holmes, the immortal character of fiction created by Sir Arthur Conan Doyle, is ageless, invincible and unchanging. In solving the significant problems of the present day he remains, as ever, the supreme master of deductive reasoning." But as Davies explains "it is unlikely that the series would have pleased Holmes' creator, but although the settings were modern, exchanging the hansom cab for the motor car, and most of the plots bore little relation to the original stories, the playing and much of the writing were in character" (69–70).

The Woman in Green was the final Holmes script by Bertram Millhauser, who had written the best of the series including *The Spider Woman* (1944) and *The Pearl of Death* (1944). The film opens with the commissioner of Scotland Yard calling his key men together to review strategies in a case the press has dubbed "the finger murders." The commissioner laments that "we're confronted with a series of the most atrocious murders since Jack the Ripper." And, indeed, London is in a state of panic as an unknown killer selects young women at random, slaughtering them before severing their right thumbs for some sort of grotesque souvenir. Holmes, however, believes in something other than a new Jack the Ripper loose in London. He tells Watson that he is "convinced that these murders are only incidental to some larger and more diabolical scheme, [and] if my assumptions are correct, this little scheme has behind it the most brilliant and ruthless intellect the world has ever known." Eventually Holmes discovers that the killings are part of an elaborate blackmail scheme by a femme fatale named Lydia Marlowe (Hillary Brooke), but the scheme itself is engineered by none other than the most ruthless intellect in the world, Professor Moriarty (Henry Daniell). The victims of the murder spree are nothing more than innocent tools in Moriarty's plan. Simply, he needs the fingers to effect his plan, as Holmes explains: "The severed finger is what links the blackmail victim to the murder. He wakes, finds the grisly thing in his pocket and doesn't know how it got there. He has no idea he has been hypnotized, for all he knows he may have committed the atrocious crime during some dreadful lapse in sanity."

A few months later, on January 7, 1946, Rathbone and Bruce were again on the trail of a Ripper-like killer as part of their radio series *The New Adventures of Sherlock Holmes*, sponsored by Petri Wine and airing over the Mutual Broadcasting System. "The Strange Case of the Murder in Wax," written by Denis Green and Anthony Boucher, is the story of several murders of young women in Hampstead Heath. Holmes has been called in on the case, and he and Watson track the killer to a London wax museum where a fire breaks out and the killer is engulfed in flame.

On February 14, 1955, Holmes and Watson were involved in "The Case of the Thistle Killer," yet another series of Ripper-style killings which were plaguing London. This time, however, the investigation was conducted over television, in *The New Adventures of Sherlock Holmes* starring Ronald Howard as Holmes and H. Marion Crawford as Watson with Archie Duncan as Inspector Lestrade. The half-hour series was independently produced in France by Sheldon Reynolds; the series was broadcast in New York by NBC television, but syndicated nationally as *Sherlock Holmes* through Motion Pictures for

Top and bottom: The press are at it again in both Roy William Neill's Sherlock Holmes adventure *The Woman in Green* (1945) and the "Thistle Killer" episode of the NBC television series *The New Adventures of Sherlock Holmes.*

Main titles for Roy William Neill's Sherlock Holmes adventure in which the great detective investigates the grisly "finger murders."

Television, Inc., and later by Guild Films, Inc. The original script by Charles and Joseph Early detailed the efforts of Holmes and Watson to capture a serial killer named Phoenix (Richard Watson) who had strangled five women in five nights, leaving as a sign three thistles near each body.

In 1960, movie distributor Joseph E. Levine made use of the name of Sir Arthur Conan Doyle as part of the extensive publicity campaign for *Jack the Ripper*. Levine cited at various times Conan Doyle's supposed opinion that the Ripper was connected to the medical profession (Haydock 210). This certainly raises an important question: Just what did Sir Arthur Conan Doyle, the creative force behind Sherlock Holmes himself, believe about Jack the Ripper? Many writers reflecting on the Ripper slayings ascribe to Conan Doyle the presumption that the Ripper may have been a woman, or what is known as the "Jill the Ripper" theory. Tom Cullen, in part, provides the basis used by Ripper historians who credit Doyle with holding the "Jill the Ripper" theory. As part of his research for *When London Walked in Terror*, Cullen made contact with Sir Arthur's son, Adrian Conan Doyle, to confirm Sir Arthur's attitude toward the Ripper. Adrian Doyle's response is worth noting here:

> More than thirty years having passed, it is difficult to recall his views in detail on the Ripper case. However, I do remember that he considered it

Top and bottom: Opening title sequence for the Ripper-like story in the syndicated version of *The New Adventures of Sherlock Holmes.*

likely that the man had a rough knowledge of surgery and probably clothed himself as a woman to avoid undue attention by the police and to approach his victims without arousing suspicion on their part [191].

Paul Begg, Martin Fido, and Keith Skinner, in *The Jack the Ripper A to Z*, also state that Doyle "proposed that a midwife in a bloodstained apron would pass unquestioned, suggesting that a male murderer might have disguised himself as a woman" (221).

Donald Rumbelow, however, in *Jack the Ripper: The Complete Casebook*, cites a July 4, 1894, interview with a reporter for the *Portsmouth Evening News* in which Conan Doyle recalled a visit to the Black Museum where he had once viewed the Ripper exhibits. Rumbelow writes that Conan Doyle, outlined the steps Holmes would undoubtedly have taken in an effort to run the Ripper to earth, and reports that, as to his own opinion, Conan Doyle merely suggested that the Ripper had probably been in America and was "a man accustomed to the use of a pen" (239).

There is nothing new of any substantive nature regarding Doyle's personal views on the Ripper case in Peter Costello's *The Real World of Sherlock Holmes: The True Crimes Investigated by Arthur Conan Doyle*. Costello sets aside one chapter to explore what he calls Conan Doyle's fascination with the Ripper case. He reconstructs a walking tour of the East End organized in the spring of 1905 for Doyle and a small group of friends from the Crime Club to visit the scenes of the Ripper's crimes, but nothing of the reconstruction sheds new light on Doyle's theories. Nonetheless, Costello's interpretation of how Conan Doyle would have viewed the many performances pitting Holmes against the Ripper is pertinent here; he writes that, "The fictional use of Holmes and Watson to solve the Ripper murders — or indeed commit them — indulged in by modern writers as eminent in their field as Ellery Queen would undoubtedly have shocked and dismayed Conan Doyle" (69), but Costello never amplifies reasons for the statement.

Despite these chronicles of confrontation, a lingering question has always stumped Sherlockians: Given that Holmes and the Ripper were contemporaries, why did they not meet? It remains a tenet of faith among Sherlockians that a confrontation between Holmes and the Ripper could only have ended one way — in triumph for Holmes. But occasionally an explanation is offered as to why Holmes and the Ripper did not make contact. In 1970, Billy Wilder's *The Private Life of Sherlock Holmes* was released to mostly indifferent reviews and sparse audiences. Film critic Leonard Maltin, in the 1987 edition of his *Movie and Video Guide*, nonetheless regards *The Private Life of Sherlock Holmes* as a "neglected film whose reputation should soar in future years," and who points out that the film, released at 125 minutes, had originally been intended as a three-and-a-half-hour feature (789). Chris Steinbrunner and Norman Michaels, in *The Films of Sherlock Holmes*, add that one scene in particular was tragically excised from the final movie. Written as an epilogue, the scene brings Inspector Lestrade (George Benson) to Baker Street seeking Holmes' (Robert Stephens) help in running to ground the killer of three Whitechapel prostitutes. Holmes, however, is deep in grief over the death of Ilse von Hoffmanns-thal (Genevieve Page) and is not emotionally up to the challenge. Dr. Watson, (Colin Blakely) deflects Lestrade with the explanation that Holmes is engaged on another case. Steinbrunner and Michaels opine that the sequence was "An ingenious explanation as to why Holmes never apprehended London's most notorious criminal" (220). A novelization of *The Private Life of Sherlock Holmes*, penned by Sherlockians Michael and Mollie Hardwick, retained this poignant epilogue, leaving the reader wistfully regretful that "Holmes is … working on another case just now."

VI

JACK THE RIPPER IN AMERICA

Seemingly, the English have been of a divided mind when it comes to Jack the Ripper, and in such a context it is appropriate to take time to review the meaning and value of Jack the Ripper in popular entertainment. For the English there is the understandable national pride of having bred the most notorious serial killer in recorded history, and certainly this may not represent an achievement for which a nation takes a bow, but it remains nonetheless an unstated pride of ownership. Conversely, there has always been the belief that the Ripper could not have been English by birth or heritage because, as many believe even today, no Englishman could reasonably have been guilty of such barbaric acts; hence, Jack the Ripper must have been of foreign extraction. To further this claim of foreign extraction, questions by the police and inquest queries often attempted to elicit statements from witnesses as to a foreign accent or foreign appearance. "Foreigners" were frequently regarded as prime suspects although in the midst of the Ripper hysteria everyone seemed vulnerable to suspicion at one time or another. Even Queen Victoria, in a letter to the Home Secretary, advised the authorities to search cattle and passenger boats in an effort, presumably, to find foreign nationals in hiding who might be guilty of the heinous crimes. Sir Melville Macnaughton, in an often cited report dated February 23, 1894, listed three key suspects in the Ripper murders: M. J. Druitt, Aaron Kosminski and Michael Ostrog. Of the three, only Druitt was English with Kosminski a Polish Jew and Ostrog a Russian.[1]

Further evidence of the foreign killer theory is provided by the *London Times* of September 11, 1888, which quotes a description of the Ripper that the

[1]*Robert Anderson, then head of the Criminal Investigation Division (CID) of Scotland Yard, claimed, without evidence, that Jack the Ripper was a "low class Jew" in his* The Lighter Side of My Official Life *published in 1910. In addition, Chaim Bermant, in chapter nine of his* Point of Arrival: A Study of London's East End *(1975), concludes that the Ripper was, indeed, a Jew. Interestingly, Martin L. Friedland, in* The Trials of Israel Lipski *(1984), suggests that the repeated efforts to identify Jack the Ripper as a Jew was a ruse to halt Jewish immigration in England.*

Times indicated had been "circulated throughout the metropolitan police district and all police stations throughout the country:"

> Description of a man who entered a passage of the house at which the murder was committed of a prostitute [Annie Chapman] at 2 a.m. on the 8th.— Age 37; height, 5 ft. 7 in.; rather dark beard and moustache. Dress-shirt, dark vest and trousers, black scarf, and black felt hat. Spoke with a foreign accent.

Ripperologist Tom Cullen leaves no doubt as to his personal belief in the speciousness of such a description. In fact, Cullen states that "I am inclined to believe that this description was entirely made up out of some policeman's head" (61). More likely, we would argue, it was a description fabricated by a committee of officials hoping to stave off criticism of police inaction.

Cullen acknowledges the widespread suspicion that the Ripper was of foreign extraction, and three-quarters of a century later Cullen conducted a series of background interviews to find out just what kind of foreign extraction was considered. In one example, Cullen cites eyewitness testimony by Mrs. Annie Tapper, who volunteered information that when she was a girl of nine working in an East End shop she met Jack the Ripper when he purchased a bunch of grapes. She stated that, "He was tall and dark — foreign looking I would say — with a black pointed beard." More important, Mrs. Tapper went on to say that Jack the Ripper carried the ubiquitous Gladstone bag (20).

What is striking about these descriptions is that rather than provide a portrait of a serious suspect they provide an engaging look into the minds of the so-called witnesses. Both the police description offered in September 1888 and the Tapper description provided to Cullen in the 1960s are marvelous descriptions of Jack the Ripper, but they are pretty much just that — descriptions of an image. If historians ever do catch up with Jack the Ripper, the likelihood is that he will not resemble Annie Tapper's Ripper nor be of any nationality but that of British origin. What is important is that both the police account and Annie's Ripper tell us much about the Ripper not in terms of who he was, but in terms of who we would like him to be. Specifically, in the anonymous police description the words dark or black are used no fewer than four times, and the description concludes with the assertion that the suspect spoke with a foreign accent (to whom the suspect spoke thereby revealing a "foreign accent" is conveniently ignored). No witness known to history ever stepped forward to claim ownership of this description, and that in itself lends an air of mystery about the description. The description identifies the suspect as a figure in black of some foreign extraction, or, appropriate to our claim, a phantom. Before we dismiss the Tapper description as merely a fanciful recollection by an elderly woman, we need to acknowledge the lady's own credibility in that what she details is very much the image of the Ripper, not the flesh and blood killer.

In these instances, the teller of the tales wanted the Ripper to be foreign, and "foreign" was often included in the depiction of the Ripper image. The sense of foreign becomes a significant mien in Ripper lore, but it is emphasized that foreign at this juncture is not used solely in the sense of xenophobia, which such contemporary descriptions as the police account were no doubt fostering, but rather in the sense of "remoteness" or "estrangement," especially an estrangement from civilized society. Since Jack the Ripper was never apprehended his appearance and motivation are whatever the public — and artists — choose to envisage or interpret. Collectively, the world has agreed upon a single iconographic image of the Ripper: a tall figure in black, wearing a cape and top hat, toting a Gladstone bag, and making his way within a milieu of a narrow, fog-enveloped alleyway. Time and time again illustrations, movie and television presentations, and literary descriptions that complement the Ripper story, whatever their social or political slant, have rarely drifted from this description. As such, Jack the Ripper is far from the flesh and blood criminal who committed crimes in Whitechapel; instead, he remains a symbol, a straw figure upon which civilization continues to project, metaphorically, its own inadequacies. In this regard Jack becomes a convenient sign of inhumanity for groups incapable of or unwilling to acknowledge their own inadequacies. Xenophobia certainly plays a role here, but so does the simple fact that Jack-as-a-figure is serving as a most convenient representation for inhumanity, and as such he is able to deflect barbarousness from the civilized onto an "other," be it a "foreigner" in a social and political sense, or be it an abstract form. This image for deflection is so strong that it has caused Cullen to observe that "the image of Jack the Ripper which East London retains as I discovered from these interviews is straight out of Victorian melodrama" (19). Hence, the image, or form, of Jack the Ripper is truly what matters in the modern age.

Since there is no flesh and blood convict to measure such a description against, the public mind has, again, turned to artistic expression. This form that gives life to Jack the Ripper remains unchanged, but the content of that Ripper form has changed over the years to fit social and political leanings, as we have seen in such films as James Hill's *A Study in Terror* and Bob Clark's *Murder by Decree*. As tolerance for violence has increased, as reflected on movie and television screens, the Ripper's penchant for blood and gore has unfortunately kept pace as well. The result is simply that the form of the Ripper has permanently overshadowed the person.

Of all the theories of foreign suspects, Americans, who then as now have a perceived national proclivity toward violent behavior, came in for more than their share of suspicion. Curiously enough, if a segment of English citizenry has always been convinced that the Ripper was foreign to English shores, a complementary segment of the American public has historically been willing to embrace Jack the Ripper as one of its own. Beginning with Robert Bloch's

"Yours Truly, Jack the Ripper," the Ripper is seen as not only a transition piece which opened the floodgates allowing the Ripper to transcend time, but it also escorted the Ripper onto American soil in grand style. As noted, Bloch placed the Ripper in Chicago in 1943, and if Jack the Ripper was out of time, his violent homicidal behavior was not out of context. The Chicago of Al Capone, the St. Valentine's Day Massacre, and Eliot Ness and the Untouchables was the perfect venue for such a violent figure (coincidentally, Chicago would also serve as the site of the Ripper's appearance in "The Ripper" episode of *Kolchak: The Night Stalker*). Moreover, there is a certain American logic to some of the most preposterous incorporations of the Ripper myth, primarily those in *Bridge Across Time* and *Jack's Back*. Jack the Ripper haunting the streets of Lake Havasu, Arizona, in *Bridge Across Time* (because the city had acquired the old London Bridge) may stretch fantasy to absurd lengths, but his murderous actions seem somehow a natural part of an American environment if only for the frontier milieu of the Arizona desert. And if *Jack's Back* serves as a thinly veiled excuse for yet another film of gratuitous sex and violence, the film at the same time unwittingly incorporates a disquieting logic: if Jack the Ripper were to return, where could he more profitably ply his craft than in the streets of an American city.

Indeed, the single most important statement made by Nicholas Meyer's 1979 *Time After Time*, certainly one of the finer Ripper presentations of recent years, is that the Ripper would truly find himself at home in the America of the late twentieth century. When the Ripper tells H. G. Wells "I'm home," he does so in an American hotel room standing next to a television set; the Ripper has found a home in the context of a culture in which violence is an accepted part of every day life. The chill we feel rising over us like a floodtide comes from the certain knowledge that the Ripper is stating the naked truth.

The appearance of a series of letters purportedly sent by Jack the Ripper during the course of the killings led inevitably to speculation that the Ripper was an American. Employing such perceived Yankee expressions as "boss," "right away," "shan't quit" and "fix me," the letters were interpreted in many quarters as coming from the hand of an American writer. If we accept the letters as genuine we have to accept the reasonable possibility that the Ripper may have had American ties. If, however, we accept the theory that the key letters were the work of one or more so-called journalists out to embellish the story of the Whitechapel killings, we are left to confront the fact that the trickster, like Annie Tapper, was acting out of a preconceived and stereotyped view that the Ripper was a foreigner. Who more likely than an American with a heritage of frontier violence on whom to lay blame.

Let us consider one more eyewitness account of the Ripper's physical stature and accessories. The description was provided by George Hutchinson, a police informant who provided the authorities with a description of a man who apparently engaged the professional services of Mary Jane Kelly only a

David Warner as Jack the Ripper holds a TV remote and declares to H. G. Wells that "I'm home" in the violence ridden latter part of the twentieth century in the closing moments of Nicholas Meyer's *Time After Time* (1979).

matter of two or three hours before her murder.[2] Hutchinson made his statement to the police on November 12, 1888, on the 13th he was interviewed by the press, and on the 14th his account was published in the *London Times*. After explaining how he knew Mary Jane Kelly, he recounted how he had come to be in the vicinity of Thrawl street where he encountered Kelly and observed her in the company of what he called a suspicious, well-dressed man. Hutchinson reported that:

> The man was about five feet six inches in height, and thirty-four or thirty-five years of age, with dark complexion and dark moustache turned up at the ends. He was wearing a long dark coat trimmed with astrakhan, a white collar with black necktie, in which was affixed a horseshoe pin. He looked like a *foreigner*. I went up the court and stayed there a couple of minutes but did not see any light in the house or hear any noise. I was out last night until three o'clock looking for him. I could swear to the man anywhere. The man I saw carried a small parcel about eight inches long

[2]*Not to be confused with the escaped lunatic George Hutchinson of Elgin, Illinois, mentioned later in this chapter.*

and it had a strap round it. He held it tightly grasped in his left hand. It looked as though it was covered with *dark American cloth* [emphasis added]. He carried in his right hand, which he laid upon the woman's shoulder, a pair of brown kid gloves. He walked very softly. I believe that he lives in the neighborhood, and I fancied that I saw him in Petticoat Lane on Sunday morning but I was not certain [Barker 205–206].

Once again we have a Ripper stereotype: dark, foreign, carrying a bag. Reportedly, when Hutchinson spoke to the police, he had described the suspect as appearing Jewish rather than foreign, but it has been suggested that the press substituted "foreigner" for "Jewish" at the behest of the police who were anxious to avoid further inflaming an ugly and ongoing anti–Semitic mood (Begg 195). Either way, the portrait served to buttress the prevalent feeling that the Ripper was alien to British tradition and culture. The speculation that the killer's bag was made of American cloth was a nice dramatic touch when juxtaposed against the background of the "Dear Boss" letter peppered with Americanisms and well-known to every follower of the investigation.

Cullen argues for the validity of the "Dear Boss" letter by glossing over the "obvious Americanisms," and suggests that the letter serves as a window into the Ripper's psychological state of mind (98). It can be argued from a slightly different perspective, however. The letter allows us a snapshot of the writer's psychology, but it is the psychology of a trickster, not a murderer. This trickster, by the providential application of the name "Jack the Ripper" and the flourish of taunting the authorities, can be said to spawn the myth of Jack the Ripper itself. By employing a few tellingly American expressions, the writer sought to feed the generalized English bias against outsiders, but at the same time was able to generate the Ripper form — the mystery figure, the phantom individual with no face, but with a very descriptive name.

Two examples of the Americanization of Jack the Ripper are worth noting here. Cullen cites the curious story of the attempt by the British press to link the Ripper murders to a series of grizzly killings in Austin, Texas, three years before the Whitechapel murders. After robbing his prey, the Texas killer used an axe to dispense his victims. Cullen then cites a letter written to the *Daily Telegraph* which argued that the "Dear Boss" letter demonstrated "an exact preprint of the Texas Tough's style" (98). No such "reprint" exists between the two sets of killings, however; all the comparison does is allow for a shifting of blame to an alien element.

Typical of the many reports surfacing in the press which pointed the finger of blame toward American shores was one which appeared in the *Pall Mall Gazette* of January 12, 1889. Under the headline "Is He the Whitechapel Killer?" the article reports that:

The Panama *Star and Herald* asks this startling question, while recording a telegram from Elgin, Illinois, U.S.A., which runs: — "Seven or eight years ago George Hutchinson, an inmate of Elgin lunatic asylum, was very handy with his knife. He delighted to visit the hospital slaughter-house, and made many peculiar toys from bones. After escaping from Elgin he was captured at Kankakee. He escaped from that place, and murdered a disreputable woman in Chicago, mutilating her body in a way similar to the Whitechapel cases. He was returned to Kankakee, but afterwards again escaped, and has been at large for three or four years" [Begg 196].

The fascinating point here is that while the British press picked up the question, the possibility was originally raised in the United States, verifying the willingness of at least some Americans to lay claim to the Ripper as one of their own, perhaps in the same way that Americans lay claim — often with pride — to such killers as Billy the Kid, Jesse James, and even Jeffrey Dahmer, who are all distinctly American.

An intriguing teleplay incorporating the popular suspicion that the Ripper fled to America is an episode of the CBS series *Cimarron Strip* titled "Knife in the Darkness," broadcast January 25, 1968. Frequently misidentified as an episode of a different yet similar series of ten years earlier called *Cimarron City*, "Knife in the Darkness" was an original teleplay by noted science fiction writer Harlan Ellison. Unfortunately, it was impossible to secure a print of "Knife in the Darkness" for review, and so we have relied on a copy of Ellison's final draft dated May 4, 1967. Comments and plot extrapolations are, therefore, based on the teleplay as Ellison intended it to be presented rather than the program as viewers saw it in 1968. It should be noted at the outset that there are reportedly some differences between the script and the episode; Ellison, a writer of inordinate skill and volatile temperament, has long had a justified reputation for carrying grudges whenever he felt that his writing suffered in a media translation. In Ellison's *An Edge in My Voice* (1985), he has written at some length and bitterness about what he perceives as the trashing of his original concept for "Knife in the Darkness." However that may be, "Knife in the Darkness" remains an important contribution in the Ripper canon, and certainly to the Americanization of the Ripper in particular.

Reference has already been made to Ellison relative to his 1967 *Dangerous Visions* anthology in which Robert Bloch resurrected the Ripper, as it were, in a story called "A Toy for Juliette." In the same anthology, with Bloch's blessing, Ellison penned a sequel to "Juliette" called "The Prowler in the City at the Edge of the World." In the context of an afterward to the story, Ellison speaks of being consumed by the mental image of Jack and the maniacal passion the Ripper had for his work. Like so many of us, Ellison has found himself wrapped up in the mystery of the Ripper and seeks answers both for Jack's killing spree and for the culture's infatuation with the mythos of Whitechapel. As a writer, Ellison conveys a special sense of "Jack the Ripper" to the printed page when he notes that:

> This ["The Prowler in the City at the Edge of the World"] was one of the hardest stories I ever wrote. I was furious at the limitations of the printed

page, the line for line rigidity of QWERTYUIOP. I wanted to break out, and the best I could do was use typographical tricks, which are in the final analysis little more than tricks. There must be some way a writer can write a book that has all the visual and sensory impact of a movie [*Dangerous Visions* 153].

Apparently, "Knife in the Darkness" for *Cimarron Strip* offered Ellison the opportunity to pursue his Ripper obsession into what was for Ellison a better forum by which to manifest the Ripper, that being film, and, in this case, a television film. The series, which starred Stuart Whitman, Jill Townsend, Randy Boone and Percy Herbert, was a 90-minute western set in the Oklahoma territory of the late 1880s, and it followed the struggles of Marshal Jim Crown in bringing law and order to this wild territory.

"Knife in the Darkness" opens with a teaser on a peculiarly "wild west" and American note. It is Christmas Night in 1888. In a clearing on the edge of Cimarron City revelers are dancing, whooping it up and generally displaying the holiday spirit. The trees and shrubs are adorned with holiday decorations, and there is dancing, music and singing — and plenty of liquor. The scene is far removed from any hint of tragedy or human discord, and far removed from the dismal surroundings of Whitechapel.

A transplanted Scot named MacGregor (Percy Herbert), who also serves as Marshal Crown's deputy, seems to be having the most fun of all; as the scene opens he is bundled in an amiable intoxication as he dances with a pretty dance hall girl named Josie. In the midst of all this merriment, however, tensions clearly emerge, and they all seem to coalesce around the person of Josie. When a young cowpoke named Tal St. James cuts in and takes Josie away from MacGregor, the Scot's hot temper begins to boil over until the timely intervention of Marshal Crown (Stuart Whitman), who cools MacGregor's wrath. From the sidelines a taciturn Indian named Shadow Feller follows Josie's movements with intense interest, and St. James takes careful note of Shadow Feller's attentions. Another cowboy, Blodgey, a rather rough and course figure, has also taken covetous notice of Josie, and in a moment St. James and Blodgey are fighting over possession of Josie who, disgusted by their behavior, rejects both men.

The scene now shifts. The ubiquitous London fog so associated with Jack the Ripper ominously begins drifting in on the crowd enabling a visual clue to audiences that soon Josie will meet a violent end. The camera then follows Josie, who is angry at the boorish behavior of Blodgey and St. James, as she separates herself from the scene of Christmas revelry for a stroll into the countryside which is now hidden by the fog. It is soon apparent that Josie is being followed, and she becomes conscious of an unidentified set of pursuing footsteps. Apprehension mounts as Josie returns to Cimarron City, but as she tries to find sanctuary inside the city in an alleyway her unrelenting tormentor follows and eventually runs her to the ground and brutally kills her. True to Ripper convention, the scene fades and the opening signature plays.

Following the commercial, a crowd has assembled at the scene of death and Marshal Crown has obviously taken charge. Dr. Cashio concludes his examination with the observation that it appears Josie was murdered by someone skilled in the use of a knife — a physician or a hide-hunter, perhaps. Suspicion immediately turns to St. James and Blodgey who are both members of the crowd. The two suspects, for obvious reasons, join forces in suggesting that a more likely suspect is the Indian, Shadow Feller.

St. James and Blodgey are soon drowning themselves in more liquor at a nearby saloon and continuing their vendetta against Shadow Feller. The saloon crowd, however, fails to become aroused by St. James' bigoted rhetoric. Angered by their disinterest, St. James exits, and later finds Shadow Feller at the Indian's camp in the woods. There, St. James learns that Shadow Feller is in possession of a brooch Josie had been wearing at the time of her murder. Now truly convinced that Shadow Feller murdered Josie, the drunken St. James convinces Blodgey and a couple of other cowboys to beat a confession out of Shadow Feller. But the stoic Indian refuses to confess, and for his obstinacy he is beaten to death by the vicious and bigoted ruffians.

Proud of his efforts in bringing to justice Josie's killer, Tal St. James goes in search of Marshal Crown. Crown, however, has been called to Pony Jane's Saloon where another very similar murder has just taken place. Maddie Lennert, a close personal friend of the marshal, has just become the killer's second victim. In her death, Maddie has exonerated Shadow Feller, and the killers of Shadow Feller now are taken into custody by Marshal Crown. The killer who began it all, however, remains at large.

Francis Wilde (Randy Boone), the young newspaperman and friend of Marshal Crown, suggests that the two killings in Cimarron City closely resemble a series of murders that had recently occurred in London. Wilde mentions the names of Martha Tabram and another woman named Nichols as victims of the mysterious Whitechapel killer.

Crown's investigation then leads him to interview two newcomers (i.e., foreigners) to Cimarron City: a soft-spoken young man named Enoch Shelton and an Englishman named Tipton. Tipton claims to be an investigator on the trail of Jack the Ripper, and Tipton entreats Crown to take seriously his theory that the Ripper is in America. "Do you know what you have in your streets?" Tipton asks Crown, followed by more pleading questions: "Do you understand that this one called Jack, who calls himself the Ripper, this one will live in fear forever?" Prophetic words penned by a twentieth century author in hindsight, but it doesn't mitigate the reality that the Ripper remains alive because western culture has various imaginative ways of keeping him alive.

On the surface, Tipton would seem to be the prime suspect if Crown were to accept that the murders of Josie and Maddie were, indeed, committed by Jack the Ripper. Tipton's nationality alone would point the finger of guilt — just as the English looked toward foreigners for the Ripper killings, and just as Tal St. James and his accomplices had looked to the alien Shadow Feller as their logical suspect.

The second suspect, Enoch Shelton, appears to be a young man in search of a future. He doesn't know precisely what he wants but he knows what he is rejecting — the big cities of the East where "the slums and the crime flourish and the 'good people' pretend it doesn't exist."

Soon Crown is the recipient of a mocking letter from the Ripper daring the lawman to try and catch him. Shortly thereafter, a telegram arrives from London in answer to an inquiry Francis Wilde had sent. The telegram warns that Tipton is a dangerous fellow who was considered a Ripper suspect because he had appeared at the scene of each Ripper murder.

At this point, Crown believes he has identified Jack the Ripper, and so begins a mad search for Tipton. But the search comes to an abrupt end in the Englishman's room at the Wayfarer's Inn where Crown discovers the butchered remains of Tipton. Tipton, like Shadow Feller, is exonerated by death.

The astute Marshal Crown, however, discerns that Tipton had met death moments before his body was discovered because the murder was especially messy; this suggests to Crown that the killer was in all likelihood still on the premises attempting to clean away splatters of blood.

Crown now searches the inn but finds no trace of the killer's clothing or paraphernalia. Stumped, he suddenly realizes that the one room he did not search was Dulcey Coopersmith's (Jill Townsend). Only moments before, Crown had escorted his friend to her room and had waited until he heard the bolt fastened into place. But unknown to Crown was that after locking herself in her room Dulcey had turned to find Enoch Shelton emerging from the shadows, revealing himself to be Jack the Ripper. As Crown approaches Dulcey's room, he hears a struggle, and Crown breaks down the door in answer to Dulcey's screams. The marshal and the Ripper battle each other about the room until, in a spectacular escape, the Ripper crashes through the second-story window, descends from the roof and fades into the fog. Crown and MacGregor quickly follow, but Shelton meets up first with a group of Indians, who are the brethren of the slain and falsely accused Shadow Feller. The Ripper tries to slash his way through the stoic band of Indians, but he himself is slain by the Indians.

Reference to Ripper lore is furthered in the episode's denouement. As a weakened and overly tired Crown sips coffee in the Wayfarer's Inn, an excited Francis Wilde enters holding a telegram and shouting "*The New York Times*! They said yes! They said they want all I can give 'm." A skeptical MacGregor wants to know about what ("As if I didn't know," he mumbles), and Francis answers with the best of his purple prose: "About Jack the Ripper. Dark nights. Murdered beauties. Chilling fog. Slithering shadows and the fairest flower of

New England, Miss Dulcey Coopersmith, stalked by a mad beast." Next, following a long line of Ripper convention, Crown remarks that Francis will never know for certain if Enoch Shelton was in fact Jack the Ripper. But Francis replies that "it's a great story" before tearing up the telegram and complying with Crown's sole point that there is "no verification [and] you'll never be able to prove it." The significance here, of course, is that what really matters is *the story* that Francis would have written had he not acquiesced to questions of fact. As in so many films and stories that have come before "Knife in the Darkness," the crimes themselves become the mystery of the Ripper in the sense that there is nothing to prove his existence other than the crimes. Francis is left with nothing but the story itself, and had his story been published in the *New York Times*, apparently in the script's acknowledgment of the *Times* own sensationalized interest in the Ripper, the story would have been yet another entry into creating the myth of Jack the Ripper.

The Americanization of Jack the Ripper has been an ongoing process since 1888, and Ellison's script can be seen as a dramatization of that interest. At times it seemed that the Ripper was spending as much time on the North American continent as he was in the dark alleyways of Whitechapel. Perhaps the most indicative of this tendency to relocate Jack the Ripper was the public furor over the 1891 murder of Carrie Brown, who was better known as "Old Shakespeare" to the denizens of Manhattan's Waterfront district. On April 24, 1891, Carrie Brown, aged 60 and a habitual drunk, was found brutally murdered in her room at the squalid East River Hotel.

Then police Chief Inspector Thomas Byrnes, with his department in tow, had smugly taunted the London authorities over the Ripper case, and Byrnes had bragged that if Jack the Ripper ever dared to operate in New York City he would be clapped behind bars within a matter of hours. The death of Carrie Brown, with its real and perceived similarities to the London Ripper murders, provided the New York press with a plethora of sensational headlines the least of which would taunt Byrnes as surely as the *London Times* had taunted the Metropolitan police.

The day after Old Shakespeare's gruesome murder was discovered, the New York newspapers were proclaiming the arrival of Jack the Ripper in their midst (Borchard 67). The New York press had suddenly been handed a story with headline potential extending beyond the normal parameters of a seedy local murder. The savage butchery of Carrie Brown and the horrific discovery of her mutilated remains in a meanly appointed transient's room couldn't help but suggest to the press — and to readers — that the blood lust of Jack the Ripper had crossed the Atlantic and arrived in New York.

Superficially, at least, there was resemblance to the Ripper's murder of Mary Jane Kelly on November 9, 1888. Although Jack the Ripper's last London murder had been two-and-a-half years before, the Ripper had never been out of the public's thoughts. In part, this was because the papers had never

```
                         CROWN
          You're sure he was Jack the Ripper?

                         FRANCIS
          Well, uh, sure, of course he was!

                         CROWN
          Who says?

                         FRANCIS
          Tipton said.

                         MACGREGOR
          He was a little balmy himself.   No
          one'll ever know for sure.

                         FRANCIS
          But...but...it's a great story.

                         CROWN
          No verification.   You'll never be
          able to prove it.

                                   CONTINUED
```

Portion of Harlan Ellison's script of "Knife in the Darkness," an episode of the CBS television series *Cimarron Strip,* follows the typical narrative pattern of keeping the Ripper a mystery when Marshal Crown states that "you'll never be able to prove it."

allowed the public to forget the sordid murders and because the public seemed intent on remembering the Ripper's gory legacy. There had never been a clearly defined beginning or end to the Ripper's killing spree. While modern Ripperologists generally consider the Ripper's victims to number but five luckless souls, the number has always been in dispute. Any killing which took place in or around Whitechapel following Mary Jane Kelly's murder and which bore even the slightest similarity to the Ripper's handiwork immediately reignited the popular imagination. For example, the London murder of a 26-year-old prostitute named Frances Coles on February 13, 1891—but three months before the murder of Carrie Brown — was the latest killing to cause intense speculation that the Ripper had again taken up his knife. The woman's throat had been cut, which was reminiscent of the Ripper's method, and for a time her death was popularly attributed to the Ripper.

It is no wonder, then, that the New York press was more than willing to highlight Carrie Brown's murder. Brown had been last seen alive, according to press accounts, around 11 o'clock on the night of her death. Carrie was observed in the company of a young man approximately half her age. Witnesses would later describe the man as a seafaring type, medium height, stocky and blonde. Carrie and her companion registered at the East River Hotel and were given room 31. The name provided by the young man to the hotel clerk was C. Knick, and all they took with them to their room was a tin pail filled with beer.

The next morning at around 9:30 the hotel clerk, Edward Fitzgerald, used his passkey to unlock and enter room 31. He found Carrie Brown brutally murdered; she had been choked and then viciously stabbed and slashed with a filed-down cooking knife found on the floor nearby. Upon closer examination, the authorities discovered that the sign of a cross had been carved on the victim's thigh. The press immediately yet incongruously referred to the cross as the sign of Jack the Ripper, and what followed was a journalistic frenzy. The *New York Times* never came out and flatly claimed that the Ripper was responsible for Carrie Brown's death, but the newspaper did insert enough references to the Ripper to encourage its readers to draw that conclusion. For instance, On April 25, 1891, the *New York Times* led off its initial report of Carrie Brown's murder by describing a "murder which in many details recalls the crimes with which 'Jack the Ripper' horrified London," and then described the victim and noted that the murder weapon "with which he had butchered his victim" had been left behind. Further in the story, the *Times* reported that there was no autopsy performed, and then wondered whether body parts had been removed as they had in the Jack the Ripper murders. Following the lead of the *London Times*, as noted, the *New York Times* could not help but issue a thinly veiled challenge to the New York police and, in particular, Chief Inspector Byrnes to catch the Ripper (or his imitator) quickly, especially in the light of Byrnes's previous boasting. The *Times* charged that:

> There has not been a case in years that has called forth so much detective talent. Inspector Byrnes apparently feels that the murderer must be arrested, for Inspector Byrnes has said that it would be impossible for crimes such as "Jack the Ripper" committed in London to occur in New York and the murderer not be found. He has not forgotten his words on the subject. He also remembers that he has a photographed letter sent by a person who signed himself "Jack the Ripper," dated "Hell," and received eighteen months ago. The police theory, however, is that "Jack" is not in New York, but that an imitator, perhaps a crank, committed the murder. A strict policy of not saying a word about the case was kept up last night. At midnight the temporary detective quarters at the Oak Street Station was closed for the night, but the nightsquad was told to look for a man about 5 feet 8 inches high, rather thin with a light mustachio, light hair, and hooked nose, and dressed in a dark cutaway coat and derby hat.

Clearly, the newspapers were setting up Byrnes and the New York Police Department to summarily solve the murder or face public contempt for failing to do what they had so brazenly promised to do—catch Jack the Ripper if he should ever ply his trade in New York City.

The next day, April 26, 1891, the *New York Times* reported in part that:

> The general opinion of the officers who are working on the case is that
> the murderer for whom they are looking is not the real "Jack the Ripper"
> but some weak minded ruffian who has read of the deeds of the
> Whitechapel's terror and attempted to do as he did. "Jack the Ripper"
> proper never did such a bungling job as this. In every instance he cut his
> victim's throat from ear to ear before starting to mutilate them and he
> always carried away parts of the body. This murderer did neither of these
> things. The real "Jack the Ripper" has always disemboweled his victims
> with what might be spoken of as "neatness and dispatch." This murderer
> was as clumsy as possible. From the appearance of the body his only object
> was to mutilate it wherever his knife struck. It would take a series of such
> crimes to establish the fact that the London "Jack the Ripper" is in New
> York.

Once again it appeared that the press was tightening the pressure on Byrnes
and his department to act. If indeed the killer of Carrie Brown was merely a
"weak minded ruffian" acting in imitation of the Ripper, lacking the "neatness
and dispatch" of the original killer, Byrnes and New York's finest would soon
appear doubly inept if they failed to apprehend this pale imitator. For his part,
Byrnes, according to the *Times* of the 26th, refused to say whether the old
woman was killed by the genuine "Jack the Ripper" or not.

The April 27 edition of the *New York Times* then viciously attacked Byrnes,
writing that:

> There was no startling development in the East River Hotel murder yes-
> terday. The police seem to be absolutely at sea. They will say nothing, per-
> haps because they have nothing to say. They display an irritability that is
> in itself strong evidence that they are completely baffled.

Then, suddenly the police made an arrest. On April 30, 1891, Chief Inspector Byrnes informed the newspapers that charges of murder had been lodged
against an Algerian national named Ameer Ben Ali for the brutal slaying of
Carrie Brown. The relatively quick arrest sidetracked the intense press speculation of the arrival of the Ripper in New York and more importantly allowed
Byrnes and the New York Police Department to escape from the situation they
had created for themselves.

In arresting Ameer Ben Ali — or "Frenchy" as he was quickly dubbed —
the New York police seemed to take their cue from London authorities in the
sense that their suspect was foreign and less likely to garner public sympathy
or put up a credible defense. In fact, Frenchy, who spoke no English and conveyed his emotional and erratic denials through an interpreter, reportedly
made a poor witness. Ameer Ben Ali was quickly convicted on the flimsiest of
evidence, but Frenchy was clearly not the man witnesses had seen register as
C. Knick and escort Old Shakespeare up to room 31 of the East River Hotel.
The explanation provided by the prosecution in court was that Frenchy had

taken room 33 across the hall from Carrie Brown and her companion. When the unidentified young man had departed from room 31 Frenchy crossed the hallway and murdered the old woman. The prosecution argued that a faint trail of blood stains leading between the two rooms proved their case (Borchard 70).

On July 10, 1891, Frenchy was sentenced to spend the remainder of his life behind bars at Sing Sing Prison. The case, however, was far from over. While Byrnes and the New York police had extricated themselves from an embarrassing situation, the case left so many unanswered questions that private inquiries continued. The case of Ameer Ben Ali is cited by Edwin M. Borchard in *Convicting the Innocent: Errors of Criminal Justice* as a classic example of the failure of American justice. So egregious were the errors in Ameer Ben Ali's case that when vindicating evidence was presented to New York's Governor Odell he granted clemency. Among the pieces of evidence presented to the governor were sworn affidavits by several neutral observers who stated flatly that no faint trail of blood connected rooms 31 and 33 at the East River Hotel after the murder of Carrie Brown. As Borchard observes, "the application for executive clemency was based solely upon the ground that Frenchy was innocent" (72).

In the final analysis, no matter who killed Carrie Brown, Jack the Ripper had been introduced by implication onto American soil. A segment of the public would credit Old Shakespeare's death to Jack the Ripper; since Jack the Ripper had always been more myth than reality — the public may be right.

A 1930 work by Theodora Benson, which is included in Allan Barnard's classic Ripper anthology *The Harlot Killer*, reinterprets the death of Old Shakespeare as the Ripper's reply to the boasts of Inspector Byrnes and the New York police. "In the Fourth Ward" is Benson's attempt at unraveling Carrie Brown's murder, and she writes that Ben Higgs was a young boy in 1891 when the ship he had been sailing with since Liverpool, the *Isabella C. Paterson*, docked in New York. An older seaman, Thomas Goolden, more or less took young Higgs under his protection. It is Goolden who appears and rescues Higgs after he is tied up and robbed in the basement of the same hotel where Old Shakespeare was killed. In cutting Higgs free from his ropes, Goolden leaves unaccountable traces of blood on Ben's hands and wrists. Goolden then disappears and fails to report back to the *Isabella C. Paterson* in time to sail. The next morning the city is speculating on the arrival of Jack the Ripper in New York. Ben Higgs is left with his suspicions:

> That poor old hag Shakespeare had been carved up as neat as you please, just like a Jack the Ripper murder. They arrested and put in prison a half-wit known as Frenchy, though he swore he was innocent; there were plenty that said he'd been framed and that the Ripper had accepted Byrnes' challenge and come over and the police doesn't own it.

If these events seem somehow removed from present concerns (the Ripper killings of 1888, Old Shakespeare's murder in 1891, and Theodora Benson's short story of 1930), they nonetheless constitute lineal passages in the public's unquenchable thirst for Ripper blood. Moreover, they all helped to provide the impetus and background for a musical by Randy Courts and Mark St. Germain called *Jack's Holiday* which debuted at Manhattan's Playwright's Horizons in March 1995. The play tells the story of Jack (Allen Fitzpatrick) who arrives in New York City in 1891 as a member of a British theatre troupe. Jack is appalled to discover the same rancid social, economic and political conditions here which drove him to action in London. The inevitable happens and the Ripper resumes his work among the prostitutes. Taunting letters and body parts repetitively serve as trademarks of Jack's work, but there is a clever sidebar to the narrative in the figure of Will Bolger, a novice journalist for whom the Ripper story serves as a sort of trial by fire into the newspaper profession.

Jan Stuart, in a review for *Newsday* (March 6, 1995), referred to *Jack's Holiday* as "a ponderous, at times incoherent mix of Grand Guignol and media jokes," and added that, in reference to Bolger, that "ever since a pair of investigative reporters upstaged a soiled White House regime in *All the President's Men*, anti-social behavior has taken a back seat to the white collar saints who bring it to light" (B7). Accordingly, the irony of the musical's narrative, which Courts and St. Germain presumably did not intend, lies in the fact that the Ripper has always owed his fame to the machinations of journalists who were more interested in writing a story that would sell rather than in necessarily uncovering truth. In Ellison's "Knife in the Darkness" script, on the other hand, Francis does yield to fact; he tears up the telegram and leaves the Wayfarer's Inn despondent over not being able to write the sordid story. It may be painful, but Francis prefers fact over story. If in the final analysis Jack the Ripper is a lie, and the murders were committed by nothing more than a misogynistic thug, it remains the press that had manufactured and sustained the "lie" by forever focusing on the figure of Jack the Ripper and not the thug.

Creative presentations of the Ripper in America have traditionally represented Jack as a British émigré. Jack's feelings of kinship and belonging in the States are shown to be an outgrowth of the cult of violence which has historically pervaded the American culture. If the British have long held the suspicion that the Whitechapel killer was an alien creature who had somehow sneaked into their midst and, unfortunately, bloodied their national image, the United States has seemed a likely point of origin. The lack of a viable American suspect has hindered prosecution by the media, as it were, but that regrettable oversight was remedied in 1996 with a new addition to the Ripper canon in a book by Stewart Evans and Paul Gainey published in America under the title *Jack the Ripper: First American Serial Killer.*

Many Americans probably received their first introduction to the Evans and Gainey theory on September 4, 1995, when the NBC morning show *Today* devoted several minutes to an interview with the writers. Interviewed by Cokie Roberts, Evans and Gainey argued their case against a quack American herb doctor named Francis Tumblety whose "feelings towards women were remarkable and bitter in the extreme," according to Chief Inspector John Littlechild. Evans, an avid collector of crime memorabilia, says that he purchased some letters from a writer named George R. Sims, and among the letters was one from Littlechild, who had headed a secret department at Scotland Yard. Littlechild named Tumblety as his personal candidate for Jack the Ripper, and Littlechild's letter, not unlike the 1894 Macnaughton report, which listed three possible suspects, deserves serious consideration coming as it does from an individual with some claim to participation in the investigation. Unfortunately, Evans and Gainey, in their euphoria at believing that they had solved the Ripper case by adopting Littlechild's suspect as their own, diluted the power of their case against Tumblety with side excursions. During the *Today* interview, Evans and Gainey may have enhanced their theory beyond the normal bounds of their own suspect's advocates' ability when they were asked to state the case against Tumblety to an American audience almost certainly hearing Tumblety's name for the first time. Gainey was succinct and believable when he stated that:

> What happened was he [Tumblety] was arrested as Jack the Ripper. They couldn't charge him with the murders because in those days there was [*sic*] no forensic aids to help them, so what they did, they charged him with a lesser offense, a sexual offense. He went to court and they hoped this would be a holding charge so they could have him longer, to interview further. But what in fact happened was two strange men came forward and paid his surety and he was immediately bailed. What happened then was he fled to France, got on a steamer back to America and then was pursued to America by detectives from Scotland Yard led by a man called Inspector Walter Andrews. And this is particularly important because Walter Andrews was one of the top men investigating the Ripper crimes at the time of the murders. Unfortunately, Tumblety was extremely clever and manipulative, escaped again and the detectives from Scotland Yard returned to England empty-handed, their mission a failure.

A point worth noting here is that while the London police may have considered Tumblety a likely suspect, the New York police seem not to have regarded Tumblety as a serious possibility. The *New York Times* (December 4, 1888) reported upon Tumblety's arrival back in the States (and its short account made clear that Tumblety had little to fear from New York authorities) that:

> "Dr." Francis Tumblety, who left his bondsmen in London in the lurch, arrived by *La Bretagne* of the Transatlantic Line Sunday. Chief Inspector Byrnes had no charge whatever against him, but he had him followed so as to secure his temporary address, and will keep him in view as a matter of ordinary police precaution. Mr. Byrnes does not believe that he will have to interfere with Tumblety for anything he may have done in Europe,

and laughs at the suggestion that he was the Whitechapel murderer or his abettor or accomplice.

In 1996, when *Jack the Ripper: First American Serial Killer* was published in the States, anyone who had seen the *Today* interview the year before might have been excused for feeling a little perplexed when upon opening the work to Chapter One they came upon "Assassination of a President." Suddenly, Tumblety was being charged by innuendo with complicity in the Lincoln assassination. In their zeal to demonize Tumblety, and thus set him up as a worthy candidate for Jack the Ripper, Evans and Gainey unwisely chose to begin with a lengthy and uninspired examination of the plot to kill Abraham Lincoln. Only in the penultimate paragraph of that first chapter do the writers make the feeblest of attempts to imply Tumblety's participation in the conspiracy. They write that:

> In Missouri, a thirty-two-year-old herb doctor [Tumblety] was arrested, incarcerated and interrogated. Assistant War Secretary Charles Dana advised Judge Advocate General Joseph Holt that he felt the prisoner "should be confined in the penitentiary." To this advice Dana added the suggestion: "Let the Indian Doctor tell all he knows about Booth and Booth's associates." What did the "Indian Doctor" know? The files of the Bureau of Military Justice do not confide an answer to that question [14].

This single paragraph represents the authors' case against Tumblety in connection with the Lincoln assassination. Granted, for a period of time Tumblety was imprisoned in Missouri under the belief that he knew something about the conspiracy against the president, but in the wake of the political hysteria following Lincoln's murder Tumblety was far from the only individual to suffer a similar fate. Officials were making arrests to give the illusion of action. At one point, the entire cast of *Our American Cousin*, the play Lincoln was watching when he was shot, was taken into custody. Interestingly, 190 pages after their feeble claim, Evans and Gainey concede that Tumblety's arrest was ultimately demonstrated to have been the result of a mix-up in names, and they quote from an official military report clearing Tumblety of any complicity in or knowledge of the Lincoln assassination (204).

It is unfortunate that Evans and Gainey went so far afield to color readers' attitudes against Tumblety. The "quack" doctor deservedly merits appraisal as the Whitechapel murderer, but grasping at innuendo (as in the Lincoln conspiracy charges) detracts from rather than adds to Tumblety's viability as Jack the Ripper. The core of the argument against Tumblety is his pathological hatred of women, especially prostitutes. At the time of the Whitechapel murders, Tumblety was ensconced at number 22 Batty Street, a ten-minute walk from the crime scenes. Tumblety's arrest, escape and bloody clothing left behind in his Batty Street room contribute to a circumstantial case against him.

Evans and Gainey make the most of the evidence they have to work with and a fair-minded reader might well come to the conclusion that while the case against Tumblety is far from proven, the investigators have at least offered up a new and intriguing possibility to rank with·Kosminski, Druitt and Ostrog.

In point of fact, *Jack the Ripper: First American Serial Killer* was first published as *The Lodger: The Arrest and Escape of Jack the Ripper* in the United Kingdom in 1995, but the following year for the American release the more sensational title of *Jack the Ripper: First American Serial Killer* was substituted. Concurrent with the American publication Britain's UK Television Channel 4 presented an hour-long documentary on July 25, 1996, which essentially made the case against Tumblety. The producers presented what amounted in some ways to be a better constructed and more convincing version of the case than the book was able to do. Titled *Secret History: The Whitechapel Murders*, the documentary and its writer-producer, David Jessel, along with coproducer-director Stephen White, elected to disregard any effort to connect Tumblety seriously to the Lincoln conspiracy. Instead it concentrated on weaving a believable if highly speculative case in favor of Tumblety's guilt.

The documentary begins with an atmospheric recreation of the White-chapel scene, and once again the familiar story of Jack the Ripper and his unholy deeds is recounted. The unearthing of the Littlechild letter is detailed as well as its assertion that an American "quack" herbalist named Tumblety was likely Jack the Ripper. Evans and Gainey both appear and reiterate their belief in Tumblety's guilt, but *Secret History*, by its calm and reasoned approach, makes the effort to rehabilitate the book which served as the documentary's inspiration. Evans remarks that:

> The fact, of course, as a policeman I must say honestly, that there wouldn't be enough to get him [Tumblety] to a court of law and convict him of murder.

Remarkably, there is a second supposition in the Littlechild letter, a supposition which at least rivals in importance the naming of a long-forgotten suspect in the Ripper slayings. As has been previously mentioned, police authorities of that time, and many Ripperologists since, have essentially credited the invention of the name "Jack the Ripper" and the key letter taunting the police not to the killer, but to one or more so-called journalists; in particular, a journalist who is frequently left unnamed or vaguely referred to as a journalist named Best, as Begg, Fido and Skinner note (45). Such implications are greater than many Ripperologists seem to realize or are prepared to admit. The thing which has intrigued Western culture about Jack down through the years and made pursuing him seem worthwhile has been the Ripper persona, as emphasized. Here there is a killer imbued with inordinate cunning and luck who plucks from the air a name for himself which captures the imagination of the world. He sends taunting boastful letters to the authorities and backs up his boastfulness with further daring murders, all the while reducing the police to incompetence. He single-handedly defines the modern serial killer and then vanishes without a trace into the Whitechapel fog. Strip away the core of the Ripper persona and what is left is merely the crude hatchet work of an ordinary thug.

It remains for Littlechild, then, to identify the journalists probably responsible for making "Jack the Ripper" a household name. In the letter, as reported by Evans and Gainey, Littlechild writes that:

> With regard to the term "Jack the Ripper" it was generally believed at the Yard that Tom Bullen of the Central News Agency was the originator but it is probable Moore, who was his chief, was the inventor. It was a smart piece of journalistic work. No journalist of my time got such privileges from Scotland Yard as Bullen [101].

Evans and Gainey immediately point out that Littlechild most certainly meant "T. J. Bulling," not Bullen. It was T. J. Bulling of the Central News Agency who passed along the Ripper letters to the police after the Ripper had mailed them to Bulling's agency (102).

Included as part of *Secret History: The Whitechapel Murders* are insightful comments by the noted cultural historian Christopher Frayling which help to place in perspective the activities of the press during the unfolding of the Ripper story. Frayling tells us that:

> All the main elements of what came to be called "tabloid journalism" about ten years later were around by the 1880s. They really only come into focus in Autumn 1888, with the Whitechapel murders where you've got a headline story: "Another Shocking Murder!" In fact, when Polly Nichols is killed they rope in various earlier murders in the East End in order to turn it into a serial even before it's a serial. So you've got your headlines. You've got interviews with all and sundry, until the police start clamming up. You've got illustrations of Miller's Court, Hanbury Street, policeman with bulldog lamp looking for body. You've got all of those things. And in a way you can say the Ripper murders turned tabloid journalism into a cliché for the first time. One newspaper called *The Star* started life a few months earlier and really took off on the back of the murders.

Clearly, in an effort to capitalize on the Whitechapel murders, the popular media have played havoc with the truth. In the world's continuing efforts to Americanize and universalize the Ripper, reality has further been breached. The resulting image of the Ripper which infests our collective mind is merely wishful thinking.

On several occasions allusions have been made to the Ripper form, stereotype, figure or image. Our culture is enamored of that tall shadowy figure, dapper in dark tailored clothing, carrying a Gladstone bag, purposefully strolling the narrow streets of Whitechapel by night, camouflaged by fog and fear. But consider the suggestion of another image which may be closer to reality. Suppose a scruffy, unshaven ruffian was huddled inside a cheap spartan room somewhere in the vicinity of Whitechapel. Outside his window he could hear the news vendors hawking the latest reports of another Ripper killing. It had taken a while for him to realize that when the newspapers were speaking of "Jack the Riper" they were speaking of him. Yes, he had killed certain fallen women for his own reasons, but not as many as the newspapers were assigning to his hand. He had never written any letters to the press or police, and had certainly not given himself the name of "Jack the Ripper." Other killers had gone about their business in Whitechapel with scarcely a second glance from the press, public or police. Why had he suddenly become the object of national and even international attention?

And here we fade-out on a cowering, perplexed thug at a loss to understand the reasons behind his own notoriety.

VII

Post Mortem

One of the more recent works in the lore of Jack the Ripper is Richard Wallace's *Jack the Ripper: "Light-Hearted Friend"* (Gemini Press, 1996), an absurd narrative in which the Ripper is revealed to be satirist and children's author Lewis Carroll, pseudonym of the Reverend Charles Dodgson. Obviously, the Jekyll and Hyde dichotomy associated with the Ripper continues to fascinate us. But as preposterous as this and so many of the Ripper theories seem to the jaundiced eye, these speculations nonetheless have their portentous effect upon our culture. The outrageous theories reinforce the premise that somewhere along the way Jack the Ripper ceased being a murderous thug of local interest to become a symbolic representation of the darkest evil that is apparently within the most cultivated of societies. As we have become more tolerant and accepting of sexual excesses and violence — both manifested almost exclusively by popular entertainment — the Ripper has responded by becoming even more depraved as the modern media seek to interpret Jack the Ripper for their modern audiences. It is this interpretation that has served as an ideal touchstone to humankind's barbaric past.

The Ripper is the avatar of "civilized violence," as explained previously, and as such the Ripper figures in two distinct modernist views of evil. In the first view, in a modern world like that of the first half of the twentieth century, a world in which religion and science coexist, Jack the Ripper symbolizes the evil that apparently lies just beneath the human spirit; here evil must be subdued by restraint, good works, or redemption. Collectively, the myths bring this darkness into light to show it for what it truly is: a force to be reckoned with, and a force that is never offered as merely an alternative way of life. For example, Herbert Marshall's 1940 CBS radio portrayal of the Whitechapel killer in "The Lodger" for Alfred Hitchcock's *Forecast* and Laird Cregar's 1944 portrayal in John Brahm's *The Lodger* were mild yet earnest representations of evil within the acceptable limits of their own time — an era when decorum and restraint were yet admirable qualities. Evil was never glorified, but rather evil was depicted as a delicious reality so terrifying that we dared not look upon it lest we become a disciple. In this world, evil was understood and recognized as a powerful lure; print, radio, television and film made it clear through presentations that the evil dwelled within us and needed to be held in check.

A mere 30 years after Brahm's *The Lodger*, reflecting a much different time in so-called human progress, Jess Franco's 1976 *Jack the Ripper* elevated the killer to a level of depravity which, upon reflection, depicts an unjustified degradation of the human soul. It is not so much Franco's narrative that degrades the spirit as much as it is his form; decorum and restraint are hopelessly absent, leaving behind a triumph of the form that now lures us into the depiction of evil itself. At this stage, we no longer contemplate evil but participate in it, all the while justifying our participation and assuring our sensibilities by assenting to a comfortable notion that it is just a movie, just a story. The graphic and explicit misogyny expressed in the film, and our willing participation to share in that misogyny, conclusively says so much about our own heretofore uncontrollable bestial desires.

Even more insidious, coupled with this individual depravity were the political trappings of films like Bob Clark's *Murder by Decree* and David Wickes' *Jack the Ripper*. Such films alarmingly quantify our recent thinking that violence is, indeed, a sanctioned act of the very governments that we have instituted to act on our behalf and in our best interests. As the appalling becomes more acceptable the Ripper becomes more appalling.

The second view's appeal is, in a sense, represented by these films. In the latter part of the twentieth century, a world in which absolutes do not exist and everything is relative, in which the sciences of behavioral psychology and sociology displace religion, Jack the Ripper becomes an explanation for attitudes of violence in a self-proclaimed civilized society. There is no doubt that contemporary culture has raised the Ripper to a level of spiritual identity, and in a real sense Jack the Ripper has supplanted the metaphysical Satan as the manifestation of iniquity in contemporary culture. In the soul of the modern rationalist, who must somehow explain the reality of viciousness in a world of rationality, the Ripper signifies the notion that evil is not so much found *within* the soul, as his predecessors believed, as much as it is found *without*. It is not that Jack the Ripper himself was evil as much as the squalor of Whitechapel, corruption of government, repressive canon of religious values and deprivation of human rights affected the Ripper's aggression. By extension, it is the squalor of poverty; corruption of governments; excesses of capitalism; and outrages of racism, sexism, xenophobia, homophobia and the like that serve as outside forces circumscribing the modern soul. Such an interpretation allows the rational man to explain violence in a world that otherwise should be utopian. As man finds himself cornered by such evils as poverty and racism, he has no recourse but to turn to frequently appreciated if not outrightly justified outbursts of violence. In the modern world, to purge evil is not to purge the soul but rather to purge man's institutions; had Whitechapel not existed, according to the rationalist, then Jack the Ripper would not have marched against civilization.

The fact remains that no matter who or what we may blame for man's inhumanity to himself, whether it be individuals or institutions, Jack the Ripper serves as a reminder that evil is a living and perhaps endless force that thrives even in the most civilized and advanced of cultures. In Bloch's 1967 *Star Trek* "Wolf in the Fold," Captain Kirk remarked that "when man moved out into the galaxy that thing must have moved with him." Kirk's observation is penetrating when one considers that though man has not yet attained the stars, he has attained cyberspace where, as in the *Star Trek* episode itself, the Ripper is found (thankfully, not *yet* to the degree that the Ripper thrived in Bloch's episode). A casual search of the Internet will produce numerous references to Jack the Ripper, but one of the more interesting references is a warning about a Jack the Ripper computer virus discovered in 1994 that is said to infect the boot sector of IBM compatible hard drives and floppy disks. Somehow this seems appropriate since the Ripper is, indeed, a virus.

In the final analysis, Jack the Ripper remains an enigma because we, his creators, are complex and contradictory beings by nature. On one level we virtually celebrate the Ripper for the primitive forthrightness with which he rejects decorum and civilized behavior. Jack the Ripper, as the references demonstrate, is the beast hidden away in all of us filled with the primordial urges civilized individuals are required to keep safely tucked away out of sight and out of mind. We are fascinated and repelled by him at the same time; we pursue him and yet do not really want to find him for in discovering the Ripper we would be discovering some ugly truths about ourselves.

As new media forums have emerged, the Ripper has been there telling an old story of primitive savagery. Concocted on the pages of the popular press, Jack has adapted to virtually every media arena to come along in the last 100 years. We have traced at considerable length the Ripper's stardom on stage, screen, radio and television. But those are by no means the only forums Jack has conquered with his dark presence.

A Los Angeles based independent film producer, Stuart Shapiro, was inspired by the Ripper to develop a line of computer fonts called "Killer Fonts." Shapiro meticulously studied the Ripper's "Dear Boss" letter and developed a font based upon the author's handwriting. "I thought sending a letter in his [Jack's] handwriting would, well, have real impact" Shapiro told one interviewer. Shapiro has since expanded his line of Killer Fonts to include such notorious characters as John Dillinger, Lee Harvey Oswald and Billy the Kid, but the Ripper began it all. And when a supportive husband contacted Shapiro seeking a gift for his wife who had just been fired from her job, it was the Jack the Ripper font he wanted so his spouse could express herself suitably to her former boss (Warrick E-1).

Even in the sphere of comic book art the Ripper has made his mark. In the last generation, as the comic book has taken on an increasingly dark vision of the world, the medium which once restricted itself more or less to moral superheroes and amiable cartoon characters has become a voice for uttering political and social commentary of an adult and often unsettling nature. Consequently, the Ripper has found another niche for self-expression. In 1989, for instance, Batman faced the Ripper in *Gotham by Gaslight*, a DC Comics adventure featuring an alternate timeline in which the Caped Crusader must save Gotham from the ravages of the celebrated serial killer after Jack arrives in town to carry on his trade.

Stephen Knight's theory of governmental corruption, duplicity and cover-up in the Ripper case provided an ideal backdrop for the new breed of graphic artists to express the same distrust of government mirrored in such presentations as *Murder by Decree* and David Wickes' *Jack the Ripper*. Comic artists Bruce Balfour and Paul Mendoza offered a three-part series succinctly called *Jack the Ripper* which ran between October 1989 and February 1990. Published by Eternity Comics and Malibu Press, this short-term series followed the essentials of Stephen Knight's theory. Inspector Abberline does not solve the Ripper case but does induce a husband and wife team — the Harlows — to involve themselves in the case, and it is the Harlows who ultimately manage to identify the killer.

The most notable example of the Ripper in comic book form was *From Hell*, a ten-part series published by Kitchen Sink Press which ran between 1991 and 1996. Once again Stephen Knight's theory was used as a textural framework. Starkly drawn black and white images by Eddie Campbell accompanied by Alan Moore's hard-edged words make for uneasy reading.

In 1996, Jack inspired a new CD-ROM game called RIPPER produced by Take 2 Interactive. Directed by Phil Parmet and starring Karen Allen, Christopher Walken and Burgess Meredith, RIPPER takes place in New York City in the year 2040. A serial killer dubbing himself "the Ripper" is systematically replicating the original Jack the Ripper murders and sending menacing letters boasting of his accomplishments. The interactive nature of CD-ROM technology has now made it possible for participants to more deeply immerse themselves in the game of chasing Jack the Ripper than ever before.

Juxtaposed against this continual recycling of the Ripper myth by ever changing forms of media expression is the unchanging nature of Jack's personal message to all of us. The Ripper fascinates us because violence continues to tantalize us just as it has done since the days of the cavemen. We have invented and embellished so much of the Ripper story over the years that anyone setting out on the trail of Jack the Ripper must first stop and ask himself which Ripper he is pursuing. Are we after the flesh and blood killer who took the lives of an undetermined number of East End prostitutes in 1888? Or are we in pursuit of the archetypical fiend carrying that Gladstone bag who lives on and on without end? Almost certainly we will never discoverer the identity of the former — to uncover the latter we need to investigate ourselves.

As stated initially, it has not been intended to offer yet another theory as to the literal identity of Jack the Ripper. That path has been traveled by scholarly Ripperologists, along with numerous crackpots, to interesting but hardly gratifying conclusions. The sole purpose was to offer a comprehensive analysis of Jack the Ripper as he has been — and will continue to be — depicted in mythmaking, whether through the oral tradition, print, mechanical or electronic means. A simple conclusion then: the many attempts to identify Jack the Ripper by name have missed the point, for it is the unshakable hold that the Ripper has exerted over our popular culture that is the real story. If Jack the Ripper should ever be identified beyond a reasonable doubt it would be like identifying the Unknown Soldier. In a very real sense — the symbol is more important than the man.

Appendix:
Media Representations
of Jack the Ripper

Major Films

Information provided from various sources include film titles and credits, press-books, posters, television listings, and reference works. Titles marked by an asterisk (*) are made-for-television movies. Italicized titles are original language titles when known.

Blade of the Ripper (*Lo Strano Vizio della Signora Ward*)

Production: Unknown, *Director:* Sergio Martino, *Producers:* Antonio Crescenzi and Sergio Martino, *Story and Screenplay:* Ernesto Gastaldi and Eduardo Manzanos Brochero, *Music:* Nora Orlandi, *Directors of Photography:* Emilio Foriset and Miguel F. Mila, *Distribution:* Unknown.

Cast: George Hilton (George), Alberto De Mendoza (Neil), Cristina Airoldi (Carol), Ivan Rassimov (Jean), Edwige Fenech (Julie).

An Italian-Spanish coproduction in color; released 1971; U.S. distribution unknown; also known by the titles *Next!* and *The Strange Vice of Mrs. Ward.*

Bluebeard

Production: Producers Releasing Corporation (PRC), *Director:* Edgar G. Ulmer, *Producer:* Leon Fromkess, *Screenplay:*

Pierre Gendron, *Story:* Arnold Phillips and Werner H. Furst, *Music:* Erdody, *Director of Photography:* Jockey A. Feindel and Eugen Schufftan, *Film Editor:* Carl Pierson, *Art Director:* Paul Palmentola and Angelo Scibetta, *Distribution:* PRC Pictures.

Cast: John Carradine (Gaston Morel), Jean Parker (Lucille), Nils Asther (Inspector Lefevre), Ludwig Stossel (Lamarté), George Pembroke (Inspector Renaud), Teal Loring (Francine), Sonia Sorel (Renée), Iris Adrian (Mimi), Henry Kolker (Deschamps), Emmett Lynn (Le Soldat), Patti McCarty (Babette), Anne Sterling (Jeanette), Carrie Devan (Constance).

A U.S. production in black and white; released November 11, 1944; 71 minutes.

Bridge Across Time*

Production: Fries Entertainment, *Director:* E. W. Swackhamer, *Producers:* Jack Michon and Richard Maynard, *Writer:*

William F. Nolan, *Music* Lalo Schifrin, *Director of Photography:* Gil Hubbs, *Film Editors:* Tom Fries and Leslie Dennis, *Art Direction:* William McAllister, *Distribution:* NBC Television Network.

Cast: David Hasselhoff (Don Gregory), Stepfanie Kramer (Angie), Randolph Mantooth (Joe), Adrienne Barbeau (Lynn Chandler), Clu Gulager (Chief Pete Dawson), Lindsay Bloom (Elaine Gardner), Ken Swofford (Ed Neville), Rose Marie (Anna Belloc), Lane Smith (Anson Whitfield), David Fox-Brenton (Mr. Latting), Michael Boyle (Dave Williamson), Barbara Bingham (Alice Williamson), Cameron Milzer (Lab Technician), Charles Benton (Mr. Daly), Nancy Shillen (Amy Phelps), Ray Favero (Waiter), Jim Hodge (Mayor McCoy), Peter Vernon (Lord Mayor of London), Paul Rossilli (Roger Eddington/The Ripper).

A U.S. made-for-television film in color; broadcast November 22, 1985; 100 minutes; also known by the titles *Arizona Ripper* and *Terror at London Bridge*.

Dr. Jekyll and Sister Hyde

Production: Hammer Film Productions Ltd., *Director:* Roy Ward Baker, *Producers:* Brian Clemens and Albert Fennell, *Story and Screenplay:* Brian Clemens, *Music:* David Whitaker, *Director of Photography:* Norman Warwick, *Film Editor:* James Needs, *Art Direction:* Robert Jones, *Distribution:* American International Pictures.

Cast: Ralph Bates (Dr. Jekyll), Martine Beswicke (Sister Hyde), Gerald Sim (Professor Robertson), Lewis Fiander (Howard), Susan Broderick (Susan Spencer), Dorothy Alison (Mrs. Spencer), Paul Whitsun-Jones (Sergeant Danvers), Ivor Dean (Burke), Tony Calvin (Hare), Virginia Wetherall (Betsy).

A British production in color; released 1971; MPAA rating "PG" for violence; nudity cut for U.S. version; 93 minutes.

Ellery Queen: Don't Look Behind You*

Production: Universal Television, *Director:* Barry Shear, *Executive Producer:*

Edward J. Montagne, *Producer:* Leonard J. Ackerman, *Teleplay:* Ted Leighton, *Story:* Ellery Queen, "Cat of Many Tails," *Music:* Jerry Fielding, *Photography:* William Margulies, *Editor:* Sam E. Waxman, *Art Director:* Alexander A. Meyer.

Cast: Peter Lawford (Ellery Queen), Harry Morgan (Inspector Richard Queen), E. G. Marshall (Dr. Cazalis), Skye Aubrey (Christy), Stephanie Powers (Celeste), Coleen Gray (Mrs. Cazalis), Morgan Sterne (Police Commissioner), Bill Zuckert (Sgt. Velie), Bob Hastings (Hal Hunter), Than Wyenn (Registrar), Buddy Lester (Policeman), Bill Lucking (Lt. Summers), Pat Delaney (Miss Price), with Tim Herbert, Robin Raymond, Victoria Hale and Billy Sands.

A made for television production; originally aired on NBC, November 19, 1971; 120 minutes.

Hands of the Ripper

Production: Hammer Film Productions Ltd., *Director:* Peter Sasdy, *Producer:* Aida Young, *Screenplay:* L.W. Davidson, *Story:* Edward Spencer Shew, *Music:* Christopher Gunning, *Director of Photography:* Kenneth Talbot, *Film Editor:* James Needs, *Art Direction:* Roy Stannard, *Distribution:* Universal Pictures.

Cast: Eric Porter (Dr. John Pritchard), Angharad Rees (Anna), Jane Merrow (Laura), Keith Bell (Michael Pritchard), Derek Godfrey (Dysart), Dora Bryan (Mrs. Golding), Marjorie Rhodes (Mrs. Bryant), Norman Bird (Police Inspector), Margaret Rawlings (Madame Bullard), Marje Lawrence (Doly), Lynda Baron (Long Liz).

A British production in color; released 1971; MPAA rating "R" for violence; 85 minutes.

Hangover Square

Production: 20th Century–Fox, *Director:* John Brahm, *Producer:* Robert Bassler, *Screenplay:* Barré Lyndon, *Based on the novel by:* Patrick Hamilton, *Music:* Bernard Herrmann, *Director of Photography:* Joseph LaShelle, *Film Editor:* Harry Reynolds, *Art Direction:* Lyle Wheeler and

Maurice Ransford, *Distribution:* 20th Century–Fox Film Corporation.

Cast: Laird Cregar (George Harvey Bone), Linda Darnell (Netta Longdon), George Sanders (Dr. Allan Middleton), Glenn Langan (Carstairs), Faye Marlowe (Barbara Chapman), Alan Napier (Sir Henry Chapman), Frederic Worlock (Superintendent Clay), Leyland Hodgson (Sergeant Lewis).

A U.S. production in black and white; released February 1945; 77 minutes.

Jack the Ripper*

Production: Hal Roach Studios, *Director:* David MacDonald, *Producer:* Hal Roach, Jr., *Screenplay:* Michael Plant, *Music:* Edwin Astley, *Director of Photography:* Stephen Dade, *Film Editor:* Ann Chegwidder, *Art Direction:* Denys Pavitt, *Distribution:* Medallion TV Enterprises.

Cast: Boris Karloff (Host), Niall MacGinnis (Walter Durst), Dorothy Alison (Judith Durst), Clifford Evans (Inspector McWilliam), Robert Brown (Constable), Mai Bacon (Fat Woman), Robert Brooks Turner (Warden), Nora Swinburne (Mrs. Willowdon), Charles Carson (Dr. Hatherley).

A U.S. production in black and white with Jack the Ripper story filmed at Associated British Studios, England; released 1958; 110 minutes; the Jack the Ripper story is just one of four pilot episodes strung together as a TV feature; originally a proposed television anthology series titled *The Veil*.

Jack the Ripper

Production: Mid-Century Film Productions Ltd., *Producer-Director:* Robert S. Baker and Monty Berman, *Screenplay:* Jimmy Sangster, *Story:* Peter Hammond and Colin Craig, *Music:* Jimmy McHugh and Pete Rugolo, *Director of Photography:* Monty Berman, *Film Editor:* Peter Benzencenet, *Art Direction:* William Kellner, *Distribution:* Joseph E. Levine and Embassy Pictures through Paramount Pictures.

Cast: Lee Patterson (Sam Lowry), Eddie Byrne (Inspector O'Neill), Betty McDowall (Anne Ford), Ewen Solon (Sir David Rogers), John LeMesurier (Dr. Tranter), George Rose (Clarke), Philip Leaver (Music Hall Manager), Barbara Burke (Kitty Knowles [Mary Clarke]), Anne Sharpe (Helen), Denis Shaw (Simes), Endre Muller (Louis Benz), Esma Cannon (Nelly), George Woodbridge (Blake), Bill Shine (Lord Sopwith), Marianne Stone (Drunken Woman), Garard Green (Dr. Urquhart), Jack Allen (Assistant Commissioner), Jane Taylor (Hazel), Dorinda Stevens (Margaret), Hal Osmonde (Snakey), George Street (Station Sergeant), Olwen Brooks (Mrs. Boulton), Helena Digby (First Victim), with The Montparnasse Ballet.

A British production (1958) in black and white with brief scene of Ripper's death (blood oozing through floorboards of elevator) in color most likely in U.S. version only; released February 1960; 88 minutes; British version carries musical score by Stanley Black.

Jack the Ripper*

Production: Euston Films, Thames Television, Hill-O'Connor Television, Lorimar-Telepictures, *Producer-Director:* David Wickes, *Screenplay:* Derek Marlowe and David Wickes, *Narrative Concept by* David Wickes, *Music:* John Cameron, *Director of Photography:* Alan Hume, *Film Editor:* Keith Palmer, *Production Design:* John Blezard, *Distribution:* CBS Television Network.

Cast: Michael Caine (Inspector Frederick Abberline), Lewis Collins (Inspector George Godley), Susan George (Catharine Eddowes), Jane Seymour (Mary Jane Kelly), Armand Assante (Richard Mansfield), Ray McAnally (Sir William Gull), Harry Andrews (Coroner Wayne Baxter), Lysette Anthony (Mary Jane Kelly), Roger Ashton Griffiths (Rodman), Peter Armitage (Sergeant Kerby), Desmond Askew (Copy Boy), Ann Castle (Lady Gull), Dierdre Costello (Annie Chapman), Angela Crow (Liz Stride), Marc Culwick (Prince Albert Victor), Hugh Fraser (Sir Charles Warren), Bruce

Green (Pizer), Richard Morant (Dr. Acland), David Swift (Lord Salisbury).

A British-American television miniseries in color; broadcast October 21 and 23, 1988, commemorating the Ripper's centenary; 160 minutes.

Jack the Ripper (*Der Dirnenmörder von London*)

Production: Cinemac, *Writer-Director:* Jess Franco, *Producers:* Erwin C. Dietrich and Max Dara, *Director of Photography:* Peter Baumgartner, *Music:* Walter Baumgartner, *Distribution:* Unknown.

Cast: Klaus Kinski (The Doctor), Josephine Chaplin (Cynthia), Herbert Fux (Inspector Selby) with Ursula von Wiese, Lina Romay, Andreas Mankopff, Hans Gaugler, Francine Custer, Olga Gebhard and Nicola Weisse.

A German-Swiss coproduction in color; released 1976; U.S. distribution uncertain; 95 minutes.

Jack the Ripper (*Jack el Destripador de Londres*)

Production: CineFilms and International Apollo Films, *Director:* José Luis Madrid, *Producer* Jim Delaveña, *Screenplay:* Sandro Continenza, José Luis Madrid and Jacinto Molina, *Director of Photography:* Diego Uberda, *Music:* Piero Piccioni, *Distribution:* Unknown.

Cast: Franco Borelli, Victor Iregua, Patricia Loran, Rensso Marinano, Irene Mir, Jacinto Molina, Andrew Reese, Orchidea de Santis.

A Spanish-Italian coproduction in color; released 1971; U.S. distribution unknown; some sources say producer Jim Delaveña is a pseudonym for José Luis Madrid; 87 minutes.

Jack's Back

Production: Elliott Kastner/André Blay in association with Palisades Entertainment presents a Cassian Elwes production, *Writer-Director:* Rowdy Herrington, *Producers:* Tim Moore and Cassian Elwes, *Music:* Danny Di Paolo, *Director of*

Photography: Shelly Johnson, *Film Editor:* Harry B. Miller III, *Production Design:* Piers Plowden, *Distribution:* Paramount Pictures.

Cast: James Spader (John/Rick Wesford), Cynthia Gibb (Chris Moscari), Jim Haynie (Sergeant Gabriel), Dr. Robert Picardo (Dr. Carlos Battera), Rod Loomis (Dr. Sidney Tannerson), Rex Ryon (Jack Pendler), Chris Mulkey (Scott Morofsky), Wendell Wright (Capt. Walter Prentis), John Wesley (Sam Hilliard).

A U.S. production in color; MPAA rating "R" for violence and profanity; released 1988; 97 minutes.

The Lodger

Production: 20th Century–Fox, *Director:* John Brahm, *Producer:* Robert Bassler, *Screenplay:* Barré Lyndon, *Based on the novel by:* Mrs. Marie Belloc Lowndes, *Music:* Hugo J. Friedhofer, *Director of Photography:* Lucien Ballard, *Film Editor:* J. Watson Webb, Jr., *Art Direction:* James Basevi and John Ewing, *Distribution:* 20th Century–Fox Film Corporation.

Cast: Merle Oberon (Kitty Langley), George Sanders (Inspector John Warwick), Laird Cregar (Mr. Slade), Sir Cedric Hardwicke (Robert Burton), Sara Allgood (Ellen Burton), Aubrey Mather (Superintendent Sutherland), Queenie Leonard (Daisy), Doris Lloyd (Jennie), David Clyde (Sergeant Bates), Lumsden Hare (Doctor Sheridan), Frederic Worlock (Sir Edward), Colin Campbell (Harold), Olaf Hytten (Harris), Harold de Becker (Charlie), with Billy Bevan, Forrester Harvey, Skelton Knaggs, Edmond Breon, Gerald Hamer, Montague Shaw and Cyril Delavanti.

A U.S. production in black and white; released January 7, 1944; 84 minutes.

The Lodger: A Story of the London Fog

Production: Gainsborough, *Director:* Alfred Hitchcock, *Producer:* Michael Balcon, *Screenplay:* Alfred Hitchcock and Eliot Stannard, *Based on the novel by:* Marie Belloc Lowndes, *Director of*

Photography: Baron Ventigmilia, *Editor and Titles:* Ivor Montagu, *Art Direction:* C. Wilfred Arnold and Bertram Evans, *Distribution:* Unknown.

Cast: Ivor Novello (The Lodger/Jonathan Drew), June (Daisy Bunting), Marie Ault (Mrs. Bunting), Arthur Chesney (Mr. Bunting), Malcolm Keen (Joe Chandler).

A British production in black and white; silent; released 1926; U.S. distribution uncertain; 88 minutes.

Man in the Attic

Production: Panoramic Productions and Leonard Goldstein, *Director:* Hugo Fregonese, *Producer:* Robert L. Jacks, *Screenplay:* Robert Presnell, Jr., and Barré Lyndon, *Based on* The Lodger *by:* Marie Belloc Lowndes, *Music:* No credits, *Director of Photography:* Leo Tover, *Film Editor:* Marjorie Fowler, *Art Direction:* Lyle Wheeler and Leland Fuller, *Distribution:* 20th Century–Fox Film Corporation.

Cast: Jack Palance (Mr. Slade), Constance Smith (Lily Bonner), Frances Bavier (Helen Harley), Rhys Williams (William Harley), Lillian Bond (Anne Rowley), Isabel Jewell (Katy), Lisa Daniels (Mary Lenihan), Byron Palmer (Inspector Paul Warwick), Tita Phillips (Daisy), with Harry Cording, Leslie Bradley, Lester Matthews and Sean McClory.

A U.S. production in black and white; released December 1953; 84 minutes.

The Monster of London City *(Das Ungeheuer von London City)*

Production: CCC Filmkunst GmbH, *Director:* Edwin Zbonek, *Producer:* Artur Brauner, *Screenplay:* Robert A. Stemmle, *Based on the novel by:* Bryan Edgar Wallace, *Music:* Martin Böttcher, *Director of Photography:* Siegfried Hold, *Editor:* Walter Wischniewsky, *Art Direction:* Hans-Jurgen Kiebach and Ernst Schomer, *English Language Version:* Les Films Jacque Willemetz with dialogue by Elsa Motta, *Distribution:* Walter Manley Enterprises through Parade Releasing Organization.

Cast: Hansjörg Felmy (Richard Sand), Marianne Koch (Ann Morley), Dietmar Schoenherr (Dr. Michael Greeley), Hans Nielsen (Inspector Dorne), Fritz Tillman (Sir George Edwards), Peer Schmidt (Teddy Flynn), Gudrun Schmidt (Evelyn Nichols), Kai Fischer (Helen Capstick).

A German production in black and white (1964) in unknown anamorphic process; released in U.S. 1965 on double bill with *The Phantom of Soho*; 87 minutes.

Murder by Decree

Production: Ambassador Films in cooperation with the Canadian Film Development Corporation; Famous Players Ltd.; WOW!! Entertainment, Inc.; Decree Productions, and Saucy Jack, Inc. *Director:* Bob Clark, *Producers:* René Dupont and Bob Clark, *Original Screenplay:* John Hopkins, *Music:* Carl Zittrer and Paul Zaza, *Director of Photography:* Reginald Morris, *Film Editor:* Stan Cole, *Art Direction:* Harry Pottle, *Distribution:* Robert A. Goldstone through Avco Embassy Pictures.

Cast: Christopher Plummer (Sherlock Holmes), James Mason (Dr. Watson), David Hemmings (Inspector Foxborough), Susan Clark (Mary Kelly), Anthony Quayle (Sir Charles Warren), John Gielgud (Prime Minister), Frank Finlay (Inspector Lestrade), Donald Sutherland (Robert Lees), Genevieve Bujold (Annie Crook), Roy Lansford (Sir Thomas Smiley), Peter Jonfield (William Slade), Teddi Moore (Mrs. Lees), Catherine Kessler (Carrie).

A Canadian-British production in Metrocolor; released 1978; MPAA rating "PG" for violence; 120 minutes.

Pandora's Box

Production: Nero-Film, *Director:* G. W. Pabst, *Producer:* George C. Horsetzky and Seymour Nebenzahl, *Screenplay:* Ladislaus Vajda, *Based on the plays* Erdgeist *and* Die Büchse der Pandora *by:* Frank Wedekind, *Director of Photography:* Günther Krampf, *Film Editor:* Joseph R.

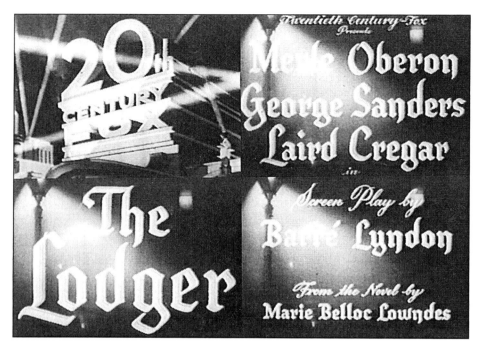

Main titles to John Brahm's atmospheric production of Barré Lyndon's adaptation of Belloc Lowndes' *The Lodger.*

Fiesler, *Art Direction:* Andrei Andreiev, *Distribution:* Moviegraph, Inc.

Cast: Louise Brooks (Lulu), Fritz Kortner (Dr. Peter Schön), Franz Lederer (Alwa Schön), Carl Goetz (Schigolch/ Papa Brommer), Alice Roberts (Countess Anna Geschwitz), Daisy D'Ora (Marie de Zarniko), Siefried Arno (the stage director), Gustav Diessl (Jack the Ripper).

A German production (1928) in black and white; silent; 131 minutes but some sources say the film was cut to 120 minutes; some sources say the film was released in the U.S. in 1929.

The Phantom Fiend

Production: Woolf and Freeman Film Services Ltd., *Director:* Maurice Elvey, *Producer:* Julius Hagan, *Screenplay:* Miles Mander and Paul Rotha, *Adaptation by:* H. Fowler Mear, *Based on* The Lodger *by:*

Marie Belloc Lowndes, *Directors of Photography:* Sidney Blythe, Basil Emmott, and William Luff, *Art Direction:* James Carter, *Film Editor:* Jack Harris, *Distribution:* Olympic Pictures Corporation.

Cast: Ivor Novello (Angeloff), Elizabeth Allen (Daisy Bunting), Jack Hawkins (Joe Martin), Kynaston Reeves (Bob Mitchell), Barbara Everest (Mrs. Bunting), A. W. Bascomb (Mr. Bunting), Shayle Gardner (Detective Snell).

A British production in black and white; released September 8, 1932; 85 minutes; released in U.S. April 19, 1935, with running time of 67 minutes; some sources indicate a 1955 reissue at 67 minutes.

The Ripper

Production: United Entertainment Pictures, *Director:* Christopher Lewis, *Producer:* Linda Lewis, *Story and Screenplay:* Bill Groves, *Distribution:* Unavailable.

Cast: Tom Savini (The Spirit of Jack the Ripper), Wade Tower (Steve) with Andrea Adams, Tom Schreier and Mona Van Pernis.

A U.S. production in color; story involves how an antique ring that belonged to Jack the Ripper turns a college professor into a modern-day Ripper; released 1985.

The Ripper*

Production: Michael R. Joyce Productions, Mutual Film Company and Starz! Pictures, *Director:* Janet Meyers, *Executive Producers:* Mark Gordon and Gary Levinsohn, *Supervising Producer:* Michael R. Joyce, *Producer:* Allison Lyon Segan, *Co-Producer:* Anthony Winley, *Writer:* Robert Rodat, *Director of Photography:* Martin McGrath, *Editor:* Elba Sanchez-Short, *Distribution:* Starz! Pictures.

Cast: Patrick Bergin (Inspector Hansen), Gabrielle Anwar (Florry), Samuel West (Prince Eddie), Michael York (Sir Charles Warren), Essie Davis (Lady Evelyn Bookman), with Adam Couper, Olivia Hamnett, Karen Davitt, Damien Pree, Stewart Morritt, Kevin Miles, John Gregg, Frank Whitten, Peter Collingwood, Josephine Keen, Lisle Jones, Anthony Morton, Christopher Kemp, Stephen Sheehan, Caroline Huff, Denzil Howson, Justin Paslow, Jessica Muschamp, John Turner, Anny Fodor.

A U.S.-Australian coproduction in color; broadcast December 6, 1997, on Starz! cable network; 100 minutes.

Room to Let

Production: Exclusive Films Ltd. *Director:* Godfrey Grayson, *Producer:* Anthony Hinds, *Screenplay:* John Gilling and Godfrey Grayson, *Based on the BBC feature by:* Margery Allingham, *Music:* Frank Spencer, *Director of Photography:* Cedric Williams, *Film Editor:* James Needs, *Art Direction:* Denis Wreford, *Distribution:* Exclusive Films Ltd.

Cast: Jimmy Hanley (Curly Minter), Valentine Dyall (Dr. Fell), Christine Silver (Mrs. Musgrave), Constance Smith (Molly Musgrave), Merle Tottenham (Alice), Charles Hawtrey (Michael Atkinson), Reginald Dyson (Sergeant Cranbourne), Aubrey Dexter (Mr. Harding), J. Anthony la Penna (James Jasper, or J. J.).

A British production (1950) in black and white; U.S. distribution uncertain; 68 minutes.

The Ruling Class

Production: Avco-Embassy Pictures, *Director:* Peter Medak, *Producers:* Jules Buck and Jack Hawkins, *Screenplay:* Peter Barnes, *Director of Photography:* Ken Hodges, *Film Editor:* Ray Lovejoy, *Distribution:* Avco-Embassy Pictures.

Cast: Peter O'Toole (14th Earl of Gurney), Alastair Sim (Bishop Lampton), Arthur Lowe (Tucker), Harry Andrews (13th Earl of Gurney), Coral Browne (Lady Claire Gurney), Michael Bryant (Dr. Herder), Nigel Green (McKyle), William Mervyn (Sir Charles Gurney), Carolyn Seymour (Grace Shelley), James Villiers (Dinsdale), Hugh Burden (Matthew Peake), Graham Crowden (Truscott), Kay Walsh (Mrs. Piggott-Jones), Patsy Byrne (Mrs. Treadwell).

A British production in color; released 1972; 154 minutes.

A Study in Terror

Production: Compton-Cameo-Tekli and Sir Nigel Films, *Director:* James Hill, *Producer:* Henry E. Lester, *Executive Producer:* Herman Cohen, *Story and Screenplay:* Donald and Derek Ford, Harry Craig, *Music:* John Scott, *Director of Photography:* Desmond Dickinson, B.S.C., *Film Editor:* Henry Richardson, *Art Direction:* Alex Vetchinsky, *Distribution:* Columbia Pictures Corporation.

Cast: John Neville (Sherlock Holmes), Donald Houston (Dr. Watson), John Fraser (Lord Carfax), Anthony Quayle (Dr. Murray), Robert Morley (Mycroft Holmes), Barbara Windsor (Annie Chapman), Adrienne Corri (Angela), Peter Carsten (Max Steiner) Frank Finlay

Title card for mystery writer Margery Allingham's pastiche of Belloc Lowndes' *The Lodger*.

(Inspector Lestrade), Judi Dench (Sally), Cecil Parker (Prime Minister), Georgia Brown (Singer), Barry Jones (Duke of Shires), Kay Walsh (Cathy Eddowes), Edina Ronay (Mary Kelly), Terry Downes (Chunky), Charles Regnier (Joseph Beck), Dudley Foster (Home Secretary), John Cairney (Michael Osborne), Christiane Maybach (Polly Nichols), Avis Bunnage (Landlady), Barbara Leake (Mrs. Hudson), Patrick Newell (P. C. Benson), Norma Foster (Liz Stride).

A British production in Columbia Color by Pathé; released November 1965; 94 minutes.

Time After Time

Production: Herb Jaffe Production, *Director:* Nicholas Meyer, *Producer:* Herb Jaffe, *Screenplay:* Nicholas Meyer, *Story:* Karl Alexander and Steve Hayes, *Music:* Miklos Rozsa, *Director of Photography:* Paul Lohmann, *Film Editor:* Donn Cambern, *Art Direction:* Edward C. Carfagno, *Distribution:* Warner Brothers.

Cast: Malcolm McDowell (Herbert G. Wells), David Warner (Dr. John Lesley Stevenson [Jack the Ripper]), Mary Steenburgen (Amy Robbins), Charles Cioffi (Lieutenant Mitchell), Laurie Main (Inspector Gregson), Andonia Katsaros (Mrs. Turner), Patti D'Arbanville (Shirley), Keith McConnell (Harding), Geraldine Baron (Carol), James Garrett (Edwards), Byron Webster (McKay), Leo Lewis (Richardson), Joseph Maher (Adams).

A U.S. production in Metrocolor with prints by Technicolor and in Panavision; released 1979; MPAA rating "PG" for violence and subject matter; 112 minutes.

Waxworks (*Das Wachsfigurenkabinett*)

Production: Neptun-Film, *Director:* Paul Leni, *Screenplay:* Henrik Galeen, *Photography:* Helmar Lerski, *Art Direction:* Paul Leni and Ernst Stern, *Distribution:* some sources say Viking Pictures.

Cast: Emil Jannings (Haroun Al-Raschid), Conrad Veidt (Ivan the Terrible), Werner Krauss (Spring-heeled/Jack the Ripper), with Wilhelm Dieterle, Olga Belajeff, Ernst Legal, John Gottowt and Georg John.

A German production (1924) in black and white; silent; 65 minutes; some sources say the film was released in U.S. in 1929 as *Three Wax Men.*

The Woman in Green

Production: Universal Pictures, *Producer-Director:* Roy William Neill, *Original Screenplay:* Bertram Millhauser, *Musical Direction:* Mark Levant, *Director of Photography:* Virgil Miller, *Film Editor:* Edward Curtiss, *Art Direction:* John B. Goodman and Martin Obzina, *Distribution:* Universal Pictures.

Cast: Basil Rathbone (Sherlock Holmes), Nigel Bruce (Dr. Watson), Hillary Brooke (Lydia Marlowe), Henry Daniell (Professor Moriarty), Paul Cavanagh (Sir George Fenwick), Matthew Boulton (Inspector Gregson), Eve Amber (Maude), Frederic Worlock (Onslow), Tom Bryon (Williams), Sally Shepherd (Crandon), Mary Gordon (Mrs. Hudson), Dennis Hoey (Inspector Lestrade), Percival Vivian (Dr. Simnell), Olaf Hytten (Norris), Harold de Becker (Shabby Man), Tommy Hughes (Newsman).

A U.S. production in black and white; released July 27, 1945; 68 minutes.

Major Radio Programs

Production and cast information on radio programs is incredibly scant. The following material was culled from various radio logs in newspapers, reference books and other source material.

The CBS Radio Mystery Theatre "The Lodger"

Network: CBS, *Director:* Himan Brown, *Writer:* George Lowther, *Cast:* Kim Hunter as Mrs. Nell Pearson, *Host:* E. G. Marshall, *Airdate:* May 13, 1974.

The CBS Radio Mystery Theatre "The Strange Case of Lucas Lauder"

Network: CBS, *Director:* Himan Brown, *Writer:* George Lowther, *Cast:* Robert Lansing as Lucas Lauder, *Host:* E. G. Marshall, *Airdate:* February 28, 1975.

Crime Classics "Good Evening, My Name Is Jack the Ripper"

Network: CBS, *Director:* Elliott Lewis, *Writers:* Morton Fine and David Friedkin, *Musical Compositions:* Bernard Herrmann, *Cast:* Lou Merrill as Thomas Hyland, Betty Hartford as Mary Jane Kelly, *Airdate:* June 30, 1954.

Ellery Queen "Nick the Knife"

Network: CBS, *Writers:* Anthony Boucher and Manfred B. Lee, *Cast:* Sydney Smith as Ellery Queen, Santos Ortega as Inspector Queen, Gertrude Warner as Nikki Porter, Ted de Corsia as Sergeant Velie, *Airdate:* August 1, 1945.

Forecast "The Lodger"

Network: CBS, *Director:* Alfred Hitchcock, *Cast:* Herbert Marshall as Mr. Sleuth/The Lodger, *Airdate:* July 22, 1940.

Hollywood Star Time "The Lodger"

Network: CBS, *Director:* Robert L. Redd, *Cast:* Vincent Price as The Lodger, *Airdate:* May 19, 1946.

Inner Sanctum "The Song of the Slasher"

Network: Blue Network, *Producer-*

Director: Himan Brown, *Writer:* Milton Lewis, *Cast:* Unavailable, *Announcer:* Ed Herlihy, *Airdate:* April 24, 1945.

The Kate Smith Show "Yours Truly, Jack the Ripper" skit
Network: CBS, *Guest Star:* Laird Cregar, *Date:* January 7, 1944.

Mollé Mystery Theatre "Yours Truly, Jack the Ripper"
Network: NBC *Airdate:* March 6, 1945.

Mollé Mystery Theatre "The Creeper"
Network: NBC, *Host:* Bernard Lenrow as "Geoffrey Barnes, Connoisseur of Mysteries," *Airdate:* March 29, 1946.

Mystery in the Air "The Lodger"
Network: NBC, *Director:* Cal Kuhl *Cast:* Peter Lorre as Mr. Sleuth/The Lodger, Agnes Moorehead as Ellen Bunting, *Announcer:* Harry Morgan, *Airdate:* August 14, 1947.

Mystery Playhouse "Yours Truly, Jack the Ripper" (Mollé re-broadcast)
Network: Syndicated, *Host:* Peter Lorre, *Airdate:* March 6, 1945.

The New Adventures of Sherlock Holmes "The Strange Case of the Murder in Wax"
Network: Mutual, *Director:* Edna Best, *Writers:* Denis Green and Anthony Boucher, *Cast:* Basil Rathbone as Sherlock Holmes, Nigel Bruce as Dr. Watson, *Announcer:* Harry Bartell, *Airdate:* January 7, 1946.

Nightbeat Untitled "Slasher" broadcast
Network: NBC, *Director:* Warren Lewis, *Cast:* Frank Lovejoy as Randy Stone, *Airdate:* November 10, 1950.

The Shadow "The Creeper"
Network: Syndicated, *Cast:* Orson Welles as The Shadow/Lamont Cranston, Agnes Moorehead as Margo Lane, *Announcer:* Ken Roberts, *Airdate:* Summer 1938.

"Smiler with the Knife: The Mystery of Jack the Ripper"
Network: BBC, *Writer:* Tony Van den Bergh, *Airdate:* April 12, 1967.

Stay Tuned for Terror "Yours Truly, Jack the Ripper"
Network: Syndicated, *Producer-Director:* John Neblett, *Narrator:* Craig Dennis, *Airdate:* March 6, 1945.

Suspense "The Lodger"
Network: CBS, *Director:* William Spier, *Writer:* Robert Tallman, *Cast:* Robert Montgomery as narrator and Mr. Sleuth/The Lodger, *Airdate:* December 14, 1944.

Suspense "The Lodger"
Network: CBS, *Director:* William N. Robson, *Writer:* Robert Tallman, *Cast:* Robert Montgomery as narrator and The Lodger, Jeanette Nolan as Ellen Bunting, Peggy Webber as Daisy, *Airdate:* February 14, 1948.

Suspense "The Whole Town's Sleeping"
Network: CBS, *Writer-Director:* Anthony Ellis, *Story:* Ray Bradbury, *Cast:* Jeanette Nolan as Lavinia Nebbs, William Conrad as the Narrator, *Airdate:* June 14, 1955.

Suspense "The Whole Town's Sleeping"
Network: CBS, *Director:* William N. Robson, *Story:* Ray Bradbury, *Write:* Anthony Ellis, *Cast:* Agnes Moorehead as Lavinia Nebbs, William Conrad as the Narrator, *Airdate:* August 31, 1958.

Unsolved Mysteries "Jack the Ripper"
No additional information available.

Major Television Programs

Information was compiled from program credits, various television listings in newspapers, and several diverse reference books on television history.

A&E Biography "Jack the Ripper"

Network: Arts and Entertainment Network, *Production:* Alvin H. Perlmutter, Inc., in association with A&E Network, *Producer:* Deborah Richardson, *Executive Producer:* Michael Cascio, *Editor:* Kendrick Simmons, *Music:* Robert Secret, *Host:* Peter Graves, *Airdate:* May 23, 1995.

Cast: Brian Saxton (Narrator), Lillian Harlan (Voice of Polly, Prostitute & Queen's Letter), Sean Kavanaugh-Dowsett (Voice of Dear Boss & Lusk Letters), Cristoph Wolkenstein (Voice of Joseph Barnett).

Alfred Hitchcock Presents "The Hands of Mr. Ottermole"

Network: CBS, *Production:* Shamley Productions and Revue Studios, *Director:* Robert Stevens, *Producer:* Joan Harrison, *Teleplay:* Francis Cockrell, *Story:* Thomas Burke, *Airdate:* May 5, 1957.

Cast: Theodore Bikel (The Sergeant/Ottermole), Rhys Williams (Mr. Summers/The Journalist), A. E. Gould-Porter (Mr. Whybrow), Torin Thatcher (Constable), Barry Harvey (Whybrow's Nephew), John Trayne (Policeman), with Charles Davis, Nora O'Mahoney, Nelson Welch, Mollie Roden, James McCallom, Hilda Plowright and Gerald Hamer.

The Avengers "Fog"

Network: ABC, *Production:* Associated British Corporation, *Director:* John Hough, *Writer:* Jeremy Burnham, U.S. *Airdate:* June 23, 1969.

Cast: Patrick Macnee (John Steed), Linda Thorson (Tara King), Nigel Green (Sir Geoffrey Armstrong), Guy Rolfe (Mark Travers), Patrick Newell (Mother), Terence Brady (Carstairs), Paul Whitsun-Jones (Sanders), David Lodge (Maskell), Norman Chappell (Fowler) with David Bird, Frank Sieman, Patsy Smart, Virginia Clay, John Garrie, Bernard Severn, Frederick Peisley, Stan Jay, Arnold Diamond, William Lyon Brown and John Barrard.

A British series, *The Avengers* met with widespread acclaim when it was released to American audiences through an arrangement with ABC in the mid-1960s.

Babylon 5 "Comes the Inquisitor"

Network: Warner Brothers, *Production:* Rattlesnake Productions and Warner Brothers, *Creator:* J. Michael Straczynski, *Executive Producers:* J. Michael Straczynski and Doug Netter, *Producer:* John Copeland, *Conceptual Consultant:* Harlan Ellison, *Director:* Michael Vejar, *Teleplay:* J. Michael Straczynski, *Airdate:* Late October [approximately the 25th] 1995.

Cast: Bruce Boxleitner (Captain John Sheridan), Mira Furlan (Delenn), Jerry Doyle (Security Chief Garibaldi), Andreas Katsulas (G'Kar), Wayne Alexander (Sebastian), Jack Kehler (Mr. Chase), Diane Adair (Narn Mother), Ardwright Chamberlain (Kosh), Jim Chiros (Centauri #1), Joshua Cox (Tech #1), Mark Hendrinckson (Narn #1), Michael Francis Kelley (Guard), Kim Strauss (Narn #2), Craig Thomas (Human).

Cimarron Strip "Knife in the Darkness"

Network: CBS, *Executive Producer:* Phillip Leacock, *Producer:* Doug Benton, *Writer:* Harlan Ellsion, *Airdate:* January 25, 1968.

Cast: Stuart Whitman (Marshal Jim Crown), Percy Herbert (MacGregor), Randy Boone (Francis Wilde) and Jill Townsend (Dulcey).

Fantasy Island "With Affection, Jack the Ripper"

Network: ABC, *Production:* Spelling-Goldberg Productions, *Director:* Mike

Vejar, *Producers:* Don Ingalls and Carl Pingatore, *Writers:* Don Ingalls and Ron Friedman, *Airdate:* November 29, 1980.

Cast: Ricardo Montalban (Mr. Roarke), Hervé Villechaize (Tattoo), Wendy Schaal (Julie), Lynda Day George (Lorraine Peters), Alex Cord (Robert West), Victor Buono (Dr. Albert Z. Fell), Angela Slater (Gracie), Ken Barry (Stanley Hocker), Meredith MacRae (Deena De Winter), Carolyn Jones (Jessie De Winter), Lyle Waggoner (Monty), Frank Birney (Headwaiter).

Two episodes consistently comprised this series; "With Affection, Jack the Ripper," which involved a beautiful criminologist seeking to discover the identity of Jack the Ripper, was followed by "Gigolo."

The Green Hornet "Alias the Scarf"

Network: ABC, *Production:* Greenway Productions and 20th Century–Fox Television, *Director:* Allen Reisner, *Executive Producer:* William Dozier, *Producer:* Richard Bluel, *Writer:* William L. Stuart, *Airdate:* February 24, 1967.

Cast: Van Williams (The Green Hornet/Britt Reid), Bruce Lee (Kato), Wende Wagner (Lenore Case), Walter Brooke (District Attorney F. P. Scanlon), Lloyd Gough (Mike Axford), John Carradine (James Rancourt), Patricia Barry (Hazel Schmidt), Ian Wolfe (Peter Willman), Paul Gleason (Paul Garret).

In Search of "Jack the Ripper"

Network: Syndicated, *Production:* Alan Landsburgh Productions, *Host/Narrator:* Leonard Nimoy, *Airdate:* 1978; no other information available.

Kolchak: The Night Stalker "The Ripper"

Network: ABC, *Production:* Universal Television, *Director:* Allen Baron, *Producer:* Paul Playdon, *Writer:* Rudolph Borchert, *Airdate:* September 13, 1974.

Cast: Darren McGavin (Carl Kolchak), Simon Oakland (Tony Vincenzo), Jack Grinnage (Ron Updyke), Beatrice Colen (Jane Plum), Ken Lynch (Captain Warren), Mickey Gilbert (Jack the Ripper), Roberta Collins (Detective Cortazza), Marya Small (Masseuse), Ruth McDevitt (Elderly Woman), Donald Mantooth (Policeman), Robert Bryan Berger (Mail Boy), Clint Young (Driver).

The New Adventures of Sherlock Holmes "The Case of the Thistle Killer"

Network: NBC and syndication through Motion Pictures for Television, Inc., and Guild Films, Inc., *Production:* A Sheldon Reynolds Production, *Director:* Steve Previn, *Original Script:* Charles and Joseph Early, *Airdate:* February 14, 1955.

Cast: Ronald Howard (Sherlock Holmes), H. Marion Crawford (Dr. John H. Watson), Archie Duncan (Inspector Lestrade), Richard Watson (John Phoenix), Kenneth Richards (Sergeant), William Smith (Superintendent).

Secret History: The Whitechapel Murders

Network: UK Television Channel 4, *Production:* Just Television for Channel 4, *Director:* Stephen White, *Producers:* David Jessel and Stephen White, *Executive Producer:* Steve Haywood, *Writer:* David Jessel, *Consultants:* Stewart Evans and Paul Gainey, *Airdate:* July 25, 1996.

Cast: Nathan Osgood (Colonel Dunham), Roy Purcell (Voice of Inspector Littlechild).

Secrets and Mysteries "From Hell"

Network: ABC syndication, *Production:* Triumph Communications, *Directors:* Graeme Whifler and Erik Nelson, *Producers:* Sue Perry, Erik Nelson, Graeme Whifler, and Glenn Kirschbaum, *Writers:* Erik Nelson and Sue Perry, *Airdate:* 1987.

Cast: Edward Mulhare (Host) and John Fleck (Walter Sickert) with appearances by Robert Bloch and Donald Rumbelow.

The program is also known by the title *Secrets of the Unknown.*

Title sequence for the ABC television series also known by the title *Secrets of the Unknown.*

The Sixth Sense "With Affection, Jack the Ripper"

Network: ABC, *Production:* Universal Television, *Director:* Robert Day, *Producer:* Stan Shpetner, *Writer:* Don Ingalls, *Airdate:* October 14, 1972.

Cast: Gary Collins (Dr. Michael Rhodes), Patty Duke (Elizabeth), Robert Foxworth (Adam), Percy Rodrigues (Lieutenant Woods), Mitch Carter (Police Officer), Marilyn Nix (Secretary), Heather Lowe (First Victim), Jannis Durkin (Second Victim).

Sliders "Murder Most Foul"

Network: Fox, *Production:* St. Clare Entertainment, *Creators:* Robert K. Weiss and Tracy Torme, *Executive Producers:* Tracy Torme, Jacob Epstein and Alan Barnette, *Executive Consultants:* John Landis, Robert K. Weiss and Leslie

Belzberg, *Director:* Jeff Woolnough, *Writer:* David Peckinpah, *Airdate:* January 3, 1997.

Cast: Jerry O'Connell (Quinn Mallory), Sabrina Lloyd (Wade Wells), Cleavant Derricks (Rembrandt Brown), John Rhys-Davies (Professor Maximillian Arturo), Kari Wuher (Maggie Becket), Suzanne Mara (Doctor Punch), Frank Castina (Wonk), David Purdham (Doctor Bolivar), Brigid Brannagh (Erin), Holly R. Claman (Anne), Brian McNamara (Inspector Reed), Taylor Leigh (Mrs. Taylor), Adam Wylie (Trevor), Lester Barrie (Diggs), Derik Van Derbeken (Security Man), Carmen Nogales (Young Woman), Brandon Michael (Boy).

Star Trek "Wolf in the Fold"

Network: NBC, *Production:* Norway

Productions and Desilu Productions, *Director:* Joseph Pevney, *Producer:* Gene L. Coon, *Writer:* Robert Bloch, *Airdate:* December 22, 1967.

Cast: William Shatner (Captain James T. Kirk), Leonard Nimoy (Mr. Spock), James Doohan (Engineer Scott), DeForrest Kelley (Dr. McCoy), John Fiedler (Hengist), Charles Macauley (Jaris), Pilar Seurat (Sybo), Joseph Bernard (Tark), Charles Dierkop (Morla), Judy McConnell (Tankris), Virginia Landridge (Karen Tracy), Tania Lemani (Kara), Judy Sherven (Nurse).

Bloch's script was adapted into a short story by science fiction writer James Blish in *Star Trek 8* (pp. 112–143) published in November 1972 by Bantam Books.

Thriller "Yours Truly, Jack the Ripper"

Network: NBC, *Production:* Hubbell Robinson Productions and Revue Studios, *Director:* Ray Milland, *Producer:* William Frye, *Teleplay:* Barré Lyndon, *Music:* Jerry Goldsmith, *Story:* Robert Bloch, *Airdate:* April 11, 1961.

Cast: Boris Karloff (Host), John Williams (Sir Guy Hollis), Donald Woods (John Carmody), Edmon Ryan (Captain Pete Jago), Adam Williams (Hymie Kralek), Nancy Valentine (Arlene), Ransom Sherman (Lester Baston), Sam Gilman (Police Official), J. Pat O'Malley (Street Singer), Gloria Blondell (Maggie Rattivic), Miss Beverly Hills (Herself).

Time Cop "A Rip in Time"

Network: ABC, *Production:* Lawrence Gordon Productions, December Third Productions and Dark Horse Entertainment in association with Universal Television. *Creators:* Mike Richardson and

Mark Verheiden, *Executive Producers:* Lawrence Gordon and Robert Singer, *Co-Executive Producers:* Mike Richardson, Lloyd Levin, Art Monterastelli, *Supervising Producer:* Mark Verheiden, *Director:* Allan Arkush, *Producers:* Alfred Gough, Miles Millar and Art Monterastelli, *Teleplay:* Philip Gough and Miles Millar, *Airdate:* September 22, 1997.

Cast: T. W. King, Cristi Conaway, Don Stark, Kurt Fuller, Tom O'Brien, W. Morgan Sheppard, Anna Gavin, Ric Sarabia, Belinda Waymouth, Saige Ophelia Spinney, John Maynard, Tim O'Hare, Simon Billig, and Michael Holden.

The Twilight Zone "The New Exhibit"

Network: CBS, *Production:* Cayuga Productions and MGM Television, *Director:* John Brahm, *Producer:* Bert Granet, *Teleplay:* Charles Beaumont, *Airdate:* April 4, 1963.

Cast: Martin Balsam (Martin Senescu), Will Kuluva (Mr. Ferguson), Maggie Mahoney (Mrs. Senescu), Milton Parsons (Henri Landru), David Bond (Jack the Ripper), Robert L. McCord (Burke), Billy Beck (Hare), Bob Mitchell (Albert W. Hicks).

A number of sources indicate that the script was actually written by Jerry Sohl; Marc Scott Zicree, in *The Twilight Zone Companion* (1982), reports that the script was "actually ghostwritten, in its entirety, by Jerry Sohl, a man who had been a staff writer on *Alfred Hitchcock Presents*," primarily because Beaumont was too preoccupied with other assignments as well as too ill to complete the assignment (353). Zicree adds that the episode was "plotted by Charles Beaumont and Jerry Sohl" (351).

Miscellaneous Media

COMIC BOOKS

From Hell (1996)

Publisher: Kitchen Sink Press, *Writer:*

Alan Moore, *Illustrator:* Eddie Campbell. A 10-volume epic that bases its narrative on Knight's theory, and includes appearances by just about any significant

Screenwriter Barré Lyndon receives co-credit for Hugo Fregonese's remake of *The Lodger.* Lyndon would also write the *Thriller* television adaptation of Robert Bloch's "Yours Truly, Jack the Ripper."

personage of Victorian England (even the "Elephant Man" makes an appearance).

Gotham by Gaslight (1989)

Publisher: DC Comics; no other information available. Reportedly, a story in which Bruce Wayne is a Victorian citizen who dons his Batman guise to pursue Jack the Ripper.

Jack the Ripper (1989–1990)

Publisher: Eternity Comics and Malibu Graphics, *Written and Illustrated by:* Bruce Balfour and Paul Mendoza. A 3-volume narrative centered on two private detectives who are brought into the Ripper case by Inspector Abberline. The story bases itself on Knight's theory.

Musical

Jack's Holiday (1995)

Director: Susan H. Schulman, *Music and Lyrics:* Randy Court, *Book and Lyrics:* Mark St. Germain.

Cast: Allen Fitzpatrick (Jack), Dennis Parlato (Police Inspector), with Judy Balzer, Nicholas Coster, Alix Korey, Greg Naughton, Anne Runolfsson and Henry Stram.

Video Game

RIPPER (1996)

Production: Take 2 Interactive, *Director:* Phil Parmet, *Screenplay:* Dennis Johnson.

Cast: Christopher Walken (Detective Vince Magnotta), Karen Allen (Dr. Clare Burton), Burgess Meredith (Hamilton Wofford/Covington Wofford), Ossie Davis (Ben Dodds), John Rhys-Davies (Vigo Haman), Jimmie Walker (Soap Beatty), Peter Boyden (Vic Farley), Scott

Cohen (Jake Quinlan), MacIntyre Dixon (Gambit Nelson), Paul Giametti (Dr. Bud Cable), David Patrick Kelly (Joey Falconetti), Steven Randazzo (Sergeant Lou Brannon), Tahnee Welch (Catherine Powell), David Thornton (Twig).

Another futuristic story in which Jack the Ripper reappears in New York City of 2040. Game players become a reporter joining 30 characters in search of the Ripper. Reportedly, this video interactive game had a budget of $2.5 million or $4 million, depending on who's reporting the figures, and takes two hours to complete. True to its modernist fashion, the game is for those 17 years old and older because of graphic blood and gore, and because of what the producers describe as "strong language."

BIBLIOGRAPHY

Alexander, Karl. *Time After Time*. New York: Delacorte, 1979.

Ambler, Eric. *The Ability to Kill and Other Pieces*. London: Bodley Head, 1963.

Anderson, Robert. *Criminals and Crime: Some Facts and Suggestions*. London: Nisbet, 1903.

_____. *The Lighter Side of My Official Life*. London: Hodder, 1910.

Archer, Fred. *Ghost Detective: Crime and the Psychic World*. London: W.H. Allen, 1970.

Barclay, Glen St. John. *An Anatomy of Horror: The Masters of Occult Fiction*. New York: St. Martin's, 1978.

Baring-Gould, William S. *Sherlock Holmes of Baker Street: A Life of the World's First Consulting Detective*. New York: Bramhall House, 1962.

Barker, Richard, ed. *The Fatal Caress ... and Other Accounts of English Murders from 1551 to 1888*. New York: Duell, Sloane and Pearce, 1947.

Barnard, Allan, ed. *The Harlot Killer*. New York: Dell, 1953.

Begg, Paul, Martin Fido, and Keith Skinner. *The Jack the Ripper A to Z*. London: Headline, 1994.

Bell, Donald. "Jack the Ripper: A Final Solution?" *The Criminologist* 9:33 (1974): 40–61.

Belton, John. *The Hollywood Professionals: Howard Hawks, Frank Borzage, Edgar G. Ulmer*. Vol. 3. New York: A.S. Barnes, 1974.

Bermant, Chaim. *Point of Arrival: A Study of London's East End*. London: Eyre Methuen, 1975.

Blish, James. *Star Trek 8*. New York: Bantam Books, 1972.

Bloch, Robert. *Once Around the Bloch: An Unauthorized Autobiography*. New York: Tor, 1993.

_____. *The Night of the Ripper*. Garden City, N.Y.: Doubleday, 1984.

_____. *Yours Truly, Jack the Ripper: Tales of Horror*. New York: Belmont, 1962.

Boot, Andy. *Fragments of Fear: An Illustrated History of British Horror Films*. San Francisco: Creation, 1996.

Borchard, Edwin M. *Convicting the Innocent: Errors of Criminal Justice*. New York: Da Capo, 1970.

Boyle, Thomas. *Black Swine in the Sewers of Hampstead*. New York: Viking, 1988.

Bradbury, Ray. *Dandelion Wine*. New York: Knopf, 1957.

Brewer, J. F. *The Curse Upon Mitre Square A.D. 1530–1888*. London: Simpkin and Marshall, 1888.

Brooks, Tim, and Earle Marsh. *The Complete Dictionary to Prime Time Network TV Shows: 1946–Present*. New York: Ballantine, 1981.

Buckle, George Earle. *The Letters of Queen Victoria: A Selection from Her Majesty's Correspondence and Journal Between the Years 1886 and 1901*. 3 vols. London: Murray, 1930.

Bunson, Matthew E. *Encyclopedia Sherlockiana: The Complete A-to-Z Guide to the World of the Great Detective*. New York: Macmillan, 1994.

Buxton, Frank, and Bill Owen. *The Big Broadcast: 1920-1950*. New York: Viking, 1972.

Carnes, Mark C. *Past Imperfect: History According to the Movies*. New York: Holt, 1995.

Carter, Lin. *Lovecraft: A Look Behind the Cthulu Mythos*. New York: Ballantine, 1972.

Cawelti, John. *Adventure, Mystery, and Romance*. Chicago: University of Chicago Press, 1976.

Costello, Peter. *The Real World of Sherlock Holmes: The True Crimes Investigated by Arthur Conan Doyle*. New York: Carroll & Graff, 1991.

Coville, Gary. "Building Suspense." *N.A.R.A. News* No. 2, 1987.

_____, and Patrick Lucanio. "Jack the Ripper: His Life and Crimes in Popular Entertainment." *Filmfax* 31: 66–72, 80–82 (February-March) 1992.

Cullen, Tom. *Autumn of Terror: Jack the Ripper: His Crimes and Times*. London: Bodley Head, 1965.

_____. *When London Walked in Terror*. New York: Avon, 1968.

Daniel, Mark. *Jack the Ripper*. New York: Signet, 1988.

Davies, David Stuart. *Holmes of the Movies: The Screen Career of Sherlock Holmes*. New York: Bramhall House, 1976.

Davis, Derek. "Jack the Ripper: The Handwriting Analysis." *The Criminologist* 19:33 (1974): 62–69.

Dibdin, Michael. *The Last Sherlock Holmes Story*. New York: Pantheon, 1978.

Doll, Bill. "The Crime de la Crime." *Jack the Ripper*. New York: Frederick Fell, 1960.

Dunning, John. *Tune in Yesterday: The Ultimate History of Old-Time Radio, 1925–1976*. Englewood Cliffs, N.J.: Prentice Hall, 1976.

Ellison, Harlan, ed. *Dangerous Visions*. Garden City, N.Y.: Doubleday, 1967.

_____. *An Edge in My Voice*. Norfolk, Va.: Donning, 1985.

Evans, Stewart P., and Paul Gainey. *Jack the Ripper: First American Serial Killer*. New York: Kodansha, 1996.

Eyles, Allen, Robert Adkinson and Nicholas Fry, eds. *The House of Horror: The Story of Hammer Films*. London: Lorrimer, 1973.

Fido, Martin. *The Crimes, Detection and Death of Jack the Ripper*. New York: Barnes and Noble, 1987.

Frank, Alan. *The Horror Film Handbook*. Totowa, N.J.: Barnes and Noble, 1982.

Friedland, Martin L. *The Trials of Israel Lipski*. London: Macmillan, 1984.

Gibson, Walter B. *The Shadow Scrapbook*. New York: Harcourt Brace Jovanovich, 1979.

Gifford, Denis. *A Pictorial History of the Horror Movies*. London: Hamlyn, 1973.

Goodman, Jonathan. *Bloody Versicles: The Rhymes of Crime*. Kent, Ohio: Kent State University Press, 1993.

Haining, Peter, ed. *Weird Tales: A Selection, in Facsimile, of the Best from the World's Most Famous Fantasy Magazine*. New York: Carroll and Graff, 1990.

Hanna, Edward B. *The Whitechapel Horrors*. New York: Carroll and Graff, 1992.

Hardwick, Michael and Mollie. *The Private Life of Sherlock Holmes*. New York: Bantam, 1971.

Hardy, Phil, ed. *The Encyclopedia of Horror Movies*. New York: Harper and Row, 1986.

Harrington, Michael. "Victorian Psycho." *National Review*, June 23, 1995.

Harrison, Michael. *Clarence: The Life of the Duke of Clarence and Avondale, KG 1864–1892*. London, W.H. Allen, 1972.

_____. *Clarence: Was He Jack the Ripper?* New York: Drake, 1974.

_____. *The World of Sherlock Holmes*. New York: Dutton, 1975.

Harrison, Shirley, ed. *The Diary of Jack the Ripper*. New York: Hyperion, 1993.

Haydock, Ron. *Deerstalker!: Holmes and Watson on Screen*. Metuchen, N.J.: Scarecrow, 1978.

Hibbert, Christopher, ed. *Queen Victoria in Her Letters and Journals*. New York: Viking, 1985.

James, Stuart. *Jack the Ripper*. New York: Frederick Fell, 1960.

Johnson, Tom, and Deborah Del Vecchio. *Hammer Films: An Exhaustive Filmography*. Jefferson, N.C.: McFarland, 1996.

Jones, Robert Kenneth. *The Shudder Pulps: A History of the Weird Menace Magazines of the 1930s*. New York: New American Library, 1975.

Kelly, Alexander, and Colin Wilson. *Jack the Ripper: A Bibliography and Review of the Literature*. London: Association of Assistant Librarians, S.S.D., 1984.

Knight, Stephen. *Jack the Ripper: The Final Solution*. London: Harrap, 1976.

Lilley, Jessica. "How to Make a Monster: Herman Cohen." *Scarlet Street: The Magazine of Mystery and Horror* No. 19 (Summer 1995): 73–78, 109.

Linz, Daniel, and Edward Donnerstein. "Sexual Violence in the Media." *World Health* (April-May 1990): 26–27.

"*The Lodger* Proves Highly Amusing." *The New York Times*, January 9, 1917, 14.

Lovecraft, Howard Phillips. *Supernatural Horror in Literature*. 1945; reprinted, New York: Dover, 1973.

Lowndes, Marie Belloc. *The Lodger*. Chicago: Academy Chicago, 1988.

Lowndes, Susan, ed. *Diaries and Letters of Marie Belloc Lowndes, 1911–1947*. London: Chatto and Windus, 1971.

Lucanio, Patrick. *Them or Us: Archetypal Interpretations of Fifties Alien Invasion Films*. Bloomington: Indiana University Press, 1987.

MacAndrew, Elizabeth. *The Gothic Tradition in Fiction*. New York: Columbia University Press, 1979.

McCarthy, John, and Brian Kelleher. *Alfred Hitchcock Presents: An Illustrated Guide to the Ten-Year Television Career of the Master of Suspense*. New York: St. Martin's, 1985.

McNeil, Alex. *Total Television: A Comprehensive Guide to Programming from 1948 to the Present*. New York: Penguin, 1984.

Maltin, Leonard, ed. *Leonard Maltin's TV Movies and Video Guide*. New York: Signet, 1987.

Mank, Gregory William. *Hollywood Cauldron: Thirteen Horror Films from the Genre's Golden Age*. Jefferson, N.C.: McFarland, 1994.

Marcus, Steven. *The Other Victorians: A Study of Sexuality and Pornography in Mid–Nineteenth-Century England*. New York: Basic, 1965.

Marill, Alvin H. *Movies Made for Television: The Telefeature and the Mini-Series, 1964–1986*. New York: Baseline, 1987.

Maxford, Howard. *Hammer, House of Horror: Behind the Screams*. New York: Overlook, 1996.

Meikle, Denis. *A History of Horrors: The Rise and Fall of the House of Hammer*. Lanham, Md.: Scarecrow, 1996.

Moskowitz, Sam. *Seekers of Tomorrow: Masters of Modern Science Fiction*. Westport, Conn.: Hyperion, 1974.

Nevins, Francis M., Jr. *Royal Bloodline: Ellery Queen, Author and Detective*. Bowling Green, Ohio: Bowling Green University Popular Press, 1974.

_____, and Ray Stanich. *The Sound of Detection: Ellery Queen's Adventures in Radio*. Madison, Ind.: Brownstone, 1983.

Paley, Bruce. *Jack the Ripper: The Simple Truth.* London: Headline, 1996.

Palmer, Scott. *Jack the Ripper: A Reference Guide.* Metuchen, N.J.: Scarecrow, 1995.

Pirie, David. *A Heritage of Horror: The English Gothic Cinema 1946–1972.* New York: Avon, 1974.

Pohle, Robert W., Jr., and Douglas C. Hart. *Sherlock Holmes on the Screen: The Motion Picture Adventures of the World's Most Popular Detective.* New York: A.S. Barnes, 1977.

Queen, Ellery. *Cat of Many Tails.* Boston: Little, Brown, 1949.

_____. *A Study in Terror.* New York: Lancer, 1966.

Rothman, William. *Hitchcock — The Murderous Gaze.* Cambridge: Harvard University Press, 1982.

Rumbelow, Donald. *Jack the Ripper: The Complete Casebook.* Chicago: Contemporary, 1988.

Sharkey, Terence. *Jack the Ripper: 100 Years of Investigation.* New York, Dorset, 1987.

Smith, James L. *Melodrama.* (The Critical Idiom 28). New York: Harper and Row, 1973.

Smith, Mike. "Ripper Madness." *Travel Holiday* October 1997, 82.

Steinbrunner, Chris, and Norman Michaels. *The Films of Sherlock Holmes.* Secaucus, N.J.: Citadel, 1978.

_____, and Otto Penzler, eds. *Encyclopedia of Mystery and Detection.* New York: McGraw-Hill, 1976.

Stewart, R. W. "Something New in Radio." *The New York Times*, August 18, 1940, Sec. 9, 10.

Strachan, Ross. *Jack the Ripper: A Collector's Guide to the Many Books Published.* London: n.p., 1997.

Stuart, Jay. "On Holiday with the Ripper." *Newsday,* March 6, 1995, B7.

Sugden, Philip. *The Complete History of Jack the Ripper.* New York: Carroll and Graff, 1994.

Terrace, Vincent. *Radio's Golden Years: The Encyclopedia of Radio Programs, 1930–1960.* New York: A.S. Barnes, 1981.

Tine, Robert. *Uneasy Lies Ahead.* New York: Viking, 1982.

Toolan, David. "Voyeurs of Savage Fury." *America* (April 27, 1991): 460.

Tracy, Jack. *The Encyclopædia Sherlockiana: A Universal Dictionary of Sherlock Holmes and His Biographer John H. Watson, M.D.* Garden City, N.Y.: Doubleday, 1977.

Trow, M. J. *The Supreme Adventure of Inspector Lestrade.* New York: Stein and Day, 1985.

Tully, James. *The Secret of Prisoner 1167, Was This Jack the Ripper?* London: Robinson, 1997.

Wallace, Richard. *Jack the Ripper: "Light-Hearted Friend."* Melrose, Mass.: Gemini, 1996.

Walsh, Ray. *The Mycroft Memoranda.* New York: St. Martin's, 1984.

Warrick, Pamela. "Killer Approach to Nasty Letters." *Los Angeles Times*, April 7, 1997, Sec. E, 1.

Weaver, Tom. *Attack of the Monster Movie Makers: Interviews with 20 Genre Giants.* Jefferson, N.C.: McFarland, 1994.

Weverka, Robert. *Murder by Decree.* New York: Ballantine, 1979.

The Whitechapel Murders or The Mysteries of the East End. London: Andy Aliffe, 1996.

Zicree, Marc Scott. *The Twilight Zone Companion.* New York: Bantam, 1982.

INDEX

A & E Biography 171
Abberline, Frederick George 10, 43, 55
ABC *see* American Broadcasting Company
Accomplice Theory 20
Ackerman, Leonard J. 162
Adair, Diane 171
Adams, Andrea 167
Adrian, Iris 161
Adventure, Mystery and Romance 63
"The Adventure of the Blue Carbuncle" 116
"The Adventure of the Bruce-Partington Plans" 112
"The Adventure of the Norwood Builder" 111
"The Adventure of the Second Stain" 113
Ainley, Henry 24
Airoldi, Cristina 161
Alan Landsburgh Productions 172
Albert Victor Christian Edward, Prince *see* Clarence, Duke of
Alexander, Karl 168
Alexander, Wayne 82, 171
Alfred Hitchcock Presents 91, 171, 174
"Alias the Scarf" 97, 102, 104–107, 172
Alison, Dorothy 162–163
All the President's Men 148

Allen, Elizabeth 166
Allen, Jack 163
Allen, Karen 10n, 158, 175
Allgood, Sara 29, 164
Allingham, Margery 32, 35, 167
Alvin H. Perlmutter, Inc. 171
Ambassador Films 165
Amber, Eve 169
American Broadcasting Company 73, 80, 171–174
American International Pictures 162
An Anatomy of Horror 62
Anderson, Robert 133n
Andreiev, Andrei 166
Andrews, Harry 107, 163, 167
Andrews, Walter 149
Anthony, Lysette 163
Anwar, Gabrielle 167
Appeal of Jack the Ripper 9
Archer, Eugene 50
Arizona Ripper see *Bridge Across Time*
Arkush, Allan 174
Armitage, Peter 163
Arno, Siefried 166
Arnold, C. Wilfred 165
Arnold, Matthew 18
Arts and Entertainment Network 23, 54, 171
Askew, Desmond 163

Assante, Armand 163
Associated British Corporation 171
Associated British Studios 163
Asther, Niles 101, 161
Astley, Edwin 163
Attack of the Monster Movie Makers: Interviews with 20 Genre Giants 113
Atwill, Lionell 24, 126
Aubrey, Skye 162
Ault, Marie 165
Autumn of Terror: Jack the Ripper: His Crimes and Times 8n
Avco-Embassy Pictures 107, 165, 167
The Avengers 104–106, 171

Babylon 5 82, 171
Bacon, Mai 163
Baker, Robert S. 11, 44, 46, 48, 72, 163
Baker, Roy Ward 162
Balcon, Michael 164
Balfour, Bruce 158, 175
Ballard, Lucien 164
Balsam, Martin 58, 174
Balzer, Judy 175
Barbeau, Adrienne 162
Barclay, Glenn St. John 62
Baring-Gould, William S. 110–112

181

Barker, Clive 57
Barnard, Allan 40, 91, 147
Barnes, Peter 167
Barnes and Noble Bookstores 57n
Barnette, Alan 173
Baron, Allen 172
Baron, Geraldine 168
Baron, Lynda 77, 162
Barrard, John 171
Barrie, Lester 173
Barry, Ken 172
Barry, Patricia 103, 172
Bartell, Harry 170
Bascomb, A. W. 166
Basevi, James 164
Bassler, Robert 96, 162, 164
Bates, Ralph 162
Batman 118
Baumgartner, Peter 163
Baumgartner, Walter 163
Bavier, Frances 165
BBC *see* British Broadcasting Corporation
The Beast of Cimarron 4n
Beaumont, Charles 58, 174
Beck, Billy 174
Beckley, Paul 50
Begg, Paul 3, 8, 14, 131
Belajeff, Olga 169
Bell, Keith 162
Belton, John 101
Belzberg, Leslie 173
Ben Ali, Ameer 146–147
Benson, George 132
Benson, Theodora 147
Benton, Charles 162
Benton, Doug 171
Benzencenet, Peter 163
Berg, Alan 38
Berger, Robert Bryan 172
Bergin, Patrick 167
Berman, Monty 11, 44, 46, 48, 72, 163
Bermant, Chaim 133n
Bernard, Joseph 174
Bertillon, Alphonse 12
Bertillon System 12, 31
Best (journalist) 9
Best, Edna 170
Beswicke, Martine 162
Bevan, Billy 164

The Big Story 3
Bikel, Theodore 92–93, 171
Billig, Simon 174
Bingham, Barbara 75, 162
Bird, David 171
Bird, Norman 162
Birney, Frank 172
Black, Stanley 47, 163
Black Museum 32, 131
The Black Museum 126
Black Swine in the Sewers of Hampstead 9, 18
Blade of the Ripper 85, 161
Blakely, Colin 132
Blay, André 164
Blezard, John 163
Blish, James 174
Blitzstein, Marc 38
Bloch, Robert 3, 5, 58, 64, 65–66, 68–72, 74, 79–80, 94, 108, 136, 172, 174
Blocker, Dan 4n
Blondell, Gloria 174
Blood of the Vampire 44, 49
Bloody Versicles, the Rhymes of Crime 10
Bloom, Lindsay 162
Blue Network 169
Bluebeard 97, 101, 161
Bluel, Richard 172
Blythe, Sidney 166
Bond, David 58, 174
Bond, Lillian 165
Boone, Randy 140–141, 171
Boot, Andy 48
Borchard, Edwin M. 147
Borchert, Rudolph 73, 172
Borelli, Franco 164
Böttcher, Martin 165
Boucher, Anthony 58, 90, 110, 127, 169–170
Boulton, Mathew 169
Boxleitner, Bruce 82, 171
Boyden, Peter 175
Boyle, Michael 162
Boyle, Thomas 9, 18
Bradbury, Ray 4, 88, 170
Bradley, Leslie 165
Brady, Terence 171

Brahm, John 29–31, 33, 46, 58, 68, 155, 162, 164, 174
Brando, Marlon 107n
Brannah, Brigid 173
Brauner, Artur 165
Brecht, Bertold 38
Breon, Edmond 164
La Bretagne 149
Brewer, Jameson 58
Bridge Across Time 74, 136, 161
British Broadcasting Corporation 170
Brochero, Eduardo Manzanos 161
Broderick, Susan 162
Bronson, Charles 71
Brooke, Hillary 127, 169
Brooke, Walter 172
Brooks, Louise 39, 166
Brooks, Olwen 163
Brown, Carrie 143–147
Brown, Georgia 168
Brown, Himan 169–170
Brown, Robert 163
Brown, William Lyon 171
Browne, Coral 107, 167
Bruce, Nigel 126–127, 169–170
Bryan, Dora 162
Bryant, Michael 167
Bryon, Tom 169
Die Büchse der Pandora see *Pandora's Box*
Buck, Jules 167
Buck's Row 7
Bujold, Genevieve 165
Bulling, T. J. 152
Bundy, Ted 80, 85
Bunnage, Avis 168
Bunson, Matthew E. 122
Buono, Victor 172
Burden, Hugh 167
Burke, Barbara 49, 51, 163
Burke, Thomas 91, 171
Burnham, Jeremy 104, 171
Byrne, Eddie 49, 163
Byrne, Patsy 167
Byrnes, Thomas 143, 146

Caine, Michael 55, 163
Cairney, John 115, 168
Calamity Town 95

Calvin, Tony 162
Cambern, Donn 168
Cameron, John 163
Campbell, Collin 164
Campbell, Eddie 158, 174
Canadian Film Development Corporation 165
Cannadine, David 123, 125
Cannon, Esma 163
Capone, Al 136
Carfagno, Edward C. 168
Carradine, John 58, 97, 99–103, 161, 172
Carroll, Lewis 155
"Carrotty Nell" *see* Coles, Frances
Carson, Charles 163
Carsten, Peter 115, 167
Carter, James 166
Carter, Mitch 173
Cascio, Michael 171
"The Case of Bert Stevens, the Terrible Murderer" 111
"The Case of the Thistle Killer" 127–128, 172
Cass, Henry 44
Castina, Frank 173
Castle, Ann 163
Cat of Many Tails 95, 162
Cavanagh, Paul 169
Cawelti, John 63
Cayuga Productions 174
CBS Radio Mystery Theatre 79, 90, 169
CBS *see* Columbia Broadcasting System
CCC Filmkunst GmbH 165
Central Independent Television 126
Central News Agency 8, 152
Chamberlain, Ardwright 171
Chaplin, Josephine 52, 163
Chapman, Annie 7–8
Chapman, George *see* Klosowski, Severin
Chappell, Norman 171
Chegwidder, Ann 163
Chesney, Arthur 165

Chicago, Illinois 139
Chiros, Jim 171
Cimarron City 3n–4n, 139
Cimarron Strip 3, 139–140, 144, 171
CineFilms 163
Cinema Releasing 58
Cinemac 163
Cioffi, Charles 168
Claman, Holly R. 173
Clarence, Duke of 14, 43, 54
Clarence, Was He Jack the Ripper? 111
Clark, Bob 42, 46, 110, 125, 165
Clark, Susan 165
Clay, Virginia 171
Clemens, Brian 162
Clyde, David 164
Cockrell, Francis 91–94, 171
Cohen, Herman 113–114, 116–118, 121, 167
Cohen, Scott 175, 176
Cole, Stan 165
Colen, Beatrice 172
Coles, Frances 8, 19, 144
Collingwood, Peter 167
Collins, Gary 75, 173
Collins, Lewis 163
Collins, Roberta 172
Columbia Broadcasting System 3, 27, 69, 90–91, 163, 169–171, 174
Columbia Pictures 114, 167
"Comes the Inquisitor" 82, 171
Compton-Cameo-Teki 113, 167
Conan Doyle, Adrian 12, 113–114, 129
Conan Doyle, Arthur 11–12, 14, 73, 131
Conrad, Joseph 18
Conrad, William 88, 170
Continenza, Sandro 163
Convicting the Innocent: Errors of Criminal Justice 147
Conway, Cristi 174
Coon, Gene L. 174
Copeland, John 171

Cord, Alex 172
Cording, Harry 165
Corri, Adrienne 115, 167
Costello, Diedre 163
Coster, Nicholas 175
Couper, Adam 167
Courts, Randy 148, 175
Cox, Joshua 171
Craig, Colin 49, 163
Craig, Harry 114, 167
Crawford, H. Marion 127, 172
The Crawling Eye 44, 48–49
Cream, Thomas Neill 7–8, 42–43
"The Creeper" 86–87, 170
Cregar, Laird 29–31, 68, 96, 155, 163–164, 170
Crescenzi, Antonio 161
Crime Classics 39–40, 169
Crime Club 131
Criminal Investigation Division (CID) 133n
The Criminologist 14
Crook, Annie 43, 54
Crow, Angela 163
Crowden, Graham 167
Cthulhu Mythos 57
Cullen, Tom 1, 8, 12, 15, 31, 129, 134
Cult films 66
Culwick, Marc 163
Curse Upon Mitre Square A.D. 1530–1888 16, 21, 58, 75
Curtiss, Edward 169
Custer, Francine 163

Dade, Stephen 163
Daily News 9
Daily Telegraph 15, 138
Dandelion Wine 88
Dangerous Visions 71, 139
Daniell, Henry 127, 169
Daniels, Lisa 165
Dannay, Frederic 121
Dara, Max 163
D'Arbanville, Parri 168
Dark Horse Entertainment 174
Darnell, Linda 96, 163
Das Eachsfigurenkabinett see *Waxworks*

Davidson, L. W. 76, 162
Davies, Stuart David 121, 126
Davis, Charles 171
Davis, Essie 167
Davis, Ossie 10n, 175
Davitt, Karen 167
Day, Robert 75, 173
DC Comics 158, 175
Dean, Ivor 162
"Dear Boss" Letter 9
de Becker, Harold 164, 169
December Third Productions 174
De Corsica, Ted 169
Decree Productions 165
Deeming, Frederick 42
Delaney, Pat 162
Delavanti, Cyril 164
Deleveña, Jim 164
De Mendoza, Alberto 161
Demme, Jonathan 61
Dench, Judi 168
Dennis, Craig 69, 170
Dennis, Leslie 162
Derricks, Cleavant 173
de Santis, Orchidea 164
Desilu Productions 174
Devan, Carrie 161
Dexter, Aubrey, 33, 167
Diamond, Arnold 171
Dibdin, Michael 109
Dickinson, Desmond 167
Dierkop, Charles 174
Diessl, Gustav 39, 166
Dieterle, Wilhelm 169
Dietrich, Erwin C. 163
Digby, Helena 163
Di Paolo, Danny 164
Dixon, MacIntyre 176
Dr. Jekyll and Sister Hyde 162
Dodgson, Charles see Carroll, Lewis
Doll, Bill 10, 12, 15, 44
Donnerstein, Edward 60
Doohan, James 71, 174
D'Ora, Daisy 166
Douglas Family 113
"Dover Beach" 18
Downes, Terry 168
Doyle, Jerry 171
Dozier, William 102, 172

Dracula 59
Dragnet 40
Die Dreigroschenoper see The Three Penny Opera
Druitt, Montague John 42–43, 133, 151
Duke, Patty 75, 173
Duncan, Archie 127, 172
Dunn, George 4n
Dupont, René 165
Durant, Ariel 72
Durant, Will 72
Durkin, Jannis 173
Dutton, Thomas 10
Dyall, Valentine 32, 35, 167
Dyson, Reginald 132, 67

Early, Charles 129, 172
Early, Joseph 129, 172
Earth Spirit 38
East River Hotel 143, 145–147
Easy Rider 117
Eddowes, Catharine 8, 17, 21, 81
An Edge in My Voice 139
Edward VII 14
Elgin lunatic asylum 138
Elwes, Cassian 164
Eliot, T. S. 62
Ellery Queen (radio) 4, 90, 169
Ellery Queen (television) 96
Ellery Queen, Don't Look Behind You 95, 162
Ellery Queen's Mystery Magazine 110
Ellis, Anthony 88, 170
Ellison, Harlan 3, 71, 82, 139, 144, 171
Elvey, Maurice 29, 166
Embassy Pictures 144, 63
Emmott, Basil 166
The Encyclopedia of Horror Movies 59, 122
Encyclopedia Sherlockiana 122
Epstein, Jacob 173
Erdgeist see Earth Spirit
Erdody 161
Eternity Comics 158, 175
Euston Films 163

Evans, Bertram 165
Evans, Clifford 42, 163
Evans, Stuart 148–152, 172
Everest, Barbara 166
Ewing, John 164
Exclusive Films Ltd. 32, 167
"Eyrie" 68

Famous Players Ltd. 165
Fantasy Island 82, 171
Favero, Ray 162
Feindel, Jockey A. 161
Felmy, Hansjörg 16, 165
Fenady, Andrew 58
Fenady, Georg 58
Fenech, Edwige 161
Fennell, Albert 162
Ferguson, Bob 114, 118
Fiander, Lewis 162
Fido, Martin 3, 8, 14, 23, 131
Fiedler, John 72, 174
Fielding, Jerry 162
Fiesler, Joseph R. 166
Films of Sherlock Holmes 131
Fine, Morton 40, 169
Fingerprinting 12, 31
Finlay, Frank 116, 165, 167
Fischer, Kai 165
Fitzgerald, Edward 145
Fitzpatrick, Allen 148, 175
"The Five Orange Pips" 112
Fleck, John 172
Fodor, Anny 167
Fog 104–107, 171
Fog (film) 113
Ford, Derek 113–114, 167
Ford, Donald 113–114, 167
Forecast 3, 27, 37, 155, 169
"Foreigners" 133, 135, 138
Foriset, Emilio 161
Foster, Dudley 116, 168
Foster, Norma 168
Fowler, Marjorie 165
Fox Network 173
Fox-Brenton, David 75, 162
Foxworth, Robert 75, 173
Fragments of Fear 48
Francisci, Pietro 44

Franco, Jess 51–53, 60, 163
Frank, Alan 77
Fraser, Hugh 163
Fraser, John 115, 167
Frayling, Christopher 152
Freemasons 43, 54
Frees, Paul 47
Fregonese, Hugo 31, 33–34, 165, 175
"Frenchy" *see* Ben Ali, Ameer
Friedhofer, Hugo J. 164
Friedkin, David 40, 169
Friedland, Martin L. 133n
Friedman, Ron 82, 172
Fries, Tom 162
Fries Entertainment 161
From Hell 158, 174
"From Hell" 172
"From Hell" letter 9
Fromkess, Leon 161
Frye, William 174
Fuller, Kurt 82, 174
Fuller, Leland 165
Furlan, Mira 82, 171
Furst, Werner H. 161
Fux, Herbert 52, 163

Gacy, John Wayne 80
Gainey, Paul 148–152, 172
Gainsborough 164
Galeen, Henrick 169
Gardner, Shayle 166
Garrett, James 168
Garrie, John 171
Gastaldi, Ernesto 161
Gavin, Anna 174
Gaygler, Hans 163
Gebhard, Olga 163
Gein, Ed 58
Gendron, Pierre 161
"Genre" 57
George, Linda Day 172
George, Susan 163
Geschwitz, Anna 166
Giametti, Paul 176
Gibb, Cynthia 79, 164
Gielgud, John 124, 165
Gifford, Denis 62
Gilbert, Mickey 73–74, 172
Gilling, John 167
Gilman, Sam 174

Gleason, Paul 172
The Godfather 107n
Godfrey, Derek 77, 162
Goetz, Carl 166
Goldsmith, Jerry 70, 174
Goldstein, Leonard 165
Goldstone, Robert A. 165
"Good Evening, My Name Is Jack the Ripper" 39–40, 169
Goodman, John B. 169
Goodman, Jonathan 10
Gordon, Lawrence 174
Gordon, Mark 167
Gordon, Mary 126, 169
Gotham by Gaslight 158, 175
"Gothic" defined 60, 62–63
The Gothic Tradition in Fiction 62
Gottlieb, Franz-Joseph 16
Gottowt, John 169
Gough, Alfred 81, 174
Gough, Lloyd 172
Gould-Porter, A. E. 171
Granet, Bert 174
Grauer, Ben 3
Graves, Peter 171
Gray, Coleen 162
Grayson, Godfrey 32–33, 167
Green, Bruce 163, 164
Green, Denis 127, 170
Green, Garard 163
Green, Nigel 104–107, 167, 171
The Green Hornet 97, 104, 172
Greenway Productions 172
Gregg, John 167
Griffiths, Roger Ashton 163
Grinnage, Jack 172
Groves, Bill 166
Guild Films, Inc. 129, 172
Gulager, Clu 162
Gull, William 54–55, 82
Gunning, Christopher 162

Hagan, Julius 166
Haining, Peter 57

Hal Roach Studios 42, 163
Hale, Victoria 162
Hamer, Gerald 164, 171
Hamilton, Patrick 162
Hammer Films 32, 76, 162
Hammond, Peter 49, 163
Hamnett, Olivia 167
Hanbury Street 152
"The Hands of Mr. Otter-mole" 91–94, 171
Hands of the Ripper 76–77, 162
Hangover Square 96, 99–100, 162
Hanley, Jimmy 32, 167
Hardwick, Cedric 29, 164
Hardwick, Michael 132
Hardwick, Mollie 132
Hardy, Phill 59, 122
Hare, Lumsden 164
Harlan, Lillian 171
The Harlot Killer 40, 91, 110, 147
Harrington, Michael 5
Harris, Jack 166
Harrison, Joan 171
Harrison, Michael 111
Hart, Douglas C. 113, 117
Hartford, Betty 39, 169
Harvey, Barry 171
Harvey, Forester 164
Hasselhoff, David 75, 162
Hastings, Bob 162
Hawkins, Jack 166, 167
Hawtrey, Charles 167
Hayes, Steve 168
Haymarket Theatre 24
Haynie, Jim 79, 164
Hayward, Louis 59
Haywood, Steve 172
"The Hell-Bound Train" 64
Hemmings, David 124, 165
Hendrickson, Mark 171
Herb Jaffe Productions 168
Herbert, Don 58
Herbert, Percy 140, 171
Herbert, Tim 162
Hercules 44
Herlihy, Ed 170
Herrington, Rowdy 78, 164

Herrmann, Bernard 96, 162, 169
"High Rip" Gangs 8
Hill, James 46, 73, 118, 167
Hill-O'Connor Television 163
Hilton, George 161
Hinds, Anthony 167
"His Last Bow" 113
"History of the White-chapel Murders" 11
Hitchcock, Alfred 3, 25–27, 29, 37, 91, 94, 155, 164, 169
Hitchcock, the Murderous Gaze 25
Hodge, Jim 162
Hodges, Ken 167
Hodgson, Leyland 163
Hoey, Dennis 126, 169
Hold, Siegfried 165
Holden, Michael 174
Hollywood Cauldron 29, 96
The Hollywood Professionals 101
Hollywood Star Time 35–36, 169
Holmes, Mycroft 113
Holmes, Sherlock 109
Holmes of the Movies 121
Holy Trinity Priory 16
Hopkins, John 122, 165
"Horror" defined 60, 62–63
Horrors of the Black Museum 116
Horsetzky, George C. 165
Hough, John 105, 171
The Hound of the Baskervilles (film, 1959) 113
Houston, Donald 113, 167
Howard, Ronald 127, 172
Howson, Denzil 167
Hubbell Robinson Productions 69, 174
Hubbs, Gil 162
Huff, Caroline 167
Hughes, Tommy 169
Hume, Alan 163
Hunter, Kim 90, 169
Hutchinson, George (escaped lunatic) 137n, 138–139
Hutchinson, George (police informant) 136–138
Hutton, Jim 96
Hytten, Olaf 164, 169

The Identity of Jack the Ripper 14
In Search of "Jack the Ripper" 172
"In the Fourth Ward" 147
Ingalls, Don 75, 82, 172–173
Inner Sanctum 87, 169
International Apollo Films 163
Internet 157
Iregua, Victor 164
"Is Jack the Ripper in New York?" 11, 24

J.F. (John Francis) 16, 18, 21, 58
"Jack El Destripador" 110
Jack Shepphard 8
"Jack the Ripper" (Arts and Entertainment Biography) 23, 54
Jack the Ripper (BBC documentary, 1973) 43, 54
Jack the Ripper (comic book series) 158, 175
Jack the Ripper (film, 1958) 11, 15, 44, 46, 49–51, 73, 80, 129, 163
Jack the Ripper (film, 1976) 51–53, 60–61, 156, 163
Jack the Ripper (*Jack el Destripador de Londres*) 163
"Jack the Ripper" (radio) 170
Jack the Ripper (telefilm, 1988) 42–43, 54–54, 60, 156, 158, 164
"Jack the Ripper" (television) 42, 163
"Jack the Ripper" (television biography) 171
Jack the Ripper: The Complete Casebook 131
Jack the Ripper: The Final Solution 14, 125
Jack the Ripper: First American Serial Killer 148, 150–51
Jack the Ripper: "Light Hearted Friend" 155
Jack the Ripper: A New Theory 12, 14, 90
"Jack the Ripper: A Solution" 14
The Jack the Ripper, A–Z 14n, 131
Jack the Ripper computer virus 157
Jack the Ripper or When London Walked in Terror 12, 90
Jack's Back 78–79, 136, 164
Jack's Holiday 148, 175
Jacks, Robert L. 165
Jaffe, Herb 168
"Jane the Ripper" *see* "Jill the Ripper"
Jannings, Emil 169
Jay, Stan 171
Jessel, David 151, 172
Jewell, Isabel 165
JFK 54
"Jill the Ripper" 12, 42, 129
John, Georg 169
John Merrick 73
Johnson, Dennis 10n, 175
Johnson, Shelly 164
Jones, Barry 115, 167
Jones, Carolyn 172
Jones, Elwyn 122
Jones, Lisle 167
Jonfield, Peter 165
Joyce, Michael R. 167
June 165
Jung, C. G. 102
Just Television for Channel 4 172

Kankakee, Illinois 139
Karloff, Boris 42, 70, 163, 174
Kastner, Elliott 164
The Kate Smith Show 68, 170
Katsaros, Andonia 168
Katsulas, Andreas 171
Kauffer, E. McKnight 11, 25

Kavanaugh-Dowsett, Sean 171
Keen, Josephine 167
Keen, Malcolm 165
Kehler, Jack 171
Kelley, DeForrest 174
Kelley, Michael Francis 171
Kellner, William 163
Kelly, Alexander 3
Kelly, David Patrick 176
Kelly, Mary Jane 8, 12, 14, 20, 39–40, 136–137, 144
Kemp, Christopher 167
Kennedy, John F. 14
Kessler, Catherine 165
Kiebach, Hans-Jurgen 165
"Killer Fonts" 157
King, Stephen 57, 62
King, T. W. 174
Kinski, Klaus 51–52, 163
Kirk, Phyllis 96
Kirschbaum, Glenn 172
Kitchen Sink Press 158, 174
Klinger, Michael 113–114
Klosowski, Severin 42
Knaggs, Skelton 164
Knick, C. 145, 146
"Knife in the Darkness" 3, 139–140, 144, 148, 171
Knight, Stephen 14, 125, 158
Koch, Marianne 16, 165
Kolchak — The Night Stalker 73, 136, 172
Kolker, Henry 161
Korey, Alix 175
Kortner, Fritz 166
Kosminski, Aaron 133, 151
Kramer, Stephanie 75, 162
Krampf, Günther 165
Krauss, Werner 169
Kuhl, Carl 170
Kuluva, Will 174

Landis, John 173
Landridge, Virginia 174
Langan, Glenn 163
Lansford, Roy 165
Lansing, Robert 79, 169
la Penna, J. Anthony 33, 167

LaShelle, Joseph 162
The Last Sherlock Holmes Story 109
Lawford, Peter 96, 162
Lawrence, Marjie 77, 162
Lawrence, Quentin 44, 49
Lawrence Gordon Productions 174
Leacock, Phillip 171
Leake, Barbara 168
"Leather Apron" 26–27
Leaver, Philip 163
Lederer, Franz 166
Lee, Bruce 172
Lee, Manfred B. 90, 121, 169
Lees, Robert 42, 75
Legal, Ernst 169
Leigh, Taylor 173
Leighton, Ted 95–96, 162
Lemani, Tania 174
LeMesurier, John 163
Leni, Paul 58, 169
Lenrow, Bernard 170
Leonard, Queenie 164
Lerski, Helmar 169
Les Films 165
Lester, Buddy 162
Lester, Henry E. 113–114, 167
Levant, Mark 169
Levin, Lloyd 174
Levine, Joseph E. 10, 44, 129, 163
Levinsohn, Gary 167
Lewis, Christopher 166
Lewis, Elliott 39, 169
Lewis, Leo 168
Lewis, Linda 166
Lewis, Milton 87, 170
Lewis, Warren 170
Lewton, Val 63
The Life of the Duke of Clarence and Avondale 1864–1892 111
Lighter Side of My Official Life 133n
Lilley, Jessica 113–114, 116
Linz, Daniel 60
Littlechild, John 149, 152
Littlechild letter 149, 151
Lizzie Borden Case 11
Lloyd, Doris 164
Lloyd, John 122

Lloyd, Sabrina 173
Lodge, David 171
The Lodger (film, 1926) 11, 22, 24, 26–27
The Lodger (film, 1944) 33, 46, 58, 68–69, 96, 99, 155–156, 164
The Lodger (novel) 3, 21, 23–24, 35, 59, 80, 90–91
The Lodger (play) 24
The Lodger (radio) 3, 27, 35–37, 68, 90, 169–170
The Lodger: The Arrest and Escape of Jack the Ripper see *Jack the Ripper: First American Serial Killer*
Lohmann, Paul 168
London Times see *Times of London*
Loomis, Rod 79, 164
Loran, Patricia 164
Lorimar-Telepictures 163
Loring, Teal 161
Lorre, Peter 36, 69, 170
Los Angeles Times 118
The Lost World (film, 1960) 113
Lovecraft, H. P. 57–58, 63–64
Lovejoy, Frank 88, 170
Lovejoy, Ray 167
Lowe, Arthur 167
Lowe, Heather 173
Lowndes, Marie Belloc 3, 21–24, 26, 32, 35, 44, 50, 80, 90–91, 104, 107, 164–166
Lowther, George 79, 90, 169
Lucanio, Patrick 60
Lucking, Bill 162
Lucretia Borgia 123
Lüdke, Bruno 8
Luff, William 166
Lulu 38
Lusk, George 9
Lux Radio Theatre 35
Lyceum Theatre 15, 55
Lynch, Ken 74, 172
Lyndon, Barré 29, 31, 69–70, 96, 99–100, 162, 165, 174–75
Lynn, Emmett 161

M*A*S*H 117
McAllister, William 162
McAnally, Ray 163
McAndrew, Elizabeth 62
Macauley, Charles 174
McCallom, James 171
McCall's 88
McCarth, Patti 161
McCloy, Sean 165
McClure's 21
McConnell, Judy 174
McConnell, Keith 168
McCord, Robert L. 174
McCormick, Donald 8, 14
McDevitt, Ruth 172
MacDonald, David 163
McDowell, Betty 163
McDowell, Malcolm 80, 168
McGavin, Darren 73, 172
MacGinnis, Niall 42, 163
McGrath, Martin 167
McHugh, Jimmy 46–47, 163
"Mack the Knife" 38
McKenzie, Alice 8
McNamara, Brian 173
Macnaughton, Melville 133
Macnaughton Report 149
Macnee, Patrick 104, 106, 171
MacRae, Meredith 172, 175
Madrid, José Luis 163–164
The Magazine of Fantasy and Science Fiction 65
Maher, Joseph 168
Mahoney, Maggie 174
Main, Laurie 168
Malibu Press 158, 175
Maltin, Leonard 131
Man in the Attic (film) 31, 34, 165
Mander, Miles 166
Mank, Gregory William 29, 96
Mankopff, Andreas 163
Mantooth, Donald 172
Mantooth, Randolph 162
Mara, Suzanne 173
Marcus, Steven 109
Margulies, William 162

Marie, Rose 162
Marinano, Rensso 164
Marlowe, Derek 54, 163
Marlowe, Faye 163
Marshall, E. G. 90, 162, 169
Marshall, Herbert 27, 155, 169
Martino, Sergio 161
Mason, James 123, 165
Mather, Aubrey 164
Matters, Leonard P. 14, 49
Matthews, Henry 20
Matthews, Lester 165
Maybach, Christiane 168
Maynard, John 174
Maynard, Richard 161
Mear, H. Fowler 166
Medak, Peter 167
Medallion TV Enterprises 163
Meiringen, Switzerland 109
Melodrama 118
Mendoza, Paul 158, 175
Meredith, Burgess 10n, 158
Merrill, Lou 40, 169
Merrow, Jane 162
Mervyn, William 167
Meyer, Alexander A. 162
Meyer, Nicholas 46, 73, 80, 168
Meyers, Janet 167
MGM Television 174
Michael R. Joyce Productions 167
Michael, Brandon 173
Michaels, Norman 131–132
Michon, Jack 161
Mid–Century Film Productions Ltd. 163
Mila, Miguel F. 161
Miles, Kevin 167
Milland, Ray 46, 69–70, 174
Millar, Miles 81, 174
Miller, Harry B. III 164
Miller, Virgil 169
Miller's Court 32, 152
Millhauser, Bertram 127, 169
Milne, Tom 59, 76

Milzer, Cameron 162
Mir, Irene 164
Miss Beverly Hills 70, 174
Mitchell, Bob 174
Mitchum, Robert 89
Molina, Jacinto 163–164
Mollé Mystery Theatre 69, 87, 94, 170
The Monster of London City 15–16, 46, 55, 165
Montagne, Edward J. 162
Montagu, Ivor 164
Montalban, Ricardo 83, 172
Monterastelli, Art 81, 174
Montgomery, George 4n
Montgomery, Robert 37, 170
The Montparnasse Ballet 163
Moore (Central News Agency chief) 152
Moore, Alan 158, 174
Moore, Teddi 165
Moore, Tim 164
Moorehead, Agnes 36, 89, 170
Morant, Richard 164
Morgan, Harry 96, 162, 170
Morley, Robert 113, 167
Morris, Reginald 165
Morritt, Stewart 167
Morton, Anthony 167
Moskowitz, Sam 68
Motion Pictures for Television, Inc. 127, 172
Motta, Elsa 165
Moviegraph, Inc. 166
Mulhare, Edward 172
Mulkey, Chris 164
Muller, Endre 49–50, 163
Murder by Decree 42–43, 46, 59, 96, 110–111, 117, 122–125, 135, 156, 158, 165
"Murder Most Foul" 173
Muschamp, Jessica 167
Mutual Broadcasting System 127, 170
Mutual Film Company 167
Mylett, Rose 8
Mystery in the Air 36, 170
The Mystery of Jack the Ripper 14, 49

Mystery Playhouse 69, 170

Napier, Alan 163
National Association of Broadcasters 36, 71, 87
National Broadcasting Company 69, 94, 162, 170, 172–74
National Police Gazette 10–11
National Review 5
Naughton, Greg 175
NBC *see* National Broadcasting Company
Nebenzahl, Seymour 165
Neblett, John 68–69, 170
Needs, James 162, 167
Neil, John 7
Neill, Roy William 126, 128, 129, 169
Nelson, Erik 172
Neptune-Film 169
Nero-Film 165
Ness, Eliot 136
Netter, Doug 171
Neville, John 113, 118–119, 167
Nevins, Francis M. 95
The New Adventures of Sherlock Holmes (radio) 127, 170
The New Adventures of Sherlock Holmes (television) 127–128, 172
"The New Exhibit" 58, 174
New York Herald Tribune 50
New York Times 10, 50, 107n, 118, 142–143, 145–146, 149
Newell, Patrick 168, 171
Newsday 148
Newsweek 61–62, 107n
Next see Blade of the Ripper
Nichols, Mary Ann "Polly" 7–8, 141, 152
"Nick the Knife" 4, 90, 169
Nielsen, Hans 165
Night Gallery 75
The Night of the Ripper 71–72

Night Stalker see *Kolchak — The Night Stalker*
Nightbeat 87, 170
Nimoy, Leonard 172, 174
Nix, Marilyn 173
Nogales, Carmen 173
Nolan, Jeanette 37, 89, 170
Nolan, William F. 74–75, 162
Norway Productions 173
Novello, Ivor 26–27, 29, 165–166

Oakland, Simon 172
Oberon, Merle 29, 164
O'Brien Tom 174
Obzina, Martin 169
Occult 62
O'Connell, Jerry 173
Odell, Governor 147
O'Hare, Tim 174
"Old Shakespeare" *see* Brown, Carrie
Olympic Pictures Corporation 166
O'Mahoney, Nora 171
O'Malley, J. Pat 70, 174
Orlandi, Nora 161
Ortega, Santos 169
Osgood, Nathan 172
Osmonde, Hal 163
Ostrog, Michael 133, 151
O'Toole, Peter 107, 167
Our American Cousin 150

Pabst, G.W. 38–39, 165
Page, Genevieve 132
Palance, Jack 31, 33, 165
Palisades Entertainment 164
Pall Mall Gazette 138
Palmentola, Paul 161
Palmer, Byron 165
Palmer, Keith 163
Pandora's Box (film, 1928) 38, 165
Panoramic Productions 165
Parade Releasing Organization 165
Paramount Pictures 44, 163, 164

Paranormal Phenomena 62
Parker, Cecil 115, 167
Parker, Jean 99, 161
Parlato, Dennis 175
Parmet, Phil 158, 175
Parsons, Milton 174
Paslow, Justin 167
Past Imperfect: History According to the Movies 123
Pathé 168
Patterson, Lee 49, 163
Paul, Adolf 16
Pavitt, Denys 163
The Pearl of Death 127
Pearson, Heskeath 112
Peckinpah, David 173
Pedachenko, Alexander 14
Peisley, Frederick 171
Pembroke, George 161
"Penny Dreadfuls" 57
Penzler, Otto 21, 23
Pernis, Mona Van 167
Perry, Sue 172
Pevney, Joseph 174
Phantom Fiend 29, 166
Phantom of Soho (film) 16, 165
Phanton von Soho, Das (film) see *The Phantom of Soho*
Phillips, Arnold 161
Phillips, Tita 165
Picardo, Robert 79, 164
Piccioni, Piero 163
Pierson, Carl 161
Pingatore, Carl 172
Pirie, David 48, 51
Pizer, John 26
Plant, Michael 42, 163
Playdon, Paul 172
Playwright's Horizons 148
Plowden, Piers 164
Plowright, Hilda 171
Plummer, Christopher 123–124, 165
Pohle, Robert W., Jr. 113, 117
Point of Arrival: A Study of London's East End 133n
Police Procedural 40
Popular Culture and Jack the Ripper 3–4

Porter, Eric 76, 162
Portsmouth *Evening News* 12, 131
Pottle, Harry 165
Powers, Stephanie 162
PRC Pictures (Producers Releasing Corporation) 97, 161
Pree, Damien 167
Presnell, Robert Jr. 31, 165
Previn, Steve 172
Price, Vincent 35, 71, 169
Prince Jack 14
The Private Life of Sherlock Holmes (film) 131
Private Life of Sherlock Holmes (novel) 132
"The Prowler in the City at the Edge of the World" 139
Psycho 58, 73
Purcell, Roy 172
Purdham, David 173

Quality of Murder 58
Quayle, Anthony 115, 165, 167
Queen, Ellery 121, 162

Randazzo, Steven 176
Ransford, Maurice 163
Rassimov, Ivan 161
Rathbone, Basil 126–127, 169–170
Rattlesnake Productions 171
Rawlings, Margaret 77, 162
Rawlins, John 126
Raymond, Robert 162
The Real World of Sherlock Holmes: The True Crimes Investigated by Arthur Conan Doyle 131
Redd, Robert L. 35, 169
Rees, Angharad 76, 162
Reese, Andrew 164
Reeves, Kynaston 166
Regnier, Charles 168
Reisner, Allen 102, 172
Revue Studios 69, 171, 174
Reynolds, Harry 162
Reynolds, Sheldon 127, 172

Rhodes, Marjorie 162
Rhys-Davies, John 10n, 173, 175
Richards, Kenneth 172
Richardson, Deborah 171
Richardson, Henry 167
Richardson, Mike 174
"A Rip in Time" 81, 83, 174
The Ripper (CD-ROM) 10n
The Ripper (1892) 16
The Ripper (film, 1985) 166
The Ripper (film, 1997) 167
RIPPER (game) 158, 175
The Ripper (television) 73, 136, 172
The Ripper File 122
"Ripper rip-offs" 86
Ripperologists 1
Roach, Hal, Jr. 163
Roberts, Alice 166
Roberts, Cokie 149
Roberts, Ken 170
Robson, William N. 37, 170
Rodat, Robert 167
Roden, Mollie 171
Rodrigues, Percy 173
Rolfe, Guy 106, 171
Romay, Lina 163
Ronay, Edina 168
Room to Let (film) 31–33, 35, 167
Rose, George 163
Rossilli, Paul 74, 162
Rotha, Paul 166
Rothman, Henry 25
Royal Academy of Music 38
Royal Bloodline 95
Rozsa, Miklos 168
Rugolo, Pete 46–47, 163
Ruling Class 107, 167
Rumbelow, Donald 1, 3n, 8, 12, 14n, 15–16, 20, 54, 72, 79, 131, 172
Runolfsson, Anne 175
Ruscoll, Joseph 87
Ryan, Edmon 69, 174
Ryon, Rex 78, 164

St. Clare Entertainment 173
St. Germain, Mark 148, 175
St. Valentine's Day Massacre 136
Salisbury, Lord 20
Sanchez-Short, Elba 167
Sanders, George 29, 96, 163–164
Sands, Billy 162
Sangster, Jimmy 48–49, 163
Sarabina, Ric 174
Sasdy, Peter 76–77, 162
"Saucy Jack" 9
Saucy Jack, Inc. 165
Savini, Tom 167
Saxton, Brian 171
Scarlet Street 113
Schaal, Wendy 172
Schifrin, Lalo 162
Schmidt, Gudrun 165
Schmidt, Peer 165
Schoenherr, Dietmar 16, 165
Schomer, Ernst 165
Schreier, Tom 167
Schufftan, Eugen 161
Schulman, Susan H. 175
Scibetta, Angelo 161
Scorsese, Martin 62
Scotland Yard 11–12
Scott, Hohn 167
The Screen Guild Players 35
Secret, Robert 171
Secret History: The Whitechapel Murders 151–152, 172
Secrets and Mysteries 65, 80, 172
Secrets of the Unknown see *Secrets and Mysteries*
Seekers of Tomorrow: Masters of Modern Science Fiction 68
Segan, Allison Lyon 167
Sennett, Mack 63
Seurat, Pilar 174
The Seven Percent Solution 73
Severn, Bernard 171

Seymour, Carolyn 107, 167
Seymour, Jane 163
The Shadow 86, 170
"The Shambler from the Stars" 64
Shamley Productions 171
Shapiro, Stuart 157
Sharpe, Anne 163
Shatner, William 71, 172
Shaw, Denis 163
Shaw, George Bernard 73, 112
Shaw, Montague 165
Shear, Barry 96, 162
Sheehan, Stephen 167
Shepherd, Sally 169
Sheppard, W. Morgan 174
Sherlock Holmes and the Secret Weapon 126
Sherlock Holmes and the Voice of Terror 126
Sherlock Holmes in Washington 126
Sherlock Holmes of Baker Street: A Life of the World's First Consulting Detective 110
Sherlock Holmes on the Screen 113
Sherman, Ransom 174
Sherven, Judy 174
Shew, Edward Spencer 76, 162
Shillen, Nancy 162
Shine, Bill 49, 163
Shpetner, Stan 173
Sickert, Joseph 14, 43, 54, 122, 125
Sieman, Frank 171
The Sign of Four 111
The Silence of the Lambs 61
Silver, Christine 32, 167
Sim, Alistair 167
Sim, Gerald 162
Simmons, Kendrick 171
Sims, George R. 149
Sing Sing Prison 147
Singer, Robert 174
The Sir Arthur Conan Doyle Theatre 113
Sir Nigel Films 113, 167
Sixteen-Stringed Jack 8

The Sixth Sense 75, 173
Skinner, Keith 3, 8, 14, 131
Slater, Angela 172
Sliders 173
Slippery Jack 8
Small, Marya 172
Smart, Patsy 171
"Smiler with the Knife: The Mystery of Jack the Ripper" 42, 170
Smith, Constance 31–33, 165, 167
Smith, Emma Elizabeth 7–8, 40
Smith, James L. 118–119
Smith, John 4n
Smith, Lane 162
Smith, Sydney 169
Smith, William 172
"So the Story Goes" 69
Sohl, Jerry 58, 174
Solon, Ewen 49, 51, 163
"The Song of the Slasher" 87, 169
Sorel, Sonia 161
"Sorry, Wrong Number" 37
Spader, James 78, 164
Spatter and splatter movies 4
Spelling-Goldberg Productions 171
Spencer, Frank 167
The Spider Woman 127
Spier, William 170
Spiering, Frank 14
Spinney, Saige Ophelia 174
Spring-Heeled Jack 8, 58
Stack, Robert 42
Stanley, Dr. 14, 42
Stannard, Eliot 164
Stannard, Roy 162
The Star 152
Star and Herald 138n
Star Trek 8, 71–72, 157, 173, 174
Stark, Don 174
Starz! Pictures 167
Stay Tuned for Terror 68–69, 170
Steenburgen, Mary 168
Steinbrunner, Chris 21, 23, 131–132

Stemmle, Robert A. 15, 165
Stephen, J. K. (James Kenneth) 111
Stephens, Robert 132
Sterling, Anne 99, 161
Stern, Ernst 169
Sterne, Morgan 162
Stevens, Dorinda 163
Stevens, Robert 92–95, 171
Stevenson, Robert Louis 15
Stewart, William 12, 14, 90
Stone, Marianne 163
Stone, Oliver 54, 60
Story of Civilization 72
Stossel, Ludwig 161
Stowell, Thomas 14, 43, 54
Straczynski, J. Michael 82, 171
Stram, Henry 175
The Strange Case of Dr. Jekyll and Mr. Hyde 15, 55
"The Strange Case of Lucas Lauder" 79, 90, 169
"The Strange Case of the Murder in Wax" 127, 170
The Strange Vice of Mrs. Ward see *Blade of the Ripper*
Strano Vizio della Signora Ward, Lo see *Blade of the Ripper*
Straub, Peter 57
Strauss, Kim 171
Street, George 163
Stride, Elizabeth 8
Stuart, Jan 148
Stuart, William L. 102, 172
A Study in Scarlet (1887) 11, 112, 114–119, 121
A Study in Terror (film, 1965) 73, 111, 113–114, 117–119, 121–122, 135, 167
A Study in Terror (novel) 46
Supernatural Horror in Literature 63

Suspense 37, 88, 170
Sutherland, Donald 165
Swackhamer, E. W. 161
Swallow Gardens
Swift, David 164
Swinburne, Nora 163
Swofford, Ken 162
Symbolic Jack the Ripper
3

"Tabloid journalism"
152
Tabram, Martha 7–8, 40,
141
Take 2 Interactive 10n,
158, 175
Talbot, Kenneth 162
Tallman, Robert 37, 170
Tapper, Annie 134
Tate, Phyllis 38
Taylor, Jane 163
Tchkersoff, Olga 12
Tenser, Tony 113–114
Terror at London Bridge
see *Bridge Across Time*
Terror in the Wax Museum
58
"Texas Tough" 138
Thames Television 163
Thatcher, Torin 94, 171
The Thin Man 87, 96
This Is Nora Drake 87
Thomas, Craig 171
Thomas, Kevin 118
Thornton, David 176
Thorson, Linda 104, 171
Thrawl Street 137
Three-Fingered Jack 8
The Three Penny Opera
38
Three Wax Men 169
Thriller 46, 69, 174–175
Tillman, Fritz 16, 165
Time After Time 46, 80,
83, 108, 136–137, 168
Time Cop 81, 174
Times of London 7, 9, 14,
110, 133, 137, 143, 145
Today 148–150
Toolan, David 60
Torme, Tracy 173
Tottenham, Merle 167
Totter, Audrey 4n
Tover, Leo 165

Tower, Wade 167
Townsend, Jill 140–141,
171
"A Toy for Juliette" 71,
139
Trayne, John 171
The Trials of Israel Lipski
133n
Triumph Communica-
tions 172
Tumblety, Francis 149,
151
Turn of the Screw 63
Turner, John 167
Turner, Robert Brooks
163
20th Century–Fox 29, 31,
35–37, 68, 96, 126,
162–165
20th Century–Fox Televi-
sion 172
The Twilight Zone 58, 174
*The Twilight Zone Com-
panion* 174

Uberda, Diego 163
UK Television Channel 4
151, 172
Ulmer, Edgar G. 97, 102,
161
*The Ungeheuer von Lon-
don City* see *The Mon-
ster of London City*
(film, 1964)
United Entertainment
Pictures 166
Universal Pictures 126,
162, 169
Universal Television 69,
162, 172–174
Unsolved Mysteries 40, 42,
170
Uppskarare see *The Ripper* (1892) 16

Vachell, Horace Annesley
24
Vajda, Ladislaus 165
Valentine, Nancy 69, 174
Van den Bergh, Tony 42,
170
Van Derbeken, Derik 173
Veidt, Conrad 169
The Veil 42, 163

Vejar, Michael 171–172
Ventigmilia, Baron 164
Verheiden, Mark 174
Vernon, Peter 162
Vetchinsky, Alex 115, 167
Victoria, Queen 20, 116,
133
"Victorian Psycho" 5
Viking Pictures 169
Villechaize, Hervé 172
Villiers, James 167
Vivian, Percival 169
"Voyeurs of Savage Fury"
60

Waddell, Bill 126
Waggoner, Lyle 172
Wagner, Wendy 172
Walken Christopher 10n,
158, 175
Walker, Jimmie 10n, 175
Wallace, Bryan Edgar
15–16, 55, 165
Wallace, Edgar 15
Wallace, Richard 155
Walsh, Kay 167–168
Walter Manley Enter-
prises 165
Warner, David 80, 137,
168
Warner, Gertrude 169
Warner Bros. 168, 171
Warwick, Norman 162
Watson, Richard 129, 172
Waxman, Sam E. 162
"Waxwork Motif" 58, 102
Waxworks 58, 169
Waymouth, Belinda 174
Wayne, David 96
Weaver, Tom 113–114, 118
Webb, J. Watson, Jr. 164
Webb, Jack 40
Webber, Peggy 37, 170
Webster, Byron 168
Wedekind, Frank 38, 165
Weiler, A. H. 118
Weill, Kurt 38
Weird Tales 57, 59, 64,
68–69
Weiss, Robert K. 173
Weisse, Nicola 163
Welch, Nelson 171
Welch, Tahnee 176
Welles, Orson 86, 170

Wesley, John 164
West, Samuel 167
The West End Horror 73
Wetherall, Virginia 162
Wheeler, Lyle 162, 165
When London Walked in Terror 12, 129
Whifler, Graeme 172
Whitaker, David 162
White, Stephen 151, 172
Whitechapel 2, 23, 32, 144
Whitman, Stuart 140, 171
Whitsun-Jones, Paul 162, 171
Whitten, Frank 167
Who Is He? (play) 24
"The Whole Town's Sleeping" 4, 88, 170
Wickes, David 42, 54, 163
Wiese, Ursula von 163
Wilde, Oscar 73
Wilder, Billy 131
Willemen, Paul 59, 76
Willemetz, Jacque 165
Williams, Adam 69, 174
Williams, Cedric 167
Williams, John 70, 174

Williams, Rhys 92, 165, 171
Williams, Van 103, 172
Wilson, Colin 2, 8
Windsor, Barbara 115, 167
Winley, Anthony 167
"With Affection, Jack the Ripper" 75, 83, 171, 173
"Wolf in the Fold" 71–72, 79, 83, 157, 173
Wolfe, Ian 103, 172
Wolkenstein, Cristoph 171
The Woman in Green 126–128, 169
Wood, Edward D. 66
Woodbridge, George 49, 163
Woodfield, Randall 85
Woodhall, Edwin T. 12, 90
Woods, Donald 70F, 174
Woolf and Freeman Film Services, Ltd. 166
Woolnough, Jeff 173
World Health 60
The World of Sherlock Holmes 111
Worlock, Frederic 163–164, 169

WOW!! Entertainment, Inc. 165
Wreford, Denis 167
Wright, Wendell 164
Wuher, Kari 173
Wyenn, Than 162
Wylie, Adam 173

York, Michael 167
Young, Aida 162
Young, Clint 172
"Yours Truly, Jack the Ripper" (radio) 68–69, 91, 170
"Yours Truly, Jack the Ripper" (television) 46, 59, 69, 174–175
"Yours Truly, Jack the Ripper" (short story) 3, 60, 62, 64, 71, 74, 79, 83, 108, 136

Zaza, Paul 165
Zbonek, Edwin 15, 46, 55, 165
Zicree, Marc Scott 174
Zittrer, Carl 165
Zuckert, Bill 162